BAL GANGADHAR TILAK

HIS WRITINGS AND SPEECHES

APPRECIATION BY

BABU AUROBINDO GHOSE

GYAN

Published by

Gyan Publishing House
5, Ansari Road
Daryaganj, New Delhi-110002
Phone: 011-47034999, 9811692060
E-mail: books@gyanbooks.com

Distribution Network
gyanbooks.com
India, USA, Canada, UK, Australia, France

ISBN : 978-81-212-2214-3 (HB)
First Published, 1918

2nd Impression 2021

Printed at: Gyan Press, Delhi.

Bal Gangadhar Tilak
Appreciation By: Babu Aurobindo Ghose

Bal Gangadhar Tilak

HIS WRITINGS AND SPEECHES

APPRECIATION BY

BABU AUROBINDO GHOSE

ENLARGED EDITION

GANESH & CO., MADRAS

Bal Gangadhar Tilak

CONTENTS

Contents

BAL GANGADHAR TILAK

AN APPRECIATION

NEITHER Mr. Tilak nor his speeches really require any presentation or foreword. His speeches are, like the featureless Brahman, self-luminous. Straightforward, lucid, never turning aside from the point which they mean to hammer in or wrapping it up in ornamental verbiage, they read like a series of self-evident propositions. And Mr. Tilak himself, his career, his place in Indian politics are also a self-evident proposition, a hard fact baffling and dismaying in the last degree to those to whom his name has been anathema and his increasing pre-eminence figured as a portent of evil. The condition of things in India being given, the one possible aim for political effort resulting and the sole means and spirit by which it could be brought about, this man had to come and, once in the field, had to come to the front. He could not but stand in the end where he stands to-day, as one of the two or three leaders of the Indian people who are in their eyes the incarnations of the national endeavour and the Godgiven captains of the national aspiration. His life, his character, his work and endurance, his acceptance by the heart and the mind of the people are a stronger argument than all the reasonings in his speeches, powerful as these are, for Swaraj, Self-government, Home Rule, by whatever name we may call the sole possible present aim of our effort, the freedom of the life of India, its self-determination by the people of India. Arguments and speeches do not win liberty for a nation; but where there is a will in the nation to be free and a man to embody that will in every action of his life and to devote his days to its realisation in the face of every difficulty and every suffering, and where the will of the nation has once said, "This man and his life mean what I have in my heart and my purpose," that is a sure signpost of the future which no one has any excuse for mistaking.

That indomitable will and that unwavering devotion have been the whole meaning of Mr. Tilak's life; they are the reason of his immense hold on the people. For he does not owe his pre-eminent position to any of the causes which have usually made for political leading in India, wealth and great social position, professional success, recognition by Government, a power of fervid oratory or of fluent and taking speech; for he had none of these things to help him. He owes it to himself alone and to the thing his life has meant and because he has meant it with his whole mind and his whole soul. He has kept back nothing for himself or for other aims, but has given all himself to his country.

Yet is Mr. Tilak a man of various and no ordinary gifts, and in several lines of life he might have achieved present distinction or a pre-eminent and enduring fame. Though he has never practised, he has a close knowledge of law and an acute legal mind which, had he cared in the least degree for wealth and worldly position, would have brought him to the front at the bar. He is a great Sanskrit scholar, a powerful writer and a strong, subtle and lucid thinker. He might have filled a large place in the field of contemporary Asiatic scholarship. Even as it is, his *Orion* and his *Arctic Home* have acquired at once a world-wide recognition and left as strong a mark as can at all be imprinted on the ever-shifting sands of oriental research. His work on the Gita, no mere commentary, but an original criticism and presentation of ethical truth, is a monumental work, the first prose writing of the front rank in weight and importance in the Marathi language, and likely to become a classic. This one book sufficiently proves that had he devoted his energies in this direction, he might easily have filled a large place in the history of Marathi literature and in the history of ethical thought.

so subtle and comprehensive is its thinking, so great the perfection and satisfying force of its style. But it was psychologically impossible for Mr. Tilak to devote his energies in any great degree to another action than the one life-mission for which the Master of his works had chosen him. His powerful literary gift has been given up to a journalistic work, ephemeral as even the best journalistic work must be, but consistently brilliant, vigorous, politically educative through decades, to an extent seldom matched and certainly never surpassed. His scholastic labour has been done almost by way of recreation. Nor can anything be more significant than the fact that the works which have brought him a fame other than that of the politician and patriot, were done in periods of compulsory cessation from his life-work,—planned and partly, if not wholly executed during the imprisonments which could alone enforce leisure upon this unresting worker for his country. Even these by-products of his genius have some reference to the one passion of his life, the renewal, if not the surpassing of the past greatness of the nation by the greatness of its future. His vedic researches seek to fix its prehistoric point of departure; the *Gita-rahasya* takes the scripture which is perhaps the strongest and most comprehensive production of Indian spirituality and justifies to that spirituality by its own authoritative ancient message the sense of the importance of life, of action, of human existence, of man's labour for mankind which is indispensable to the idealism of the modern spirit.

The landmarks of Mr. Tilak's life are landmarks also in the history of his province and his country. His first great step associated him in a pioneer work whose motive was to educate the people for a new life under the new conditions, on the one side, a purely educational movement of which the fruit was the Ferguson College, fitly founding the reawakening of the country by an effort of which co-operation in self-sacrifice was the moving spirit, on the other, the initiation of the *Kesari* newspaper, which since then has figured increasingly as the characteristic and powerful expression of the political mind of Maharashtra. Mr. Tilak's career has counted three periods each of which had an imprisonment for its culminating point. His first imprisonment in the Kolhapur case belongs to this first stage of self-development and development of the Mahratta country for new ideas and activities and for the national future.

The second period brought in a wider conception and a profounder effort. For now it was to reawaken not only the political mind, but the soul of the people by linking its future to its past; it worked by a more strenuous and popular propaganda which reached its height in the organisation of the Shivaji and the Ganapati festivals. His separation from the social reform leader, Agarkar, had opened the way for the peculiar rôle which he has played as a trusted and accredited leader of conservative and religious India in the paths of democratic politics. It was this position which enabled him to effect the union of the new political spirit with the tradition and sentiment of the historic past and of both with the ineradicable religious temperament of the people of which these festivals were the symbol. The congress movement was for a long time purely occidental in its mind, character and methods, confined to the English-educated few, founded on the political rights and interests of the people read in the light of English history and European ideals, but with no roots either in the past of the country or in the inner spirit of the nation. Mr. Tilak was the first political leader to break through the routine of its somewhat academical methods, to bridge the gulf between the present and the past and to restore continuity to the political life of the nation. He developed a language and a spirit and he used methods which indianised the movement and brought into it the masses. To his work of this period we owe that really living, strong and readily organised movement in Maharashtra which has shown its energy and sincerity in more than one crisis and struggle. This divination of the mind and spirit of his people and its needs and this power to seize on the right way to call it forth prove strikingly the political genius of Mr. Tilak; they made him the one man predestined to lead them in this trying and difficult period when all has to be discovered and all has to be reconstructed. What was done then by Mr. Tilak in Maharashtra has been initiated for all India by the swadeshi movement. To bring in the mass of the people, to found the greatness of the future on the greatness of the past, to infuse Indian politics with Indian religious fervour and spirituality, are the indispensable conditions for a great and powerful political awakening in India. Others, writers, thinkers, spiritual leaders, had seen this truth. Mr. Tilak was the first to bring it into the actual field of practical politics. This second period of his labour for his country culminated in a longer and harsher imprisonment which was, as it were, the second seal of the divine hand upon his work; for there can be no diviner seal than suffering for a cause.

A third period, that of the swadeshi movement, brought Mr. Tilak forward prominently as an All-India leader; it gave him at last the wider field, the greater driving power, the larger leverage he needed to bring his life-work rapidly to a head, and not only in Maharashtra but throughout the country. The incidents of that period are too fresh in memory to need recalling. From the inception of the Boycott to the Surat catastrophe and his last and longest imprisonment, which was its sequel, the name and work of Mr. Tilak are a part of Indian history. These three imprisonments, each showing more clearly the moral stuff and quality of the man under the test and glare of suffering, have been the three seals of his career. The first found him one of a small knot of pioneer workers; it marked him out to be the strong and inflexible leader of a strong and sturdy people. The second found him already the inspiring power of a great reawakening of the Maratha spirit; it left him an uncrowned king in the Deccan and gave him that high reputation throughout India, which was the foundation-stone of his present commanding influence. The last found him the leader of an All-India party, the foremost exponent and head of a thorough-going Nationalism: it sent him back to be one of the two or three foremost men of India adored and followed by the whole nation. He now stands in the last period of his life-long toil for his country. It is one in which for the first time some ray of immediate hope and near success shines upon a cause which at one time seemed destined to a long frustration and fulfilment only perhaps after a century of labour, struggle and suffering.

The qualities which have supported him and given him his hard-earned success, have been comparatively rare in Indian politics. The first is his entirely representative character as a born leader for the sub-nation to which he belongs. India is a unity full of diversities and its strength as well as its weakness is rooted in those diversities: the vigour of its national life can exist only by the vigour of its regional life. Therefore in politics as in everything else a leader, to have a firm basis for his life-work, must build it upon a living work and influence in his own sub-race or province. No man was more fitted to do this than Mr. Tilak. He is the very type and incarnation of the Maratha character, the Maratha qualities, the Maratha spirit, but with the unified solidity in the character, the touch of genius in the qualities, the vital force in the spirit which make a great personality readily the representative man of his people. The Maratha race, as their soil and their history have made them, are a rugged, strong and sturdy people, democratic in their every fibre, keenly intelligent and practical to the very marrow, following in ideas, even in poetry, philosophy and religion the drive towards life and action, capable of great fervour, feeling and enthusiasm, like all Indian peoples, but not emotional idealists, having in their thought and speech always a turn for strength, sense, accuracy, lucidity and vigour, in learning and scholarship patient, industrious, careful, thorough and penetrating, in life simple, hardy and frugal, in their temperament courageous, pugnacious, full of spirit, yet with a tact in dealing with hard facts and circumventing obstacles, shrewd yet aggressive diplomatists, born politicians, born fighters. All this Mr. Tilak is with a singular and eminent completeness, and all on a large scale, adding to it all a lucid simplicity of genius, a secret intensity, an inner strength of will, a singlemindedness in aim of quite extraordinary force, which remind one of the brightness, sharpness and perfect temper of a fine sword hidden in a sober scabbard. As he emerged on the political field, his people saw more and more clearly in him their representative man, themselves in large, the genius of their type. They felt him to be of one spirit and make with the great men who had made their past history, almost believed him to be a reincarnation of one of them returned to carry out his old work in a new form and under new conditions. They beheld in him the spirit of Maharashtra once again embodied in a great individual. He occupies a position in his province which has no parallel in the rest of India.

On the wider national field also Mr. Tilak has rare qualities which fit him for the hour and the work. He is in no sense what his enemies have called him, a demagogue: he has not the loose suppleness, the oratorical fervour, the facile appeal to the passions which demagogy requires; his speeches are too much made up of hard and straight thinking, he is too much a man of serious and practical action. None more careless of mere effervescence, emotional applause, popular gush, public ovations. He tolerates them since popular euthusiasm will express itself in that way; but he has always been a little impatient of them as dissipative of serious strength and will and a waste of time and energy which might better have been solidified and devoted to effective work. But he is entirely a democratic politician, of a type not very common among our leaders, one who can both awaken the spirit of the mass and respond to their spirit, able to lead them, but also able to see where he must follow the lead of their predominant sense and will and feelings. He moves among his followers as one of them in a perfect equality, simple and familiar in his dealings with them by the very force of his temperament and character, open, plain and direct and though capable of great reserve, yet, wherever necessary, in his speech, admitting them into his plans and ideas as one taking counsel of them, taking their sense even while enforcing as much as possible his own view of policy and action with all the great strength of quiet will at his command. He has that closeness of spirit to the mass of men, that unpretentious openness of intercourse with them, that faculty of plain and direct speech which interprets their feelings and shows them how to think out what they feel, which are pre-eminently the democratic qualities. For this reason he has always been able to unite all classes of men behind him, to be the leader not only of the educated, but of the people, the merchant, the trader, the villager, the peasant. All Maharashtra understands him when he speaks or writes; all Maharashtra is ready to follow him when he acts. Into his wider field in the troubled swadeshi times he carried the same qualities and the same power of democratic leadership.

It is equally a mistake to think of Mr. Tilak as by nature a revolutionary leader; that is not his character or his political temperament. The Indian peoples generally, with the possible exception of emotional and idealistic Bengal, have nothing or very little of the revolutionary temper; they can be goaded to revolution, like any and every people on the face of the earth, but they have no natural disposition towards it. They are capable of large ideals and fervent enthusiasms, sensitive in feeling and liable to gusts of passionate revolt which are easily appeased by even an appearance of concession; but naturally they are conservative in temperament and deliberate in action. Mr. Tilak, though a strong-willed man and a fighter by nature, has this much of the ordinary Indian temperament, that with a large mind open to progressive ideas he unites a conservative temperament strongly in touch with the sense of his people. In a free India he would probably have figured as an advanced Liberal statesman eager for national progress and greatness, but as careful of every step, as firm and decided in it and always seeking to carry the conservative instinct of the nation with him in every change. He is besides a born Parliamentarian, a leader for the assembly, though always in touch with the people outside as the constant source of the mandate and the final referee in differences. He loves a clear and fixed procedure which he can abide by and use, even while making the most of its details,—of which the theory and practice would be always at his finger ends,—to secure a practical advantage in the struggle of parties. He always set a high value on the Congress for this reason; he saw in it a centralising body, an instrument and a first, though yet shapeless, essay at a popular assembly. Many after Surat spoke of him as the deliberate breaker of the Congress, but to no one was the catastrophe so great a blow as to Mr. Tilak. He did not love the do-nothingness of that assembly, but he valued it both as a great national fact and for its unrealised possibilities and hoped to make of it a central organization for practical work. To destroy an existing and useful institution was alien to his way of seeing and would not have entered into his ideas or his wishes.

Moreover, though he has ideals, he is not an idealist by character. Once the ideal fixed, all the rest is for him practical work, the facing of hard facts, though also the overcoming of them when they stand in the way of the goal, the use of strong and effective means with the utmost care and prudence consistent with the primary need of as rapid an effectivity as will and earnest action can bring about. Though he can be obstinate and iron-willed when his mind is made up as to the necessity of a course of action or the indispensable recognition of a principle, he is always ready for a compromise which will allow of getting real work done, and will take willingly half a loaf rather than no bread, though always with a full intention of getting the whole loaf in good time. But he will not accept chaff or plaster in place of good bread. Nor does he like to go too far ahead of possibilities, and indeed has often shown in this respect a caution highly disconcerting to the more impatient of his followers. But neither would he mistake, like the born Moderate, the minimum effort and the minimum immediate aim for the utmost possibility of the moment. Such a man is no natural revolutionist, but a constitutionalist by temper, though always in such times necessarily the leader of an advanced party or section. A clear constitution he can use, amend and enlarge would have suited him much better than to break existing institutions and get a clear field for innovations which is the natural delight of the revolutionary temperament.

This character of Mr. Tilak's mind explains his attitude in social reform. He is no dogmatic reactionary. The Maratha people are incapable of either the unreasoning or too reasoning rigid conservatism or of the fiery iconoclasm which can exist side by side,—they are often only two sides of the same temper of mind,—in other parts of India. It is attached to its social institutions like all people who lives close to the soil, but it has always shown a readiness to adapt, loosen and accomodate them in practice to the pressure of actual needs. Mr. Tilak shares this general temperament and attitude of his people. But there have also been other reasons which a strong political sense has dictated ; and first, the clear perception that the political movement could not afford to cut itself off from the great mass of the nation or split itself up into warring factions by a premature association of the social reform question with politics. The proper time for that, a politician would naturally feel, is when the country has a free assembly of its own which can consult the needs or carry out the mandates of the people. Moreover, he has felt strongly that political emancipation was the one pressing need for the people of India and that all else not directly connected with it must take a second place; that has been the principle of his own life and he has held that it should be the principle of the national life at the present hour. Let us have first liberty and the organised control of the life of the nation, afterwards we can see how we should use it in social matters; meanwhile let us move on without noise and strife, only so far as actual need and advisability demand and the sense of the people is ready to advance. This attitude may be right or wrong; but, Mr. Tilak being what he is and the nation being what it is, he could take no other.

If, then, Mr. Tilak has throughout his life been an exponent of the idea of radical change in politics and during the swadeshi agitation the head of a party which could be called extremist, it is due to that clear practical sense, essential in a leader of political action, which seizes at once on the main necessity and goes straight without hesitation or deviation to the indispensable means. There are always two classes of political mind : one is pre-occupied with details for their own sake, revels in the petty points of the moment and puts away into the background the great principles and the great necessities, the other sees rather these first and always and details only in relation to them. The one type moves in a routine circle which may or may not have an issue ; it cannot see the forest for the trees and it is only by an accident that it stumbles, if at all, on the way out. The other type takes a mountain-top view of the goal and all the directions and keep that in their mental compass through all the deflections, retardations and tortuosities which the character of the intervening country may compel them to accept ; but these they abridge as much as possible. The former class arrogate the name of statesman in their own day ; it is to the latter that posterity concedes it and sees in them the true leaders of great movements. Mr. Tilak, like all men of pre-eminent political genius, belongs to this second and greater order of mind.

Moreover in India, owing to the divorce of political activity from the actual government and administration of the affairs of the country, an academical turn of thought is too common in our dealings with politics. But Mr. Tilak has never been an academical politician, a "student of politics" meddling with action ; his turn has always been to see actualities and move forward in their light. It was impossible for him to view the facts and needs of current Indian politics of the nineteenth century in the pure serene or the dim religious light of the Witenagemot and the Magna Charta and the constitutional history of England during the past seven centuries, or to accept the academic sophism of a gradual preparation for liberty, or merely to discuss isolated or omnibus grievances and strive to enlighten the darkness of the official mind by luminous speeches and resolutions, as was the general practice of Congress politics till 1905. A national agitation in the country which would make the Congress movement a living and acting force was always his ideal, and what the Congress would not do, he, when still an isolated leader of a handful of enthusiasts in a corner of the country, set out to do in his own strength and for his own hand. He saw from the first that for a people circumstanced like ours there could be only one political question and one aim, not the gradual improvement of the present administration into something in the end fundamentally the opposite of itself, but the early substitution of Indian and national for English and bureaucratic control in the affairs of India. A subject nation does not prepare itself by gradual progress for liberty; it opens by liberty its way to rapid progress. The only progress that has to be made in the preparation for liberty, is progress in the awakening of the national spirit and in the creation of the will to be free and the will to adopt the necessary means and bear the necessary sacrifices for liberty. It is these clear perceptions that have regulated his political career.

Therefore the whole of the first part of his political life was devoted to a vigorous and living propaganda for the reawakening and solidifying of the national life of Maharashtra. Therefore, too, when the Swadeshi agitation gave first opportunity of a large movement in the same sense throughout India, he seized on it with avidity, while his past work in Maharashtra, his position as the leader of a small advanced section in the old Congress politics and his character, sacrifices and sufferings, at once fixed the choice of the New Party on him as their predestined leader. The same master idea made him seize on the four main points which the Bengal agitation had thrown into some beginning of practical form, Swaraj, Swadeshi, National Education and Boycott, and formulate them into a definite programme, which he succeeded in introducing among the resolutions of the Congress at the Calcutta session,—much to the detriment of the uniformity of sage and dignified impotence which had characterised the august, useful and calmly leisurely proceedings of that temperate national body. We all know the convulsion that followed the injection of this foreign matter; but we must see why Mr. Tilak insisted on administering annually so potent a remedy. The four resolutions were for him the first step towards shaking the

Congress out of its torpid tortoise-like gait and turning it into a living and acting body.

Swaraj, complete and early self-government in whatever form, had the merit in his eyes of making definite and near to the national vision the one thing needful, the one aim that mattered, the one essential change that includes all the others. No nation can develop a living enthusiasm or accept great action and great sacrifices for a goal that is lost to its eye in the mist of far-off centuries; it must see it near and distinct before it, magnified by a present hope, looming largely and actualised as a living aim whose early realisation only depends on a great, sustained and sincere effort. National education meant for him the training of the young generation in the new national spirit to be the architects of liberty, if that was delayed, the citizens of a free India which had rediscovered itself, if the preliminary condition were rapidly fulfilled. Swadeshi meant an actualising of the national self-consciousness and the national will and the readiness to sacrifice which would fix them in the daily mind and daily life of the people. In Boycott, which was only a popular name for passive resistance, he saw the means to give to the struggle between the two ideas in conflict, bureaucratic control and national control, a vigorous shape and body and to the popular side a weapon and an effective form of action. Himself a man of organisation and action, he knew well that by action most, and not by thought and speech alone, can the will of a people be vivified, trained and made solid and enduring. To get a sustained authority from the Congress for a sustained effort in these four directions, seemed to him of capital importance; this was the reason for his inflexible insistence on their unchanged inclusion when the programme seemed to him to be in danger.

Yet also, because he is a practical politician and a man of action, he has always, so long as the essentials were safe, been ready to admit any change in name or form or any modification of programme or action dictated by the necessities of the time. Thus during the movement of 1905—1910 the Swadeshi leader and the Swadeshi party insisted on agitation in India and discouraged reliance on agitation in England, because the awaking and fixing of a self-reliant national spirit and will in India was the one work for the hour and in England no party or body of opinion existed which would listen to the national claim, nor could exist,—as anybody with the least knowledge of English politics could have told,—until that claim had been unmistakably and insistently made and was clearly supported by the fixed will of the nation. The Home Rule leader and the Home Rule party of to-day, which is only the "New Party" reborn with a new name, form and following, insist on the contrary on vigorous and speedy agitation in England, because the claim and the will have both been partially, but not sufficiently recognised, and because a great and growing British party now exists which is ready to make the Indian ideal part of its own programme. So, too, they insisted then on Swaraj and rejected with contempt all petty botching with the administration, because so alone could the real issue be made a living thing to the nation; now they accept readily enough a fairly advanced but still half-and-half scheme, but always with the proviso that the popular principle receives substantial embodiment and the full ideal is included as an early goal and not put off to a far-distant future. The leader of men in war or politics will always distrust petty and episodical gains which, while giving false hopes, are merely nominal and put off or even endanger the real issue, but will always seize on any advantage which brings decisive victory definitely nearer. It is only the pure idealist,—but let us remember that he too has his great and indispensable uses,—who insists always on either all or nothing. Not revolutionary methods or revolutionary idealism, but the clear sight and the direct propaganda and action of the patriotic political leader insisting on the one thing needful and the straight way to drive at it, have been the sense of Mr. Tilak's political career.

The speeches in this book belong both to the Swadeshi and the Home Rule periods, but mostly to the latter. They show Mr. Tilak's mind and policy and voice with great force that will and political thought now dominant in the country which he has so prominently helped to create. Mr. Tilak has none of the gifts of the orator which many lesser men have possessed, but his force of thought and personality make him in his own way a powerful speaker. He is at his best in his own Marathi tongue rather than in English; for there he finds always the apt and telling phrase, the striking application, the vigorous figure which go straight home to the popular mind. But there is essentially the same power in both. His words have directness and force—no force can be greater—of a sincere and powerful mind always going immediately to the aim in view, the point before it, expressing it with a bare, concentrated economy of phrase and the insistence of the hammer full on the head of the nail which drives it in with a few blows. But the speeches have to be read with his life, his character, his life-long aims as their surrounding atmosphere. That is why I have dwelt on their main points;—not that all I have said is not well known, but the repetition of known facts has its use when they are important and highly significant.

Two facts of his life and character have to be insisted on as of special importance to the country because they give a great example of two things in which its political life was long deficient and is even now not sufficient. First, the inflexible will of the patriot and man of sincere heart and thorough action which has been the very grain of his character; for aspirations, emotion, enthusiasm are nothing without this; will alone creates and prevails. And wish and will are not the same thing, but divided by a great gulf: the one, which is all most of us get to, is a puny, tepid and inefficient thing and, even when most enthusiastic, easily discourage and turned from its object; the other can be a giant to accomplish and endure. Secondly, the readiness to sacrifice and face suffering, not needlessly or with a useless bravado, but with a firm courage when it comes, to bear it and to outlive, returning to work with one's scars as if nothing had happened. No prominent man in India has suffered more for his country; none has taken his sacrifices and sufferings more quietly and as a matter of course.

The first part of Mr. Tilak's life-work is accomplished. Two great opportunities have hastened its success, of which he has taken full advantage. The lavalike flood of the Swadeshi movement fertilised the soil and did for the country in six years the work of six ordinary decades; it fixed the goal of freedom in the mind of the people. The sudden irruption of Mrs. Besant into the field with her unequalled gift,—born of her untiring energy, her flaming enthusiasm, her magnificent and magnetic personality, her spiritual force,—for bringing an ideal into the stage of actuality with one rapid whirl and rush, has been the second factor. Indeed the presence of three such personalities as Mr. Tilak, Mrs. Besant and Mr. Gandhi at the head and in the heart of the present movement, should itself be a sure guarantee of success. The nation has accepted the near fulfilment of his great aim as its own political aim, the one object of its endeavour, its immediate ideal. The Government of India and the British nation have accepted it as their goal in Indian administration; a powerful party, in England, the party which seems to command the future, has pronounced for its speedy and total accomplishment. A handful of dissentients there may be in the country who still see only petty gains in the present and the rest in the dim vista of the centuries, but with this insignificant exception, all the Indian provinces and communities have spoken with one voice Mr. Tilak's principles of work have been accepted; the ideas which he had so much trouble to enforce have become the commonplaces and truisms of our political thought. The only question that remains is rapidity of a now inevitable evolution. That is the hope for which Mr. Tilak still stands, a leader of all India. Only when it is accomplished, will his life-work be done; not till then can he rest while he lives, even though age grows on him and infirmities gather,—for his spirit will always remain fresh and vigorous,—any more than a river can rest before the power of its waters has found their goal and discharged them into the sea. But whether that end,—the end of a first stage of our new national life, the beginning of a greater India reborn for self-fulfilment and the service of humanity.—come to-morrow or after a little delay, its accomplishment is now safe, and Mr. Tilak's name stands already for history as a nation-builder, one of the half-dozen greatest political personalities, memorable figures, representative men of the nation in this most critical period of India's destinies, a name to be remembered gratefully so long as the country has pride in its past and hope for its future.

AUROBINDO GHOSE.

A STANDARD CHARACTER FOR INDIAN LANGUAGES

[*Speech delivered at Benares, at the Nagari Pracharni Sabha Conference, under the Presidency of Mr. R. C. Dutt, in December,* 1905].

GENTLEMEN,—The scope and object of the Nagari Pracharni Sabha has already been explained to you by the president. I should have gladly dilated on the same. But as ten speakers are to follow me within an hour and a half, I must forego the pleasure and restrict myself, during the few minutes at my disposal to a brief mention of the points which I think ought to be kept in view in endeavouring to work on the lines adopted by the Sabha.

The first and the most important thing we have to remember is that this movement is not merely for establishing a common character for the Northern India. It is a part and parcel of a larger movement, I may say a National Movement to have a common language for the whole of India; for a common language is an important element of nationality. It is by a common language that you express your thoughts to others; and Manu rightly says that everything is comprehended or proceeded from *vak* or language. Therefore if you want to draw a nation together there is no force more powerful than to have a common language for all. And that is the end which the Sabha has kept in view.

But how is the end to be attained? We aim at having a common language not only for Northern India, but I will say, in course of time, for the whole of India including the Southern of the Madras Presidency, and when the scope of our labours is so widened our difficulties seem to grow apace. First of all we have to face what may be called the historic difficulties. The contests between the Aryans and the non-Aryans in ancient, and between the Mahomedans and the Hindus in later times have destroyed the linguistic harmony of the country. In Northern India the languages spoken by the Indian population are mostly Aryan, being derived from Sanskrit; while those in the South are Dravidian in origin. The difference exists not only in words but in the characters in which those words are written. Next to this is the difference between Urdu and Hindi to which so much prominence is given in this province. On our side we have also the Modi or the running script character as distinguished from the Balabodha or the Devanagari in which the Marathi books are ordinarily printed.

There are, therefore, two great important elements which we have to harmonise and bring together, under our common character or language before we venture to go to the Mahomedan or Persian characters. I have already said that though a common language for India is the ultimate end we have in view, we begin with the lowest step of the ladder, I mean a common character for Hindus. But here too we have to harmonise the two elements now mentioned—the Aryan or the Devanagari character, and the Dravidian or the Tamil character. It should be noted that the distinction is not one of character only inasmuch as there are certain sounds in the Dravidian languages which are not to be found in any Aryan language.

We have resolved to proceed step by step, and as explained to you by the president we have at first taken up in hand only the group of the Aryan languages *i.e.*, those derived from Sanskrit. These are Hindi, Bengali, Marathi, Gujarathi and Gurumuki. There are other sub-dialects, but I have named the principal ones. These languages are all derived from Sanskrit; and the characters in which they are written are also modifications of the ancient characters of India. In course of time each of these languages has, however, developed its own peculiarities in grammar, pronunciation and characters, though the alphabet in each is nearly the same.

The Nagari Pracharni Sabha aims at having a common character for all these Aryan languages, so that when a book is printed in that character it may be more readily intelligible to all the people speaking the Aryan languages. I think we all agree on this point and admit its utility. But the difficulty arises, when a certain character is proposed as best fitted to be the common character for all. Thus, for instance the Bengalis may urge that the characters in which they write their language are more ancient than those adopted by the Gujarathi or Marathi speaking people, and that Bengali should therefore be selected as a common character for all. There are others who think that the Devanagari, as you find it in the printed books, is the oldest character and therefore it is entitled to be the common character for all the Aryan languages.

I do not think, however, that we can decide this question on poor historic grounds. If you go to ancient inscriptions you will find that no less than ten different characters were in use at different times since the days of Ashoka and that Kharoshtri or Brahmi is believed to be the oldest of them all. Since then all letters have undergone a great deal of change; and all our existing characters are modifications of some one or other of the ancient characters. It would, I think, therefore be idle to decide the question of common character on purely antiquarian basis.

To avoid this difficulty it was at one time suggested that we should all adopt Roman characters; and one reason advanced in support thereof was that it would give a common character both for Asia and Europe.

Gentlemen, the suggestion appears to me to be utterly ridiculous. The Roman alphabet, and therefore Roman character, is very defective and entirely unsuited to express the sounds used by us. It has been found to be defective even by English grammarians. Thus while sometimes a single letter has three or four sounds, sometimes a single sound is represented by two or three letters. Add to it the difficulty of finding Roman characters or letters that would exactly represent the sounds in our languages without the use of any diacritic marks, and the ridiculousness of the suggestion would be patent to all.

If a common character is needed for us all, it should be, you will therefore see, a more perfect character than the Roman. European Sanskritists have declared that the Devanagari alphabet is more perfect than any which obtains in Europe. And with this clear opinion before us, it would be suicidal to go to any other alphabet in our search for a common character for all the Aryan languages in India. No, I would go further and say that the classification of letters and sounds on which we have bestowed so much labour in India and which we find perfected in the works of Panini is not to be found in any other language in the world. That is another reason why the Devanagari alphabet is the best suited to represent the different sounds we all use. If you compare the different characters given at the end of each book published in the

Sacred Books of the East Series you will be convinced of what I say. We have one sound for one letter and one letter for each sound. I do not think, therefore, that there can be any difference of opinion as to what alphabet we should adopt. The Devanagari is pre-eminently such an alphabet. The question is one of character or the form in writing which the letters of the alphabet assume in different provinces; and I have already said that this question cannot be solved on mere antiquarian grounds.

Like Lord Curzon's standard time we want a standard character. Well, if Lord Curzon had attempted to give us a standard character on national lines he would have been entitled to our respect far more than by giving us a standard time. But it has not been done; and we must do it ourselves giving up all provincial prejudices. The Bengalis naturally take pride in their own character. I do not blame them for it. There are others in Gujarath who say that their character is easy to write because they omit the head-line. The Maharashtras on the other hand may urge that Marathi is the character in which Sanskrit is written, and therefore, it ought to be the common character for the whole of India.

I fully appreciate the force of these remarks. But we must come to a solution of the question and for that purpose discuss the subject in a business-like and practical manner. Whatever character we adopt, it must be easy to write, elegant to the eye and capable of being written with fluency. The letters that you devise must again be sufficient to express all the sounds in different Aryan languages, nay, must be capable of being extended to express the Dravidian sounds without diacritic marks. There should be one letter for every sound and *vice versa*. That is what I mean by sufficient and complete character. And if we put our heads together it would not be difficult to devise such a character based on the existing ones. In determining upon such a character we shall have to take into consideration the fact, namely, which of the existing characters is or are used over a wider area. For a single character used over a wider area if suited in other respects will naturally claim preference to be a common character as far as it goes.

When you have appointed your committee for the purpose and found out a common character, I think we shall have to go to Government and urge upon its attention the necessity of introducing in the vernacular school books of each province a few lessons in this standard character, so that the next generation may become familiar with it from its school days. Studying a new character is not a difficult task. But there is a sort of reluctance to study a new character after one's studies are completed. This reluctance can be overcome by the way I have suggested and herein Government can help us. It is not a political question as such, though in the end everything may be said to be political. A Government that gave us a standard time and standard system of weights and measures would not, I think, object to lend its help to a scheme which aims to secure a standard character for all Aryan languages.

When this common character is established it would not be difficult to read the books printed in one dialect of the Aryan language by those who use a different dialect of the same? My own difficulty in not understanding a Bengali book is that I cannot read the characters. If a Bengali book is printed in the Devanagari characters I can follow the author to a great extent, if not wholly, so as to understand the purport of the book; for, over fifty per cent of the words used will be found borrowed or derived from Sanskrit. We are all fast adopting new ideas from the West, and with the help of the parent tongue, Sanskrit, coining new words to express the same. Here, therefore, is another direction in which we may work for securing a common language for all and I am glad to see that by preparing a dictionary of scientific terms in Hindi, the Sabha is doing a good service in this line. I should have liked to say something on this point. But as there are other speakers to follow me, I do not think I shall be justified in doing so and therefore resume my seat with your permission.

THE BHARATA DHARMA MAHAMANDALA

[*Benares, 3rd January*, 1906]

I am sorry I cannot address you in any other language except Marathi and English. English should be boycotted for religious purposes. But I cannot help and hope you will excuse me. I shall speak a few words on the importance of Hindu religion, its present condition and efforts that are being made to preserve it from decay. What is Hindu religion? If you go to the different parts of India, you will find different views about Hindu religion entertained by different people. Here you are mostly Vaishnavas or followers of Shri Krishna. If you go to the south, you will meet followers of Ramanuja and such others. What is Hindu religion then? Bharata Dharma Mahamandala cannot be a Mahamandala unless it includes and co-ordinates these different sections and parts. Its name can only be significant if different sections of Hindu religion are united under its banner. All these different sects are so many branches of the Vedic religion. The term Sanatana Dharma shows that our religion is very old—as old as the history of the human race itself. Vedic religion was the religion of the Aryans from a very early time. But you all know no branch can stand by itself. Hindu religion as a whole is made up of different parts co-related to each other as so many sons and daughters of one great religion. If this idea is kept in view and if we try to unite the various sections it will be consolidated in a mighty force. So long as you are divided amongst yourselves, so long as one section does not recognise its affinity with another, you cannot hope to rise as Hindus. Religion is an element in nationality. The word Dharma means a tie and comes from the root *dhri* to bear or hold. What is there to hold together? To connect the soul with God, and man with man. Dharma means our duties towards God and duty towards man. Hindu religion as such provides for a moral as well as social tie. This being our definition we mut go back to the past and see how it was worked out. During Vedic times India was a self-contained country. It was united as a great nation. That unity has disappeared bringing on us great degradation and it becomes the duty of the leaders to revive that union. A Hindu of this place is as much a Hindu as the one from Madras or Bombay. You might put on a different dress, speak a different language, but you should remember that the inner sentiments which move you all are the same. The study of the Gita, Ramayana and Mahabharata produce the same ideas throughout the country. Are not these—common allegiance to the Vedas, the Gita and the Ramayana—our common heritage? If we lay stress on it forgetting all the minor differences that exist between different sects, then by the grace of Providence we shall ere long be able to consolidate all the different sects into a mighty Hindu nation. This ought to be the ambition of every Hindu. If you thus work to unite, you will find within a few years one feeling and one thought actuating and dominating all people throughout the country. This is the work we have to do. The present condition of our religion is not at all one that is desirable. We think ourselves separated and the feeling of that unity which was at the root of our advancement in the past is gone. It is certainly an unfortunate circumstance that we should have so many sections and sub-sections. It is the duty of an association like the Bharata Dharma Mahamandala to work to restore the lost and forgotten union. In the absence of unity India cannot claim its place among the nations of the world. For some two hundred years India was in the same condition as it is to-day. Buddhism flourished and attacks were made on Hindu religion by Buddhists and Jains. After 600 years of chaos rose one great leader, Shankaracharya and he brought together all the common philosophical elements of our religion and proved and preached them in such a way that Buddhism was swept away from the land.

We have the grand and eternal promise Shri Krishna has given in the Gita that whenever there is a decay of Dharma, He comes down to restore it.

When there is a decay owing to disunion, when good men are persecuted, then Shri Krishna comes down to save us. There is no religion on the face of the earth except the Hindu religion wherein we find such a hopeful promise that God comes to us as many times as necessary. After Mahomed no prophet is promised, and Jesus Christ comes once for ever. No religion holds such promise full of hope. It is because of this that the Hindu religion is not dead. We are never without hope. Let heretics say what they may. A time will come when our religious thoughts and our rights will be vindicated. Each man is doing his best, and as the association is doing its best, every Hindu is welcome to assist it and carry it to its goal. If we do not find men coming forward let us hope they will do so in the next generation. We are never without hope; no other religion has such a definite and sacred promise as we have of Shri Krishna. It is based on truth and truth never dies. I say it and I am prepared to prove this statement. I believe that truth is not vouchsafed to one only. The great characteristic of truth is that it is universal and catholic. It is not confined to any particular race. Hindu religion tolerates all religions. Our religion says that all religions are based on truth, "you follow yours, I mine."

Shri Krishna says that the followers of other religions worship God though not in a proper form. Shri Krishna does not say that the followers of other religions would be doomed to eternal hell. I challenge any body to point out to me a similar text from the scriptures of other religions. It cannot be found in any other religion, because they are partial truth while our Hindu religion is based on the whole, the Sanatan truth, and therefore it is bound to triumph in the end. Numerical strength also is a great strength. Can the religion which counts its followers by crores die? Never, unless the crores of our fellow-followers are suddenly swept away our religion will not die. All that is required for our glorious triumph and success is that we should unite all the different sects on a common platform and let the stream of Hindu religion flow through one channel with mighty consolidated and concentrated force. This is the work which the Bharata Dharma Mandala has to do and accomplish. Let us be all united. Because a particular man wears a particular dress, speaks a different tongue, worships a particular *devata*, is that any reason for our withdrawing our hands of fellowship to our Hindu brother? The character of our Hindu religion is very comprehensive—as comprehensive as its literature itself; we have a wonderful literature. Wisdom, as is concentrated in Gita and epitomised in about 700 verses, that wisdom, I am confident, cannot be defeated or overcome by any philosophy, be it Western or any other. Now I turn to the forces that are arrayed against us. There are mainly two forces of (1) science and (2) Christianity. If our religion is threatened with any hostile criticism, it comes from these two. As for the first, a great change is coming over the West and truths that are discovered by them were known to our Rishis. Modern science is gradually justifying and vindicating our ancient wisdom. With the establishment of Physical Research Societies and the expansion of scientific knowledge they have come to understand that the fundamental principles of our religion are based on truth that can be proved. Take an instance. Chaitanya pervades everything. It is strictly a Hindu theory. Professor Bose has recently shown that this Vedantic doctrine is literally true according to modern science. Take the doctrine of the survival of soul independent of the body.

Doctrines of Karma and Re-incarnation go with it. Spencer never believed in these. But recently it has been our great privilege to see that Sir Oliver Lodge and Mayor and others have declared that the soul does not die with body; so much now they are convinced of. Modern science accepts the doctrine of Karma if not of re-incarnation. But it is not the belief of Christianity. They hold that God gives a new soul each and every time. Thus it would be seen that a change is coming over the West. Our enemies are fast disappearing before the teachings of modern science, take courage and work hard for the final triumph. If you make a little effort and aim at union, you have a bright future before you. Now-a-days, Vedanta is not only read but studied by Americans. No European doctor believes that the beating of the heart can be voluntarily stopped. But it has been proved to the contrary. Vedanta and Yoga have been fully vindicated by modern science and these aim at giving you spiritual union. It is our clear duty, therefore, to follow truth and re-edit our scriptures and place them before the world in the light of modern science that they may be acceptable to all. But I tell you again unity is necessary for such work. You would be wanting in duty to yourself and to your ancestors if you do not give up provincial prejudices and promote unity that underlies all sects. We have been very idle. We have grown so stupid owing to our idleness that we are required to be told by foreigners that our treasures conceal gold and not iron. Modern science and education are prepared to help you if you take advantage of them, and time will come when instead of Christians preaching Christianity here we shall see our preachers preaching Sanatan Dharma all over the world. Concentrate all your forces. The idea of a Hindu University where our old religion will be taught along with modern science is a very good one and should have the support of all. In conclusion, I would again draw your attention to bring about a harmonious union of all sects and rightly claim and obtain our rightful place among the nations of the world.

THE POLITICAL SITUATION

[*Speech delivered by Mr. Tilak, at Calcutta, under the presidency of Babu Motilal Ghose, on 7th June,* 1906].

MR. CHAIRMAN AND GENTLEMEN,—I am unable to impress you with my feeling and sentiment. I express my gratefulness on my own behalf and that of my friends for the splendid reception accorded to us. This reception is given not to me personally but as a representative of the Marathi nation. This honour is due to the Marathi nation for the services and sympathy towards the Bengali race in their present crisis. The chairman has said that times have altered and I add that the situation is unique. India is under a foreign rule and Indians welcomed the change at one time. Then many races were the masters and they had no sympathy and hence the change was welcomed and that was the cause why the English succeeded in establishing an empire in India. Men then thought that the change was for their good. The confusion which characterised native rule was in striking contrast with the constitutional laws of the British Government. The people had much hope in the British Government, but they were much disappointed in their anticipations. They hoped that their arts and industries would be fostered under British rule and they would gain much from their new rulers. But all those hopes had been falsified. The people were now compelled to adopt a new line, namely, to fight against the bureaucracy.

Hundred years ago it was said, and believed by the people, that they were socially inferior to their rulers and as soon as they were socially improved they would obtain liberties and privileges. But subsequent events have shown that this was not based on sound logic. Fifty years ago Mr. Dadabhai Naoroji, the greatest statesman of India, thought that Government would grant them rights and privileges when they were properly educated, but that hope is gone. Now it might be said that they were not fitted to take part in the administration of the country owing to their defective education. But, I ask, whose fault it is. The Government has been imparting education to the people and hence the fault is not theirs but of the Government. The Government is imparting an education to make the people fit for some subordinate appointments. Professions have been made that one day the people would be given a share in the administration of the country. This is far from the truth. What did Lord Curzon do? He saw that this education was becoming dangerous and he made the Government control more strict. He passed the Universities Act and thus brought all schools under Government control. Education in future would pin the people to service only and they now want to reform it. In

Bombay such an attempt was first made in founding the Fergusson College. In 1880 and in 1884 the Government showed willingness to hand over Government Colleges to the control of the Fergusson College but now that institution has gone partially into the hands of the Government.

Policy of justice and efficiency was the policy under which the people are now being governed. By justice is meant justice not between the rulers and the ruled but that between subjects and subjects; by efficiency the efficiency of bureaucracy. Assurances had been given which were expressly pronounced impracticable. Even Lord Curzon has declared that the Queen's Proclamation was an impossibility. This was said not by an ordinary Englishman but by a Viceroy. Bureaucracy has developed a policy beyond which they are determined not to go. It is hopeless to expect anything from the rulers. The rulers have developed a system which they are not prepared to alter in spite of the protests of the people.

Protests are of no avail. Mere protest, not backed by self-reliance, will not help the people. Days of protests and prayers have gone. Shivaji heard the protests of the people and the *jijia* tax was repealed. Good wishes between master and servant are impossible. It may be possible between equals. The people must show that they are fit for privileges. They must take such departments as finance in their own hands and the rulers will then be bound to give them to the people. That is the key of success. It is impossible to expect that our petitions will be heard unless backed by firm resolution. Do not expect much from a change in government. Three P's—pray, please and protest—will not do unless backed by solid force. Look to the examples of Ireland, Japan and Russia and follow their methods. You probably have read the speech delivered by Arthur Griffin and we must consider the way as to how to build a nation on Indian soil.

The rulers have now a definite policy and you are asking them to change it. It is only possible that they will have enlightened despotism in place of pure despotism. It is idle to expect much by educating the British public. You will not be able to convince them by mere words. The present system of administration is unsuited to this country and we must prove it. Mr. Morley has said that he was unable to overthrow the bureaucracy. The whole thing rests with the people. We must make our case not by mere words but we must prove it by actual facts. We must show that the country cannot be governed well by the present method. We must convince the Government of this.

But can this be done? We must either proceed onward or give up the cause altogether. Do not rely much upon the sympathy of the rulers. Mr. Morley has given a strange illustration of his sympathy in the partition question. Mr. Morley has said that he has full sympathy with the people but he cannot or will not undo partition. An apt illustration of this sympathy will be found in the laws of the land. Punishment of whipping is provided in the Penal Code and there is another law which provides that the sufferer will be sent to hospital for treatment. If you want that sort of sympathy Mr. Morley is ready to give it to you. If you forget your grievances by hearing words of sympathy then the cause is gone. You must make a permanent cause of grievance. Store up the grievances till they are removed. Partition grievance will be the edifice for the regeneration of India. Do not give up this partition grievance for the whole of India is at your back. It is a cornerstone and I envy the people of Bengal for laying this cornerstone.

Shivaji was born at a time when there was darkness and helplessness. I believe that Bengal will produce such a leader at this juncture who will follow the great Maharatta leader not in method but in spirit. This festival shows that Providence has not forsaken us. I hope that God will give us such a leader who would regenerate the country by his self-sacrifice, ardent devotion, disinterested action. We must raise a nation on his soil. Love of nation is one's first duty. Next comes religion and the Government. Our duty to the nation will be the first.

Swadeshi and Swadeshi will be our cry for ever

and by this we will grow in spite of the wishes of the rulers. Swadeshi and national education are the two methods.

IS SHIVAJI NOT A NATIONAL HERO ?

Hero-worship is a feeling deeply implanted in human nature; and our political aspirations need all the strength which the worship of a Swadeshi hero is likely to inspire into our minds. For this purpose Shivaji is the only hero to be found in the Indian history. He was born at a time when the whole nation required relief from misrule; and by his self-sacrifice and courage he proved to the world that India was not a country forsaken by Providence. It is true that the Mahomedans and the Hindus were then divided; and Shivaji who respected the religious scruples of the Mahomedans, had to fight against the Mogul rule that had become unbearable to the people. But it does not follow from this that, now that the Mahomedans and the Hindus are equally shorn of the power they once possessed and are governed by the same laws and rules, they should not agree to accept as a hero one who in his own days took a bold stand against the tyranny of his time. It is not preached nor is it to be at all expected that the methods adopted by Shivaji should be adopted by the present generation. The charge brought by the Anglo-Indian writers in this connection is a fiction of their own brain and is put forward simply to frighten away the timid amongst us. No one ever dreams that every incident in Shivaji's life is to be copied by any one at present. It is the *spirit* which actuated Shivaji in his doings that is held forth as the proper ideal to be kept constantly in view by the rising generation. No amount of misrepresentation can succeed in shutting out this view of the question from our vision; and we hope and trust that our Mahomedan friends will not be misled by such wily methods. We do not think that the Anglo-Indian writers will object to England worshipping Nelson or France worshipping the great Napolean on the ground that such national festivals would alienate the sympathies of either nation from the other, or would make the existence of amicable relations between the two nations an impossibility in future. And yet the same advice is administered to us in a patronising tone by these Anglo-Indian critics, being unmindful of the fact that we have now become sufficiently acquainted with their tactics to take their word for gospel truth. The Shivaji festival is not celebrated to alienate or even to irritate the Mahomedans. Times are changed, and, as observed above, the Mahomedans and the Hindus stand in the same boat or on the same platform so far as the political condition of the people is concerned. Can we not both of us derive some inspiration from the life of Shivaji under these circumstances? That is the real question at issue; and if this can be answered in the affirmative it matters little that Shivaji was born in Maharashtra. This aspect of the question has been clearly perceived and exclaimed by the leading Indian papers in Bengal such as the *Patrika* and the *Bengalee*; and there is little chance of the serpentine wisdom of the Anglo-Indian writers being blindly accepted by the parties for whom it is meant. We are not against a festival being started in honour of Akbar or any other hero from old Indian history. Such festivals will have their own worth; but that of Shivaji has a peculiar value of its own for the whole country. and it is the duty of every one to see that this characteristic of the festival is not ignored or misrepresented. Every hero, be he Indian or European, acts according to the spirit of his times; and we must therefore judge of his individual acts by the standard prevalent in his time. If this principle be accepted we can find nothing in Shivaji's life to which one can take exception. But as stated above we need not go so far. What makes Shivaji a national hero for the present is the spirit which actuated him throughout and not his deeds as such. His life clearly shows that Indian races do not so soon lose the vitality which gives them able leaders at critical times. That is the lesson which the Mahomedans and the Hindus have to learn from the history of the great Mahratta Chief; and the Shivaji festival is intended to emphasise the same lesson. It is a sheer misrepresentation to suppose that the worship of Shivaji includes invocations to fight either with the Mahomedans or with the Government. It was only in conformity with the political circumstances of the country at the time that Shivaji was born in Maharashtra. But a future leader may be born anywhere in India and who knows, may even be a Mahomedan. That is the right view of the question, and we do not think that the Anglo-Indian writers can succeed in diverting our attention from it."—(*The Mahratta, 24th June, 1906*).

HONEST SWADESHI

[*Speech delivered on Sunday, the 23rd December,* 1906, *in Beadon Square, Calcutta, under the presidency of Lala Lajpat Rai*] :—

I did not expect to have to speak on the day on which my long journey from Poona came to an end, but circumstances appear to have left me no choice. Lord Minto opened the Industrial Exhibition here the other day and, in doing so, said that honest Swadeshism should be dissociated from political aspirations. In other words the Swadeshi agitation had, within the last eighteen months, been carried on by the workers for motives other than those professed and for ends not yet disclosed. This is entirely an unfair representation of the existing state of things and can easily be demonstrated to be so. To begin with, if Lord Minto thinks the Swadeshi workers dishonest, why should he have associated himself with them by consenting to open the Exhibition? Further, if Lord Minto is honest, and our Bengal leaders who have been preaching the Swadeshi cause are dishonest, why should they have invited his Lordship to do the formal and the ceremonious act of declaring the Exhibition open? So taken either way, it will appear that his Lordship and our leaders cannot possibly hit it off together. If he did not want us, we shall certainly be able to do without him. So his consenting to perform the opening ceremony was clearly a great blunder. Then is our movement really dishonest? In Germany, France, America, Governments protect their infant industries by imposing taxes on imports. The Government of India should also have done the same as it professes to rule India in the interests of Indians. It failed in its duty, so the people are trying to do for themselves what the Government ought to have done years and years ago. No, Lord Minto dares not call the Emperor of Germany dishonest nor can he similarly characterise the presidents of the French or American Republics. How then can our leaders be called dishonest? Are they to be abused because they are endeavouring to do what the Government has culpably omitted to do? As head of a despotic Government, his Lordship cannot possibly sympathise with the political aspirations and agitations of the people, and it may be expected that he may maintain an unbroken silence about it. Had I been in his Lordship's position I would have done so, but why should Lord Minto call us dishonest? There is a harder word that is on my lips, but to say the least it is impolitic of Lord Minto to have said so. There it was said that Swadeshi was an industrial movement and has nothing to do with politics. We all know that Government is not engaged in commerce. It might have begun that way but it certainly does not trade now. Did it not protect British trade and adopt measures to promote it? If the Indian Government dissociates itself from the commercial aspirations of the British nation, then it will be time for Swadeshi workers to consider the question of dissociating their movement from politics. But so long as politics and commerce are blended together in this policy of the Government of India, it will be a blunder to dissociate Swadeshi from politics. In fact, Swadeshism is a large term which includes politics and to be a true Swadeshi one must look on all lines—whether political or industrial or economical—which converge our people towards the status of a civilised nation. Gentlemen, I insist on your emphatically repudiating the charge of dishonesty.

TENETS OF THE NEW PARTY

[*Calcutta, 2nd January*, 1907]

Two new words have recently come into existence with regard to our politics, and they are *Moderates* and *Extremists*. These words have a specific relation to time, and they, therefore, will change with time. The Extremists of to-day will be Moderates to-morrow, just as the Moderates of to-day were Extremists yesterday. When the National Congress was first started and Mr. Dadabhai's views, which now go for Moderates, were given to the public, he was styled an Extremist, so that you will see that the term Extremist is an expression of progress. We are Extremists to-day and our sons will call themselves Extremists and us Moderates. Every new party begins as Extremists and ends as Moderates. The sphere of practical politics is not unlimited. We cannot say what will or will not happen 1,000 years hence—perhaps during that long period, the whole of the white race will be swept away in another glacial period. We must, therefore, study the present and work out a programme to meet the present condition.

It is impossible to go into details within the time at my disposal. One thing is granted, *viz.*, that this Government does not suit us. As has been said by an eminent statesman—the government of one country by another can never be a successful, and therefore, a permanent Government. There is no difference of opinion about this fundamental proposition between the Old and New schools. One fact is that this alien Government has ruined the country. In the beginning, all of us were taken by surprise. We were almost dazed. We thought that everything that the rulers did was for our good and that this English Government has descended from the clouds to save us from the invasions of Tamerlane and Chengis Khan, and, as they say, not only from foreign invasions but from internecine warfare, or the internal or external invasions, as they call it. We felt happy for a time, but it soon came to light that the peace which was established in this country did this, as Mr. Dadabhai has said in one place—that we were prevented from going at each other's throats, so that a foreigner might go at the throat of us all. Pax Britannica has been established in this country in order that a foreign Government may exploit the country. That this is the effect of this Pax Britannica is being gradually realised in these days. It was an unhappy circumstance that it was not realized sooner. We believed in the benevolent intentions of the Government, but in politics there is no benevolence. Benevolence is used to sugar-coat the declarations of self-interest, and we were in those days deceived by the apparent benevolent intentions under which rampant self-interest was concealed. That was our state then. But soon a change came over us. English education, growing poverty, and better familiarity with our rulers, opened our eyes and our leaders; especially, the venerable leader who presided over the recent Congress was the first to tell us that the drain from the country was ruining it, and if the drain was to continue, there was some great disaster awaiting us. So terribly convinced was he of this that he went over from here to England and spent 25 years of his life in trying to convince the English people of the injustice that is being done to us. He worked very hard. He had conversations and interviews with Secretaries of State, with Members of Parliament—and with what result?

He has come here at the age of 82 to tell us that he is bitterly disappointed. Mr. Gokhale, I know, is not disappointed. He is a friend of mine and I believe that this is his honest conviction. Mr. Gokhale is not disappointed but is ready to wait another 80 years till he is disappointed like Mr. Dadabhai.

He is young, younger than myself, and I can very well see that disappointment cannot come in a single interview, from interviews which have lasted only for a year or so. If Dadabhai is disappointed, what reason is there that Gokhale shall not, after 20 years? It is said there is a revival of Liberalism, but how long will it last? Next year it might be, they are out of power, and are we to wait till there is another revival of Liberalism, and then again if that goes down and a third revival of Liberalism takes place; and after all what can a liberal Government do? I will quote the observation of the father of the Congress Mr. A. O. Hume. This was made in 1893. Let the Government be Liberal or Conservative, rest sure that they will not yield to you willingly anything. A Liberal Government means that the Government or the members of the Government are imbued with Liberal principles because they want to have the administration of their country conducted on those principles. They are Liberals in England, but I have seen Liberals in England come out to India to get into conservative ways. Many of the Civilian officers from schools and colleges, when they come out are very good Liberals. Coming in contact with Anglo-Indian men or when they marry Anglo-Indian women, they change their views, and by the time they leave India they are Conservatives. This has been the experience all over. So Liberal or Conservative, the point is, is any one prepared to give you those rights and concessions which intellectually a philosopher may admit to be fit to be conceded or granted to a subject nation in course of time? It is intellectual perception. A philosopher and statesman cannot be forced to do it. I laughed when I read the proceedings of the meeting in Calcutta, congratulating people on the appointment of Mr. Morley to the Secretaryship of State for

India. Passages were read from Mr. Morley's books. Mr. Morley had said so and so in Mr. Gladstone's Life; Mr. Morley had said this and had said that; he was the editor of a certain paper 30 years ago, and he said so and so. I asked myself if it would not have been better that some of the passages from the *Bhagavat Gita* were so quoted. The persons to whom I refer are gentlemen for whom I have the highest respect. But what I say is, that they utterly misunderstood the position or absolutely ignored the distinction between a philosopher and a statesman. A statesman is bound to look to the present circumstances and see what particular concessions are absolutely necessary, and what is theoretically true or wrong. He has to take into consideration both the sides. There are the interested Anglo-Indians and the Secretary of State is the head of the Anglo-Indian bureaucracy whose mouth-piece he is. Do you mean to say that when the whole bureaucracy, the whole body of Anglo-Indians, is against you, the Secretary of State will set aside the whole bureaucracy and give you rights? Has he the power? If he does, will he not be asked to walk away? So then it comes to this that the whole British electorate must be converted. So you are going to convert all persons who have a right to vote in England, so as to get the majority on your side, and when this is done and when by that majority the Liberal party is returned to Parliament bent upon doing good to India and it appoints a Secretary of State as good as Mr. Morley, then you hope to get something of the old methods. The new Party has realized this position. The whole electorate of Great Britain must be converted by lectures. You cannot touch their pocket or interest, and that man must be a fool indeed who would sacrifice his own interest on hearing a philosophical lecture. He will say it is a very good lecture; but I am not going to sacrifice my interest. I will tell you a story. One of my friends who had been lecturing in England delivered a lecture on the grievances of India. A man from the audience came and asked him how many of them there were. The lecturer replied 30 crores. The inquirer replied, 'Then you do not deserve anything.' That is the attitude with which an English workman looks at the question. You now depend on the Labour Party. Labourers have their own grievances, but they won't treat you any better. On the contrary they will treat you worse, because British labourers obtain their livelihood by sending us their goods. This is the real position. This position is gradually recognized. Younger people who have gone to England like Mr. Gokhale are not so disappointed though those who went with him were like Lala Lajpat Rai. I am entering into personalities but I cannot place these facts in an intelligent manner if I do not give the names, although all of them are my friends. This is then the state of things. The New

Party perceives that this is futile. To convert the whole electorate of England to your opinion and then to get indirect pressure to bear upon the Members of Parliament, they in their turn to return a Cabinet favourable to India and the whole Parliament, the Liberal party and the Cabinet to bring pressure on the bureaucracy to yield—we say this is hopeless. You can now understand the difference between the Old and the New Parties. Appeals to the bureaucracy are hopeless. On this point both the New and Old parties are agreed. The Old party believes in appealing to the British nation and we do not. That being our position, it logically follows we must have some other method. There is another alternative. We are not going to sit down quiet. We shall have some other method by which to achieve what we want. We are not disappointed, we are not pessimists. It is the hope of achieving the goal by our own efforts that has brought into existence this New Party.

There is no empire lost by a free grant of concessions by the rulers to the ruled. History does not record any such event. Empires are lost by luxury, by being too much bureaucratic or over-confident or from other reasons. But an empire has never come to an end by the rulers conceding power to the ruled.

You got the Queen's Proclamation. But it was obtained without a Congress. They wanted to pacify you, as you had grown too turbulent, and you.

got that Proclamation without a demand, without Congress and without constitutional agitation. That is a very good and generous declaration indeed. The Queen was very anxious that it should be couched in such terms as would create hopes in you. Now all that anxiety did not proceed from constitutional agitation. It was after 1858 that constitutional agitation began. The result was, the Proclamation remained a dead letter, because you could not get it enforced, the conditions under which it] was made having disappeared. A promise was made but you proved too weak to have it enforced. That is the reason why it was not enforced. The bureaucracy got the upper hand and they established a system of administration in which it made it impossible for the Proclamation to be acted up to. Lord Curzon poohpoohed it. Another lawyer said it was unconstitutional because it was not passed by Parliament. His name was Sir James Stephen. This was at the time of the Ilbert Bill. They want now to explain away that Proclamations. Is Mr. Morley going to fulfil it ? The explanation of the Proclamation is not the question. The question is what will compel him to fulfil it. This is the point at issue. I admit that we must ask ; but we must ask with the consciousness that the demand cannot be refused. There is great difference betwen asking and petitioning. Take the Age of Consent Bill, the Land Tax, the Tenancy Question. Whenever there was a grievance we used to hold meetings, make petitions, representations, and complaints in the Press; and once the decision of Cæsar was known, everything was silent and we accepted it loyally. Such is the experience of the Government and this is what, I believe, they wrote to Mr. Morley relating to the Partition question. They have probably told Mr. Morley that if he remained quiet for a short time, everything would be right. "The present howl is due to a few agitators, and when sufficient time has elapsed the agitation will subside and the Partition will be accepted. We know the people of India better than you do. We have ruled over them and we intend to rule over them, and if our experience is worth anything we advise you not to yield to their clamorous agitation." Mr. Morley's counsellors are Anglo-Indians, they placed this before Mr. Morley. He thinks that such consensus of opinion, administrative experience, it is impossible to over-ride. Philosopher or no philosopher, he thinks that the administrative duties require it, and he does it as honestly as any other man in the world. This is then how the matter stands. The new Party wishes to put a stop to this. We have come forward with a scheme which if you accept, shall better enable you to remedy this state of things than the scheme of the Old School. Your industries are ruined utterly, ruined by foreign rule; your wealth is going out of the country and you are reduced to the lowest level which no human being can occupy. In this state of things, is there any other remedy by which you can help yourself? The remedy is not petitioning but boycott. We say prepare your forces, organise your power, and then go to work so that they cannot refuse you what you demand. A story in *Mahabharata* tells that Sri Krishna was sent to effect a compromise, but the Pandavas and Kauravas were both organizing their forces to meet the contingency of failure of a compromise. This is politics. Are you prepared in this way to fight if your demand is refused? If you are, be sure you will not be refused; but if you are not, nothing can be more certain than that your demand will be refused, and perhaps, for ever. We are not armed, and there is no necessity for arms either. We have a stronger weapon, a political weapon, in boycott. We have perceived one fact, that the whole of this administration, which is carried on by a handful of Englishmen, is carried on with our assistance. We are all in subordinate service. The whole Government is carried on with our assistance and they try to keep us in ignorance of our power of co-operation between ourselves by which that which is in our own hands at present can be claimed by us and administered by us. The point is to have the entire control in our hands. I want to have the key of my house, and not merely one stranger turned out of it. Self-Government is our goal; we want a control over our administrative machinery. We don't want to become clerks and remain. At present, we are clerks and willing instruments of our own oppression in the hands of an alien Government, and that Government is ruling over us not by its innate strength but by keeping us in ignorance and blindness to the perception of this fact. Professor Seely shares this view. Every Englishman knows that they are a mere handful in this country and it is the business of every one of them to befool you in believing that you are weak and they are strong. This is politics. We have been deceived by such policy so long. What the New Party wants you to do is to realise the fact that your future rests entirely in your own hands. If you mean to be free, you can be free; if you do not mean to be free, you will fall and be for ever fallen. So many of you need not like arms; but if you have not the power of active resistance, have you not the power of self-denial and self-abstinence in such a way as not to assist this foreign Government to rule over you? This is boycott and this is what is meant when we say, boycott is a political weapon. We shall not give them assistance to collect revenue and keep peace. We shall not assist them in fighting beyond the frontiers or outside India with Indian blood and money. We shall not assist them in carrying on the administration of justice. We shall have our own courts, and when time comes we shall not pay taxes. Can you do that by your united efforts? If you can, you are free from to-morrow. Some gentlemen who spoke this evening referred to half bread as against the whole bread. I say I want the whole bread and that immediately. But if I can not get the whole, don't think that I have no patience.

I will take the half they give me and then try for the remainder. This is the line of thought and action in which you must train yourself. We have not raised this cry from a mere impulse. It is a reasoned impulse. Try to understand that reason and try to strengthen that impulse by your logical convictions. I do not ask you to blindly follow us. Think over the whole problem for yourselves. If you accept our advice, we feel sure we can achieve our salvation thereby. This is the advice of the New Party. Perhaps we have not obtained a full recognition of our principles. Old prejudices die very hard. Neither of us wanted to wreck the Congress, so we compromised, and were satisfied that our principles were recognised, and only to a certain extent. That does not mean that we have accepted the whole situation. We may have a step in advance next year, so that within a few years our principles will be recognised, and recognised to such an extent that the generations who come after us may consider us Moderates. This is the way in which a nation progresses. This is the way national sentiment progresses, and this is the lesson you have to learn from the struggle now going on. This is a lesson of progress, a lesson of helping yourself as much as possible, and if you really perceive the force of it. if you are convinced by these arguments, then and then only is it possible for you to effect your salvation from the alien rule under which you labour at this moment.

There are many other points but it is impossible to exhaust them all in an hour's speech. If you carry any wrong impression come and get your doubts solved. We are prepared to answer every objection, solve every doubt, and prove every statement. We want your co-operation; without your help we cannot do anything single-handed. We beg of you, we appeal to you, to think over the question, to see the situation, and realise it, and after realising it to come to our assistance, and by our joint assistance to help in the salvation of the country.

THE SHIVAJI FESTIVAL

[A speech delivered in Marathi, on the occasion of the Shivaji Coronation festival, in Poona, on the 25th June, 1907].

It is a pity the Government cannot yet understand that the object of festivals like these is not to create disturbances. Its mind is yet enveloped in undeserved suspicion. There are a dozen detectives and reporters at this very meeting. Now where is the need for all this suspicion and distrust? I am sorry that the District Magistrate himself did not take the trouble to attend. Why not take the golden opportunity to know firsthand what the advocates of the Shivaji festival have got really to say on these occasions? I, for one, am prepared to say every word that I now say even before His Excellency the Governor. I will say it before God Himself, for what I say I have honestly at heart, I will proclaim it from the housetops if required, I will avow it if a detective come to me and ask for my views. There is no occasion for expressing views by stealth or secrecy; and what need of it? Surely, Indian people are not robbers in their own country. They can certainly proclaim their aspirations and they really ought to. We do not fear a hearing, only we want a full and a fair hearing. I strongly condemn the mean attempt to lay the nets for a stray unguarded word to penalise and victimise the speaker. If Government wants to know the truth let it be prepared to hear the whole truth. Why spend two lacs on maintaining short-hand reporters and detectives, and such other men of the intelligence department? The money would be surely better spent on technical education. If we celebrate the Shivaji festival we do not do it for raising the standard of revolt. The idea will be foolish and absurd, as we all know that we have no arms, no ammunition.

An educated man, an M.A., and an L.L.B. may surely be given credit for knowing that the military strength of the Government is enormous and that a single machine-gun showering hundreds of bullets per minute will quite suffice for our largest public meetings. How can a detective find out things which never enter the perception of the educated classes? Those who are thus shadowed may however console themselves with the idea that the great God who sees everything is the people's detective upon kings and Governments, and that this divine detective must sooner or later bring the British Government to justice. The secret of all this mischief lies in the idea that the educated classes are the enemies of the Government. Mr. Morley in fact said it in so many words, and he made much of the fact that every member of the proletariat did not often completely endorse what the educated man had to say,—as if every savage or aborigine, every illiterate man of the masses, should be able to comprehend the depths of the political cunning of our bureaucracy. But what is it in the educated classes that leads Mr. Morley to mistake them for enemies? Is it the knowledge in them that so leads him? Then surely Mr. Morley himself is the enemy of knowledge. We all know that Adam, the original man, suffered because he ate the fruit of the tree of 'Knowledge' and the educated Indians are being treated similarly for the 'knowledge' which is bestowed upon them. Is the Government prepared to be classed with those who are the enemies of knowledge in this creation?

To turn to the Shivaji festival, the knowledge we have, or the knowledge which we want to inculcate among the people in this connection, relates not to the actual use of the identical measures which Shivaji for instance took but to a proper appreciation of the spirit in which he resorted to the measures suitable to his time. Festivals like these prove an incentive to the legitimate ambitions of a people with a great historic past. They serve to impart courage, such courage as an appreciation of heroes securing their salvation against odds, can give. They are an antidote to vague despair. They serve like manure to the seeds of enthusiasm and the spirit of nationality. Malice or wickedness is never the keynote, or even the minor note, of those who come together on occasions like these. I wish that every word I say on this point should be faithfully reported, and I will gladly supply omissions if the report were submitted to me for correction. The time is surely not yet for lawlessness, for we have not yet exhausted all the possibilities of what may be claimed as legitimate and lawful action. But the pity of it all is that the Government is engaged in treating even this lawful action as unlawful. Lala Lajpat Rai, for instance, had done nothing that was not lawful and yet the whole official hierarchy conspired and acted like one man to deport him. I cannot imagine a clearer sign that the greatness of the British Government is doomed, and that decay and demoralisation has set in. Mr. Morley is a great "Pandit," a learned man. There is no use denying the fact; but it was a pity that this excellent repository of learning, this great English "Pandit," is no better after all than one of our own orthodox Pandits of Benares who are strangers to worldly wisdom. It is an irony of fate that the greater the scholarship, the less the statesmanship. Mr. Morley ridicules the educated classes on the ground that they are poor. Has Mr. Morley forgotten the old days when he himself enjoyed no better lot? The educated Indian may aspire to rise to high office, but that is no more culpable in him than for this English Pandit to aspire for State Secretaryship. His analysis of the factors of the Indian population is very amusing. He claims the Princes and the Notables on his side. Surely it is not a thing to be wondered at when we know that the Indian Princes are mere puppets, whose tenure of life as Princes hangs on the breath of the British Government. The Viceroy proclaimed Ordinance I of 1907 as there were disturbances in Bengal and the Punjab; but the Maharajah of Kolhapore went one better though he had not the least excuse of any kind. Mr. Morley claims the merchant class on his side. This is not true about the whole class and it must be remembered that merchants who are engaged in British trade and who depend on the means of enjoying the luxuries of life on that trade cannot be expected to come forward boldly to speak against Government. And, lastly, he claimed the lowest and the poorest classes, the illiterate ryots, as being on the side of Government. The Hon'ble Mr. Logan echoed the same sentiment only the other day in the Bombay Legislative Council. But this is moonshine. The pretensions of this official friend of the ryot cannot be exposed and contradicted to his very face only because the ryot is illiterate and cannot know who presumed to pose as his friend. But surely these false pretensions will be doomed as soon as education is sufficiently extended, and I may perhaps say that, it is only for this reason that the Government is so cautious in extending it. The educated classes alone have the knowledge and the courage for agitation and naturally the State Secretary treats them as enemies. But I appeal to you that the educated classes need not feel despair over such a thing. The educated classes are no doubt poor but they have one compensating advantage. They possess knowledge, and knowledge is not poor inasmuch as it possesses unlimited potentiality for wealth of every sort. They may also rely upon gradually bringing to their side those classes on whose support Government now thinks it may rely. History abounds in cases of kingdoms undone by the discontent of penniless beggars. No one could be more poor than the great Chanakya of mediæval Indian History, and it is well known how Chanakya, who had no stake in the world but the little knot of his hair, exterminated the whole race of the Nandas in return for the insult that was desperately given to him. Mr. Morley of all persons should not have scorned the power of educated men because they were poor and had no earthly stake. But when thoughtful men like Mr. Morley betray such evident signs of thoughtlessness, then surely the decline of the British Raj has begun. Mr. Morley has however rendered one great service. He has disillusioned the over-credulous and optimistic souls among us, and literally proved that the greatest Radical after all is no better than the worst Conservative so far as India is concerned. The Old generation, to which I myself belong, is now nearly "hors de combat." The younger generation certainly does not share in this deluding optimism and that is a hopeful sign for India, and I look forward to their exerting themselves with courage and perseverance. Mr. Paranjpe and another speaker had referred to the theory of social contract of Rousseau, and Mr. Damale had construed the Proclamation of 1858 as a contract. For my part I think that the word "contract" cannot be made applicable to relations existing between unequals, and it is dangerous for us to be deluded into a belief that the Proclamation is anything like a contract. No doubt it was a pledge solemnly given, but in its inception it was an utterance made in only a statesmanly spirit, because it was calculated to make for peace at the time. But the finger of the tactician is discernable in it. It is essentially an English idea that a political agitation is an attempt to enforce the terms of such an agreement. The Eastern idea is different; but it is a mistake to hold that it does not warrant an agitation by the subjects to control the power of the King. The idea is no doubt true that the King is part and parcel of the Godhead, and some foolish people have tried to fling it in the face of the Indian people to detract from their demand for popular institutions. But the canons of interpretation of a text are not less important than the text itself, and the real mischief arises from not construing the text in this respect as it should be. The King or Sovereign is no doubt a part and parcel of the God-head, but according to the Vedanta, so is every member of the subject people. For is not every soul a chip from the same block of

Brahman ? It is absurd to suppose that the Indian lawgivers of old regarded a King as absolved from all duties towards his subjects. Why, Manu has distinctly laid down, for instance, that the King who punishes those whom he should not, or does not punish those whom he should, goes to hell.

And the beauty of it is that this penalty is not stipulated for in an agreement or contract but is imposed by the Rishis, that is to say, those who were absolutely disinterested in worldly affairs and to whom, therefore, the sacred work of legislation fell. The Hindu believes in a multiplicity of "Devatas" or deities, and we all know what happens to the King that becomes undutiful. The King may himself be a sort of deity, but the conflict between him and his subjects begets another deity only superior to him. And if the cause of the people be just, the second deity quietly absorbs the first. It is well-known that both Parashurama and Rama are regarded as direct incarnations of God. But it is on record that when the days of the sixth incarnation were numbered the flame (of glory and power, as the Purana graphically describes), came out from the mouth of Parashurama and entered that of Rama. And what was Parashurama but a mere human being when he was deprived of this flame, the insignia of divinity? This divine element in kingship even according to the oriental ideas is not free from its peculiar limitations, and I challenge any one to point out any text which lays down that the yoke of the tyranny of a ruler, whoever he may be, should be quietly borne. The divine King as soon as he ceases to be just ceases also to be divine. He becomes an "asura" and this depreciated divinity is forthwith replaced by a deity, the divinity in which is not so alloyed. Shivaji did not probably concern himself with the text "Na Vishnu Prithivipathi" and surely he did not know what Hobbes or Locke thought about the principles of political government much less Rousseau or the Encyclopædists who were all anxious to replace the old religious theory of kingship by the secular one of contract. He knew his Vedanta all right and also knew how to put that Vedanta to practical use. The Vedanta may indeed be capable of giving colour to foolish theories of Government, but the wise Vedantin knows how to refute those theories even in the terms of Vedanta itself. But then it may be urged, that we shall have to suffer for doing what I want you to do. But then the path of duty is never sprinkled with rose-water nor roses grow on it. It is true that what we seek may seem like a revolution in the sense that it means a complete change in the "theory" of the Government of India as now put forward by the bureaucracy. It is true that this revolution must be a bloodless revolution, but it would be a folly to suppose that if there is to be no shedding of blood there are also to be no sufferings to be undergone by the people. Why, even these sufferings must be great. But you can win nothing unless you are prepared to suffer. The war between selfishness and reason, if it is conducted only with the weapons of syllogism must result in the victory for the former, and an appeal to the good feelings of the rulers is everywhere discovered to have but narrow limits.]Your revolution must be bloodless; but that does not mean that you may not have to suffer or to go to jail. Your fight is with bureaucracy who will always try to curb and suppress you. But you must remember that consistently with the spirit of laws and the bloodlessness of the revolution, there are a hundred other means by which you may and ought to achieve your object which is to force the hands of the bureaucracy to concede the reforms and privileges demanded by the people. You must realise that you are a great factor in the power with which the administration in India is conducted. You are yourselves the useful lubricants which enable the gigantic machinery to work so smoothly.

Though down-trodden and neglected, you must be conscious of your power of making the administration impossible if you but choose to make it so. It is you who manage the rail-road and the telegraph, it is you who make settlements and collect revenues, it is in fact you who do everything for the administration though in a subordinate capacity. You must consider whether you cannot turn your hand to better use for your nation than drudging on in this fashion. Let your places be filled by

Europeans on the splendid salary of eight annas a day if possible! You must seriously consider whether your present conduct is self-respectful to yourselves or useful to the nation. You must also consider what humiliation you have to suffer when foreigners openly express their wonder at the three hundred millions of Indian bearing their present ignominious lot without any effective protest. To say this, is not to violate the spirit of laws of any constitution. Surely it does not violate the sense of God's justice as we understand it. It is but those who oppose the reasonable demands of the Indian people that offend against God's justice.

You must imitate your rulers only in one thing, namely, in maintaining an unfailing succession of public workers. If one Lala Lajpat Rai is sent abroad, another ought to be found to take his place as readily as a junior Collector steps into the shoes of a senior. It is vain to hope that your petitions will have the effect of releasing Lala, though it is well-known that the Government do not mean to keep him a prisoner all his life. His deportation is intended not so much to penalise Lala Lajpat Rai as to terrorise those that would follow his example, and if their agitation stopped as soon as one deportation took place, Government will run away with the idea that terrorism had triumphed. It is no use, in fact it is a wrong course, to declare your loyalty with the L. writ large, on an occasion like the present. Those proclaimers of loyalty may be loyal, but who is not? Government is too shrewd not to know the real sentiments of the people, how far loyal or how far disloyal. And just as they are likely to put down agitation under the deliberate pretence of mistaking it for disloyalty, so also they are shrewd enough to know the real character of the loyalty that is so proclaimed by the placards, and by the beat of drums from the housetops. What you want is courage to declare that there is no disloyalty in agitating for constitutional rights and you will go on demanding them, though threatened that such demands will be treated as signs of disloyalty. What you want is bread for the masses and honourable rights for the masses as well as classes. That is not being disloyal, and I for one do not care that it is likely to be deliberately mistaken for disloyalty. The time has certainly come when you must be prepared to clearly formulate and persistently demand the more important rights and privileges. I say again to the reporters that every word that I am uttering, I am uttering deliberately and that a faithful report of those words will rather help than retard the cause I have at heart. With regard to Mr. Kinckaid's lecture on the Peshwas I have to point out that on the whole he has taken a correct view of that period of the Mahratta history, though I differ from him in one respect. The rule of the Peshwas came to an end not because they were usurpers of the political power, but because in the very nature of things a single family or dynasty cannot produce an unbroken succession of men possessed of such incomparable valour, ability and statesmanship as the family of Balaji Vishvanath did. There would have been even in England the same collapse of dynastic rule if the British constitution did not afford the useful ballast of the Parliament in which the sovereign power is diffused among so many individuals. We, Indians, have learnt at our own cost the lesson of the importance of popular and representative Government, and that is exactly the reason why our aspirations seem to be diverted from the patent oriental ideal.

NATIONAL EDUCATION

[*Extract from the Speech delivered in* 1908, *Barsi*, (*Original in Marathi*)]:—

I shall speak here this evening on national education. We are not accustomed to this term, hence it needs a little explanation. To be able to read and write alone is no education. These are simply the means of its attainment. That which gives us a knowledge of the experiences of our ancestors is called education. It may, however, be through books or through anything else. Every business needs education and every man has thus to give it to his children. There is no business indeed which does not require education. Our industries have been taken away by other people, but we do not know it. A potter knows how to shape a pot of China-clay but does not know what this clay is made of; hence his industry is lost. Similarly is the necessity of religious education. How can a person be proud of his religion if he is ignorant of it? The want of religious education is one of the causes that have brought the missionary influence all over our country. We did not think of it until very lately, whether we get the right sort of education or not. The tradesmen who are present here this evening send their sons very reluctantly to school and some of them do not send at all; because they do not get their education which they need. Besides their sons educated in the present-day system turn out fashionable. They wish to become clerks. They feel ashamed to sit on the *gaddi* where their forefathers earned the whole of their estate. The reason of this is that the education which they receive is onesided. The Government wanted Engineers, Doctors and clerks. It therefore started such schools which could supply its need. The students therefore who came out of these schools at first were bent upon services. It was the state of things sometime back that after passing three or four classes in school one could easily get on in life, but it has now become absolutely difficult, even to live from hand to mouth. We have therefore become conscious. It has become now almost clear that it is not the fault on our part that even after getting so much education we remain unable to satisfy our bare necessities; but the fault goes direct to the education that we receive. Naturally therefore the question as to how to reform the present system of education stood before us. If the Educational Department had been under our control we could have effected in it any necessary changes immediately. At first we asked the Government to transfer it to our control—the selection of the text-books for schools, for example. We feel now the necessity of such education which will prepare us to be good citizens. His Excellency the Governor of Bombay also admits the necessity of reforms in the present system of education. But he says that the Government is short of funds. I do not think this excuse reasonable, it may be true or otherwise. It is, however, true that the Government cannot think of this matter. The Government cannot give us religious education; and it is well that they are not doing it; because they are not our co-religionists. We are not given such education as may inspire patriotic sentiments amongst us. In America the Proclamation of Independence is taught in V or VI classes. In this way they train their children in politics. Some eighty or ninety years ago the industries of German declined on account of the rivalry between England and that country. But the German Government at once started scientific and mechanical education in that country. In this way Germany became so powerful in commerce that she has now become an object of dread to other countries. Properly speaking these things ought to be done by the Government itself. We pay taxes to the Government only that it may look after our welfare. But the Government wants to keep us lame. There is conflict between the commercial interests of England and India. The Government therefore cannot do anything in this matter.

There being no convenient schools in the villages, our villagers cannot train their children. We must therefore begin this work. There has been a good deal of discussion over this matter. And in the end we have come to the conclusion that for proper education national schools must be started on all sides. There are some of our private schools but owing to the fear of losing the grant-in-aid, the necessary education cannot be given there. We must start our own schools for this education. We must begin our work selflessly. Such efforts are being made all over the country. The Gurukul of Hardwar stands on this footing. Berar and Madras have also begun to move in this direction. Our *Maharashtra* is a little backward. A few efforts are being made here also; but they need encouragement from you. Money is greatly needed for this work. I am sure, if you realise the necessity and importance of this subject, you would encourage the organisers generously. So far I have told you about the subject, now I turn to tell you what we shall do in these schools of national education.

Of the many things that we will do there *religious education will first and foremost engage our attention*. Secular education only is not enough to build up character. Religious education is necessary because the study of high principles keeps us away from evil pursuits. Religion reveals to us the form of the Almighty. Says our religion that a man by virtue of his action can become even a god. When we can become gods even by virtue of our action, why may we not become wise and active by means of our action like the Europeans? Some say that religion begets quarrel. But I ask,

"Where is it written in religion to pick up quarrels?" If there be any religion in the world which advocates toleration of other religious beliefs and instructs one to stick to one's own religion, it is the religion of the Hindus alone. Hinduism to the Hindus, Islamism to the Musalmans will be taught in these schools. And it will also be taught there to forgive and forget the differences of other religions.

The second thing that we will do, will be to lighten the load of the study of the foreign languages. In spite of a long stay in India no European can speak for a couple of hours fluent Marathi, while our graduates are required as a rule to obtain proficiency in the English language. One who speaks and writes good English is said, in these days, to have been educated. But a mere knowledge of the language is no true education. Such a compulsion for the study of foreign languages does not exist anywhere except in India. We spend twenty or twenty-five years for the education which we can easily obtain in seven or eight years if we get it through the medium of our vernaculars. We cannot help learning English; but there is no reason why its study should be made compulsory. Under the Mahomedan rule we were required to learn Persian but we were not compelled to study it. To save unnecessary waste of time we have proposed to give education through our own vernaculars.

Industrial education will be the third factor. In no school this education is given. It will be given in these schools. It is an important thing. During the whole of this century we have not known how a match is prepared. In Sholapur matches are manufactured from straw ; and straw is found abundantly in our country. If therefore this industry is taken into our hands the importation of matches will largely decrease in India. It is the same with the sugar industry. We can procure here as good sugarcane as is found in Mauritius. It is seen by scientific experiments that the sugarcane found in the suburbs of Poona can produce as much sugar as is found in the sugarcane of Mauritius. Six crores of rupees are drained out every year from this country only for sugar. Why should this be ? Well. can we not get here sugarcane ? or the machinery necessary for its manufacture ? The reason is that we do not get here the education in this industry. It is not so in Germany. The Department of Industry investigates there as to which industry is decaying, and if perchance there be any, in a decaying state, substantial support at once comes forth from the Government for reviving it. The British Government, too, does the same thing in England. But our Government does not do it here. It may be a mistake or the Government may be doing it knowingly, but it is clear that we must not sit silent if the Government is not doing it. We are intending to start a large mechanical and scientific laboratory for this purpose. Sugar produces *Rab* and from *Rab* is extracted liquor, but the Government does not permit us this extraction ; hence we cannot get here cheap sugar. Mauritius imports to this country twenty thousand tons of sugar every year. All this is due to the policy of the Government, but we do not know it. The Government will be obliged to change it if we put pressure upon it. We have come to learn these things not earlier than twenty-five years after leaving the college. Our young men should know them in their prime of life.

Education in politics will be the fourth factor. We are not taught this subject in the Government schools. The student must understand that the Queen's Proclamation is the foundation of our rights. The Government is trying to shut our young men from these things. What has been proved by our revered Grand Old man—Dadabhoy Naoroji, after a ceaseless exertion for over fifty years, should be understood by our students in their youth. Every year some thirty or forty crores of rupees are drained out of India without any return. We have, therefore, fallen to a wretched state of poverty. These things, if understood in the prime of life, can make such a lasting impression over the hearts of our young men, as it would be impossible in an advanced age. Therefore this education should be given in school. Educated men of the type of Prof. Vijapurkar, have come forth to devote their lives in the cause of this education. The educationists are helping with their learning and experience, and it now remains with the well-to-do to help them with money. It is a matter of common benefit, if the future generation come out good, able to earn their bread and be true citizens. We should have been glad if the Government had done it. If the Government cannot do it, we must do. The Government will not interfere with us and if at all it does so, we should not mind it. As the dawn of the Sun cannot be stopped so it is with this. Our poverty has not yet reached its zenith. In America such work is done by a single man. But if no one man can venture to do it here, let us do it unitedly, for we are thirty crores of people. A sum of five lacs of rupees goes out every year for liquor alone from Sholapur. Can you not therefore help us in this work ? The will is wanted. Let the Government be displeased - we hope the Government will never deter us—we must do our duty. If the Government prohibits us from marriages, do we obey it ? The same is the case with education. As men do not give up building houses for fear that rats would dig holes, so we should not give up our work for fear of Government displeasure. If perchance any difficulty arises, our young men are to face it. To fear difficulties is to lose manliness. Difficulties do us immense good. They inspire in us courage and prepare us to bear them manly. A nation cannot progress if it meets no difficulties in the way. We do not get this sort of education for want of self-Government. We should not therefore await the coming of these rights, but we must get up and begin the work.

THE DECENTRALISATION COMMISSION

The question of centralisation or decentralisation of the powers of the administrative machinery involves considerations of uniformity, smoothness and regularity of work, general efficiency, economy of time, work and money, popularity, &c.; and speaking broadly these may be classed under three different heads: (1) Efficiency, (2) Economy, and (3) Popularity.

As regards the first, I do not think it is seriously contended that the efficiency of administration has suffered merely owing to over-centralisation. On the contrary it is urged that it is worth while making the administration a great deal more popular even if it would become a trifle less efficient by decentralisation. But the cry for decentralisation has its origin in the desire of the local officers to have a freer hand in the administration of the areas committed to their care. They believe that their life has been made rather mechanical or soulless by over-centralisation; and having naturally attributed to the same cause the growing estrangement between themselves and the people they have proposed decentralisation as an official remedy to remove this admitted evil. I do not think the people, looking from their own standpoint, can accept this view. The general public is indifferent whether efficiency and economy are secured by more or less official decentralisation. It is entirely a matter between higher and lower officials, between the secretariat and the local officers, or between the Supreme and the Local Governments. The people still believe that centralisation secures greater uniformity and regularity, and reduces the chances of the conscious or unconscious abuse of power resulting from unappealable authority being vested in lower officers, and would rather oppose decentralisation in this respect. The only complaint so far as I know, against the existing centralisation or decentralisation hitherto raised by the people are (1) The combination of the Executive and the Judicial functions in the same officers, (2) Financial centralisation in the Government of India as evidenced by the Provincial Contract System, (3) Partition of Bengal and (4) Excessive growth of departmentalism encroaching upon popular rights. But these, excepting the second, do not form the subject of the official grievance against over-centralisation.

My knowledge of the internal working of the different departments of administration is too limited to make definite proposals regarding the redistribution of power and authority between various officials so as thereby to make the administration more economical than at present. I shall, therefore confine my remarks mostly to the popular aspect of the question and to the four complaints noted above.

It is idle to expect that the adoption of the loose and irregular system of earlier days would remove the present estrangement between officers and people. It is true that in earlier days the relations between officers and people were more cordial; but this was not due to the looseness of the system then in vogue. In days when the system of British administration had yet to be evolved and settled, the help of the leaders of the people was anxiously sought by officers as indispensable for smooth and efficient administration of a new province. The officers then moved amongst the people and were in touch with them, not as a matter of mere goodness or sympathy but as a matter of necessity, as they themselves had yet many things to learn from these leaders; and this much satisfied the people at that time, as new aspirations were not as yet created. That state of things has ceased to exist. The creation and gradual development of the various departments, the framing of rules and regulations for the smooth working thereof, the settlement of all old disputes, the completion of the revenue survey, the disarmament of the people, the gradual waning of the influence of the old aristocracy including the higher class of watandars, the compilation of the works of ready reference on all matters embodying the experience of many years for the guidance of the officers, and other causes of the same kind, joined with the facilities for communication with the head-quarters of Government, have all tended to make the local officers more and more independent of the people and so lose touch with the latter. Over-centralisation may, at best, be one of such causes; but if so, it is to my mind very insignificant. No amount of decentralisation by itself can therefore restore that cordiality between the officers and the people which existed in the earlier days of the British rule as a necessity of those times; and though the present officers may by nature be as sympathetic as their predecessors, it is not possible to expect from them the same respect for growing popular opinion as was exhibited by their predecessors in older days. Under these circumstances such further decentralisation as would tend to vest greater powers in the lower officials will only make the system unpopular by encouraging local despotism which the people have justly learnt to look upon with disfavour. The only way to restore good relations between the officers and the people at present is, therefore, to create *by law* the necessity of consulting the people or their leaders, whom the old officials consulted, or whose advice they practically followed, as a matter of policy in earlier unsettled times. This means transfer of authority and power not between officials themselves, but from officials to the people, and that too in an ungrudging spirit. The leaders of the people must feel that matters concerning public welfare are decided by officials in consultation with them. The officers did it in earlier days as a matter of necessity, and the necessity which was the result of circumstances in those days, must, if we want the same relations to continue, be now created by laws granting the rights of self-government to the people, and thus giving to their opinion and wishes a duly recognised place in the affairs of the State. I do not mean to say that this could be done at once or at one stroke. We must begin with the village system the autonomy of which has been destroyed by the growth of departmentalism under the present rule. The village must be made a unit of self-government, and village communities or councils invested with definite powers to deal with all or most of the village questions concerning Education, Justice, Forest, Abkari, Famine Relief, Police, Medical Relief and Sanitation. These units of self-government should be under the supervision and superintendence of Taluka and District Boards which should be made thoroughly representative and independent. This implies a certain amount of definite popular control even over Provincial finance; and the Provincial Contract System will have to be revised not merely to give to the Provincial Government a greater stability and control over its finances, but by further decentralisation to secure for the popular representative bodies adequate assignments of revenue for the aforesaid purposes. This will also necessitate a corresponding devolution of independent legal powers on the popular bodies whether the same be secured by a reform of the Legislative Council or otherwise. Mere Advisory Councils will not satisfy the aspirations of the people, nor will they remove the real cause of estrangement between the officers and the people. The remedy proposed by me, I know is open to the objection that it means a surrender of power and authority enjoyed by the brueaucracy at present, and that the efficiency of the administration might suffer thereby. I hold a different view. I think it should be the aim of the British Administration to educate the people in the management of their own affairs, even at the cost of some efficiency and without entertaining any misgiving regarding the ultimate growth and results of such a policy. It is unnecessary to give, any detailed scheme regarding the organisation of Village, Taluka or District Councils proposed above for if the policy be approved and accepted there will be no difficulty in framing a scheme or making alterations therein to meet difficulties and objections as they occur in practice. As regards other complaints referred to above against the present centralisation or decentralisation of powers amongst officials, I think it is high time that the combination of Judicial and Executive functions in the same officers should be discontinued. In 'Judicial functions I include those judicial powers that are granted to revenue officers in the matter of land revenue, pensions, Inams and Saramjams except such as are necessary for the collection of revenue. There is no reason why these powers should be retained by executive officers if they are to be divested of jurisdiction in criminal matters. It is needless to say that this reform pre-supposes complete independence of judicial officers. Unnecessary growth of departmentalism is well illustrated by the latest instance of the partition of the Khandesh District. The partition of Bengal is the worst instance of the kind. These are objectionable even from an economical point of view, and in the case of the partition of Bengal the policy has deeply wounded the feelings of the people. The revenues of the country are not inelastic; but the margin, soon as it is reached, is swallowed up by the growth of departments at the sacrifice of other reforms conducive to the welfare of the people. In this connection I may here state that I advocate a re-arrangement of Provinces on considerations of linguistic and ethnological affinities and a federation thereof under a central authority. To conclude, the mere shifting of the centre of power and authority from one official to another is not in my opinion, calculated to restore the feelings of cordiality between officers and people, prevailing in earlier days. English education has created new aspirations and ideals amongst the people; and so long as these national aspirations remain unsatisfied, it is useless to expect that the hiatus between the officers and the people could be removed by any scheme of official decentralisation, whatever its other effects may be. It is no remedy, —not even palliative,—against the evil complained of, nor was it ever put forward by the people or their leaders. The fluctuating wave of decentralisation may infuse more or less life in the individual members of the bureaucracy, but it cannot remove the growing estrangement between the rulers and the ruled unless and until the people are allowed more and more effective voice in the management of their own affairs in an ever expansive spirit of wise liberalism and wide sympathy aiming at raising India to the level of the governing country.

CONGRESS COMPROMISE

Mrs. Annie Besant and the Hon. Mr. Gokhale have published their accounts, each from his own point of view, of the failure to bring about a United Congress at Madras. But there are gaps in either of these accounts; and as I was the third party in the negotiations, I am obliged to point out where these accounts fail to give a connected version of the whole story.

Both Mrs. Besant and Mr. Gokhale have omitted to mention the important fact that it was understood on both sides that the success of the compromise depended not so much upon Mr. Gokhale's willingness, but entirely upon the acceptance of the terms of the compromise by the Conventionist leaders in the city of Bombay. So all that we did in Poona was to discuss and provisionally settle what amendment in the Congress Constitution should be made, which, even if it did not come up to the marks, would make it possible for the Nationalists to join the Congress, and, secondly, what steps should be taken by the Provincial Congress Committee if the presence of the Nationalists was required at the Madras Congress sessions. I had already ascertained the views of the leading members of the Nationalist party on the subject, and further discussed and settled them at a small meeting of them at my house held on 29th November, when Mrs. Besant was, according to her first programme, to come here to visit Mr. Gokhale and myself. She, with Mr. Subba Rao, however, came a week later, and I then fully and freely explained the position of our party to both of them. Everything went on well so far; and no exception has been taken, in any of the accounts hitherto published, to the conversation I had with Mrs. Besant or Mr. Subba Rao up to this time.

The difficult task of winning over the Bombay City Conventionists was, however, now assigned to Mr. Subba Rao; and I must say here that I never hoped that it would be attended with success, and the result fully justified my fears. Mr. Subba Rao, according to his own statement in *New India* of the 8th inst., found that the Bombay Conventionist leaders were dead opposed to the extension of the franchise to public meetings or to independent constituencies, and what is pertinent to the question in hand, that "great apprehension was felt" by these Conventionists "that the Congress would be running a great risk, if Mr. Tilak and his followers came in." This, as anybody will see, was the real cause of the compromise negotiations; for, from what took place at Bankipore in 1912, it was not to be expected that Mr. Gokhale would, after this, continue to support the proposed amendment to the Constitution though it was, as now published, drafted by him.

My conversation with Mr. Subba Rao, of which

so much is made in Mr. Gokhale's statement, took place after Mr. Subba Rao returned disappointed from Bombay. This was on the 8th December, and he must have told and discussed with Mr. Gokhale, (with them he had put up) as he did with me that day, the attitude of the Bombay Conventionists with regard to the proposed amendment. When I went to see him the next morning he had at his own initiation reduced to writing the main point of our conversation, and reading them to me asked if I had any corrections to suggest. I suggested a few and he made them in his own hand; and the statement remained with him. A true copy of the written statement is now published in the press.

Mr. Gokhale says that the written statement did not come into his hands till a week later. Well, I have never questioned his word in this behalf. But he certainly knew that one was prepared on the 9th December. What he, however, did afterwards is undisputed. Relying, as he says, upon an oral report of my second conversation with Mr. Subba Rao, after his return from Bombay, Mr. Gokhale wrote a *confidential* letter to Babu Bhupendra in which Mr. Gokhale made certain charges against me, and said that he therefore withdrew his former support to Mrs. Besant's amendment. In reply Babu Bhupendra is said to have asked for a revised edition of this confidential letter in order that the same may be freely used. But before this second letter had reached Babu Bhupendra, he had to show the first letter to some of his Bengal friends to justify his sudden change of front towards the question, for he too, till then, was in favour of the amendment. The confidential letter thus became public property and the effect produced by the disclosure of its contents was that I was believed to have advocated "boycott of Government," and therefore no compromise was either possible or expedient; and, as a matter of fact the Bombay Conventionist delegates and the Servants of India delegates jointly opposed the amendment for the same reason. Mrs. Besant, who moved the amendment in the Subjects Committee, felt embarrassed and telegraphed to me that "my opponents charged me with boycott of Government" and wished in reply to know what the truth was. I promptly replied that I had never advocated "boycott of Government" and that prominent Nationalists had served and were serving in Municipal and Legislative Councils and that I had fully supported their action, both privately and publicly. When this telegraphic reply of mine was read in the Subjects Committee, Babu Bhupendra withdrew his words; and Mrs. Besant's amendment, instead of being rejected, was referred to a committee for consideration.

This is the history of the failure of the compromise in brief. But though Babu Bhupendra has withdrawn the charge he made against me on the strength of Mr. Gokhale's confidential letter, Mr. Gokhale would not follow the same course and still persists in openly maintaining the charge against me relying (1) on the oral report of Mr. Subba Rao's conversation with me after the former's return from Bombay to Poona, and (2) on some detached extracts from the newspaper reports of my speech made eight years ago. In short, he pleads justification for the charge he made against me in his confidential letter and wants to throw the whole responsibility of the failure of the compromise on my shoulders.

Now as, regards the oral reports of parts of my conversation with Mr. Subba Rao I must say that I do not accept them as correct; and they have no value as against the written statement prepared by Mr. Subba Rao. As regards the charge of advocating the boycott of Government I have already repudiated it in plain terms. It is unfair to ask me to do anything more until the confidential letter in which the charge was first made is published. For I am entitled to know the whole of the case against me before I make any further reply. The contents of Mr. Gokhale's confidential letter were allowed to filter through Mr. Basu down to the Subjects Committee and have done harm to me on my back, as also to the compromise. If Mr. Gokhale thinks that I am attributing bad faith to him, the way for him is quite clear and open. He never wanted my consent, though I am in ten minutes' drive from his residence, when he wrote his confidential letter to Babu Bhupendra, and I fail to understand why he should now ask me to read the letter and ask him to publish it. I am not going to do anything of the kind, nor send to Mr. Gokhale an accredited agent of mine for the purpose. The initiative and the responsibility of sending the letter to Mr. Basu was his, and so must be that of publishing it. It is for him to consider whether he does not owe it to himself and to me to publish both his letters, so that the public may, after my reply to them, form their own judgment in the matter.

Poona, 12-2-1915. B. G. TILAK.

HOME RULE SPEECH AT BELGAUM

[*The lecture below was delivered immediately after the meeting held under the auspices of the Historical Research Society, on the* 1st *of May,* 1916. *Rajamanya Rajashri Dada Sahib Khaparde presided.*]

When I was requested to deliver a lecture here to-day, I did not know what to lecture. I do not stand before you to-day in any way prepared for any particular subject. I had come for the Conference. Thinking that it would not be out of place if I were to say a few words to you about those subjects which were discussed during the past few days and about the object with which a Home Rule League was established here before the Congress, I have selected that subject for to-day's lecture.

What is *swarajya*? Many have a misconception about this. Some do not understand this. Some understanding it, misrepresent it. Some do not want it. Thus there are many kinds of people. I am not prepared to-day to enter into any particular discussion of any sort beyond saying a few general words on the following among other points: What is *swarajya*? Why do we ask for it? Are we fit for it or not? In what manner must we make this demand for *swarajya* of those of whom we have to make it? In what direction and on what lines are we to carry on the work which we have to carry on? It is not the case that these general words which I am going to say are the outcome of my effort and exertion alone. The idea of *swarajya* is an old one. Of course when *swarajya* is spoken of it shows that there is some kind of rule opposed to *swa*, *i.e.* ours and that this idea originates at that time. This is plain. When such a condition arrives it begins to be thought that there should be *swarajya*, and men make exertions for that purpose. You are at present in that sort of condition. Those who are ruling over you do not belong to your religion, race or even country. The question whether this rule of the English Government is good or bad is one thing. The question of 'one's own' and 'alien' is quite another. Do not confuse the two at the outset. When the question 'alien,' or 'one's own?' comes, we must say 'alien.' When the question 'good or bad?' comes, we may say 'good,' or we may say 'bad.' If you say 'bad,' then what is the improvement that must be made in it?—this question is different. If you say 'good' it must be seen what good there is under it which was not under the former rule. These are different points of view.........Formerly there were many kingdoms in our India—in some places there was Mohammadan rule, in some places there was Rajput rule, in some places there was Hindu rule and in some places there was Maratha rule—were these *swarajyas* good or bad? I again remind you that this is a question different from our theme. We shall consider it afterwards. All other rules being broken up, the universal sovereignty of the English Government has been established in India. To-day we have not to consider the history of other's down-fall. We have also not to consider how they fell. Nor am I going to speak about that. Let us turn to the present system of administration. Some able men who have been educated in England and have received college education there come to India and the State administration of India is carried on through them. 'Emperor' is a word. When you give a visible form to the sentiment which arises in your mind at the mention of the word *Raja i.e.*, King, there is the present Emperor. This sentiment itself is invisible. When a visible form is given to this invisible something there is the King - the Emperor. But the Emporor does not carry on the administration. The question of *swarajya* is not about the Emperor, not about this invisible sentiment. This must be remembered at the outset. Let there be any country, it must have a King, it must have some men to carry on its management and there must be exercised some sort of rule in it. The case of anarchical nations is different. These nations can never rise. As in a house there must be some one to look to its management—when there is no man belonging to the house an outsider is brought in as a trustee—just so is the case also with a kingdom. In every country there is a certain body for carrying on its administration and there is some sort of arrangement. An analysis must be made of both these things, *viz.*, of this arrangement and this body and, as stated yesterday by the President (the President of the Provincial Conference,) of the sentiment of 'King.' There must be a king, there must be State administration. Both these propositions are true from the historical point of view. Of a country where there is no order, where there is no king, that is, where there is no supervising body, the *Mahabharat* says: 'A wise man should not live even for a moment at that place. There is no knowing when, at that place, our lives may be destroyed, when our wealth may be stolen, when our house may be dacoited, nay, set on fire.' There must be a government. I will not say at length what there was in the Kritayuga in ancient times. The people of that time did not require a King. Every one used to carry on business looking only to mutual good. Our Puranas say that there was once a condition when there was no king. But if we consider whether such a state existed in historical times it will appear that such a condition did not exist. There must be some control or other. Control cannot be exercised always by all people assembling together at one place. Hence, sovereign authority is always divided into two parts: one the Advisory body, and the other executive body. The question about *swarajya* which has now arisen in India is not about the said invisible sentiment. This question is not about those who are to rule over us, (and) according to whose leadership, by whose order and under whose guidance, that rule is to be exercised. It is an undisputed fact that we should secure our own good under the rule of the English people themselves, under the supervision of the English nation, with the help of the English nation, through their sympathy, through their anxious care and through those high sentiments which they possess. And I have to say nothing about this (cheers). Note this first. Do not create confusion in your minds by confounding both the aspects. These two aspects are quite distinct. What we have to do we must do with the help of some one or another, since to-day we are in such a helpless condition. It is an undoubted fact that we must secure our good under protection. Had it not been for that, your independence would never have gone. If we take for granted that we have to bring about the dawn of our good with the help of the English Government and the British Empire, then one more strange thing which some people see in this, will altogether disappear. To speak in other words, there is no sedition in this. If then with the help of the English Government—if the words 'invisible English Government,' be used for the words 'English Government' there would be no mistake—if with the help of this invisible English Government, with the aid of this invisible English Government, you are to bring about the dawn of your good fortune, then, what is it that you ask?

This second question arises. The answer to it, again, lies in the very distinction of which I spoke to you. Though a Government may be invisible, still when it begins to become visible, the management of that kingdom is carried on by its hands and by its actions. This state of being visible is different from invisible Government. If you ask how, I say in the same manner as the great *Brahma* is different from *Maya*. I have taken the word visible and invisible from *Vedanta* (Philosophy). The great *Brahma* which is without attributes and form is different and the visible form which it assumes when it begins to come under the temptation of *maya*, is different. Hence these dealings which are due to *maya* are sure to change. What is the characteristic of *maya* ? It changes every moment. One Government will remain permanent (*viz.*) invisible Government; and the visible Government changes every moment. The word *Swarajya* which has now arisen relates to visible Government. Maintaining the invisible Government as one, what change, if effected in the momentarily changing visible Government, would be beneficial to our nation ? This is the question of *Swarajya*. And this being the question of *Swarajya*, there arises the further question : In whose hands should be the administration carried on in our India ? We do not wish to change the invisible Government—English Government. We say that the administration should not be in the hands of a visible entity by whose hands this invisible Government is getting work done, but should pass into some other's hands. The *Swarajya* agitation which is now carried on, is carried on in the belief that this administration if carried on by some other hands or with the help of some one else, or some other visible form would be more beneficial to the people than when carried on by those by whose hands it is now carried on. Let us take a parallel. There is an Emperor in England. An English Act contains the rule that the king commits no wrong. The king never commits a wrong (offence). His authority is limited in such a manner that he has always to be advised by a minister. The Prime Minister acts on his own responsibility. There may be a good many people here who have studied English history. This is the British constitution. When this principle was established in English History, the number of sedition cases began to fall. Here in India, we have the administrators instituting cases of sedition. Those who carry on the administration are different and the king is different. The king is one and the same. But the minister changes every five years. It would not be sedition if any were to start a discussion advocating a change of ministry. It happens every day before the eyes of the English people. The king's ministers go out of office after five years, go out of office after two years ; they may quarrel among themselves as they like. What is that to the king ? He is the great *Brahma* without attributes ? He is not affected by this. The *Swarajya* agitation now existing in

India is then about change in such a ministry. Who rules in India? Does the Emperor come and do it? He is to be taken in procession like a god on a great occasion, we are to manifest our loyalty towards him. This is our duty. Through whom, then, is the administration carried on. It is carried on through those who are now servants (*viz.*)the State Secretary, Viceroy, Governor, and below him the Collector, the Patel and lastly the police sepoy. If it be said that one Police sepoy should be transferred and another Police sepoy should be appointed would that constitute sedition? If it be said that the Collector who has come is not wanted and that another is wanted, would that constitute sedition? If it be said that one Governor is not wanted, another Governor should be appointed, would that constitute sedition? If it be said 'This State Secretary is not wanted, bring another' would that constitute sedition? Nobody has called this sedition. The same principle which is applicable to a Police sepoy is also applicable to the State Secretary. We are the subjects of the same king whose minister the State Secretary is and whose servant he is. This then being so, if any one were to say, "this State Secretary is not wanted, this Viceroy is not wanted, Fuller Saheb is not wanted in Bengal,—such resolutions have often been passed in the case of Governors, not in the present but in the past time—and were to give reasons for that, you may say about him that his head must have been turned and that the reasons he gives are not good or sufficient. But from the historical point of view, it does not follow that when he says so, that constitutes sedition (cheers). Our demand belongs to the second class. It is concerned with *swarajya*. Consider well what I say. If you think that the present administration is carried on well, then I have nothing to say. In the Congresses and Conferences that are now held you come and say: "Our Kulkarni Vatan has been taken (away), zulum has been exercised upon us in connection with the Forest Department, liquor has spread more in connection with the Abkari Department, also we do not receive that sort of education which we ought to get." What is at the root of all this? What is the benefit of merely saying this? Why do you not get education? Why are shops of the Abkari Department opened where we do not want them? In the Forest Department, laws about reserved forests and about forest of this sort or of that sort are made. Why were they made? At present, lists upon lists of grievances come before the Congress. Why was jury abolished against your will? Why was no college opened in the Karnatic up to this time? All these questions are of such a kind that there is but one answer to them. At present what do we do? Is there no College?—petition to the Collector or to the Governor, because he has power in his hands. If this power had come into your hands, if you had been the officials in their place, or if their authority had been responsible to the public opinion, these things would not have happened. No other answer than this can be given to the above. These things happen because there is no authority in your hands. The authority to decide these matters is not given to you for whose good this whole arrangement is to be made. Hence we have to ask like children. The child cries when it is hungry. It cannot say that it is hungry. The mother has to find out whether it is hungry or has a bellyache. Sometimes the remedies used prove out of place. Such has become our condition at present. In the first place you do not at all know what you want and where lies your difficulty. When you know it, you begin to speak. You have no power in your hands to cause things to be done according to your desire. Such being the condition, what has happened now? Whatever you have to do, whatever you want—if you want to dig a well in your house—you have to petition to the Collector. If you want to kill a tiger in the forest you have to petition to the Collector. Grass cannot be obtained, wood cannot be obtained from the forest freely, permission to cut grass is required—petition the Collector. All this is a helpless state. We do not want this arrangement. We want some better arrangement than this. That is *Swarajya*, that is Home Rule. These questions do not arise in the beginning. When a boy is young he knows nothing. When he grows up he begins to know and then begins to think that it would be very good if the management of the household was carried on at least to some extent according to his opinion. Just so it is with a nation. When it is able to consider for itself, when it acquires the capacity of considering for itself, then the question is likely to arise. Let us give up the thought about the invisible Government, let us come within the limits of the visible Government. We then see that the people who make this arrangement, who carry on the administration, are appointed in England according to a certain law, and rules are made within the limits of those laws as to what should be their policy. These rules may be good or bad. They may be good, they may be quite well-arranged and methodical. I do not say that they are not. But, however good may be the arrangement made by other people, still he who wants to have the power to make his own arrangement is not likely always to approve. This is the principle of *Swarajya*. If you got the powers to select your Collector, it cannot be said with certainty that he would do any more work than the present Collector. Perhaps he may not do. He may even do it badly. I admit this. But the difference between this and that is this; this one is selected by us, he is our man, he sees how we may remain pleased; while the other thinks thus: what we think to be good must appear so to others: what is there with respect to which we should listen to others: I am so much educated, I get so much pay, I possess so much ability—why would I do anything which would be harmful to others? The only answer is 'Because you have such conceit.' (Laughter.) It is only the wearer that knows where the shoe pinches. Others cannot know. This is the only cause. There is no other cause. Hence if you minutely consider the various complaints which have arisen in our country it will appear that the system which is subsisting now is not wanted by us. Not that we do not want the king, nor that we do not want the English Government, nor that we do not want the Emperor. We want a particular sort of change in the system according to which this administration is carried on and I for one do not think that if that change were made there would arise any danger to the English rule. But there is reason to think that some people whose spectacles are different from ours see it, because they say so (cheers). Hence the minds of many people are now directed to the question as to what change should be effected in the system to fit in English Rule with the popular will. We make minor demands, *viz.*, remove the liquor shop in a certain village named Ghodegoan; they say it should not be removed. Done. We say reduce the salt tax, they say we look to the amount of revenue derived from the salt duty. If the tax is reduced how should the revenue be managed? He who has to make the arrangement of administration has to do these things. When I ask for the authority to manage my household affairs, I do not say give me the income which you obtain and spend it not. We ourselves have to earn and we ourselves must expend. This is the sort of double responsibility which we want. Then we shall see what we have to do. Such is the claim at present. Bureaucrats come and say, act according to our wishes ; on the other hand we say, act according to our wishes so that all our grievances may be removed. We know that sometimes a boy obstinately asks for a cap worth 25 rupees from his father. Had he been in his father's place it is very doubtful whether he would have paid 25 rupees for the cap or not. The father refuses, but the boy is grieved at the time. And why is he grieved at it? Because he does not understand; because the management is not in his own hands. If he had he would know. In like manner the introduction of self-administration is beneficial to India. We want this thing to-day. When this only thing is obtained the remaining things come into our possession of themselves. This is at the root of the thousands of demands which we are making. When we get this key into our hands, we can open not only one but 5 or 10 doors at once. Such is the present question. In order that the attention of all may be directed to this question this Home Rule League was established here the other day. Some will be grieved at it; I do not deny it. Every one is grieved. It was said here some time back that when a boy is a minor, the father when dying appoints a *panch*. The *panch* when appointed supervises the whole of the estate. Some benefit does accrue. This is not denied. Afterwards when the boy has grown up, he sees that there is something wrong in this arrangement. 'I must acquire the right of management, then I shall carry on better management than this,' he says to himself. He is confident. It may not be that he actually carries on the management as well. If he be a prodigal, he may squander away his father's money. But he thinks he must manage his own affairs. In order to avoid any opposition the law lays down the limitation that on the boy's completing 21 years of age, the trustee should cease his supervision and give it into the boy's possession. This rule which we observe in every day life applies equally also to the nation. When the people in the nation become educated and begin to know how they should manage their affairs, it is quite natural for them that they themselves should claim to manage the affairs which are managed for them by others. But the amusing thing in the history of politics is that the above law of about 21 years has no existence in it. Even if we may somehow imagine a law enjoining that when a nation has been educated for a hundred years it should be given the right to administer itself it is not possible to enforce such a law. The people themselves must get the law enforced. They have a right to do so. There must be some such arrangement here. Formerly there was some better arrangement to a little extent. Such an arrangement does not exist now. And therein lies the reason of all our demands, of the grievances which we have, the wants which we feel and the inconveniences which we notice in the administration. And the remedy which is proposed after making inquiries is called Home Rule. Its name is *Swarajya*. To put it briefly, the demand that the management of our affairs should be in our hands is the demand for *Swarajya*. Many people have at present objections to this. I merely gave the definition in order to make the subject clear. The people on the other side always misrepresent it. If there be no mistake in the logical reasoning of what I have now said, how will any mistake arise unless some part of it is misrepresented ? Hence, those people who want to point out a mistake misrepresent some sentences out of this and find fault with them saying this is such a thing, that is such a thing. It is not the duty of a wise man to impute those things to us which we never demand at all ; to censure us and ridicule us before the people. Need I say more about this ? (Cheers.) If any one of you has such a misconception let him give it up. At least remember that what I tell you is highly consistent. It is in accordance with logical science. It agrees with history. I said that king means invisible king or Government—this is no offence whatever. There are deities between. Very often God does not get angry ; these deities get angry without reason. We must first settle with them. So if there has arisen any misconception let it be removed. All I have said is for that purpose. Now I tell you the nature of our demand. Even before that, let us consider a little the question whether we are fit for carrying on the administration or not. Sometime ago I gave you the instance of *panch* and their ward. There generally it happens that as the boy grows up more and more, those who think that the management should not pass into his hands report, one that his head has now begun to turn, another that he is not mad but that he appears to be half mad and so on. The reason of this is that the management should remain in their own hands for a couple of years more. A third says: 'True, you may give authority into his hands but do you know that he has got bad habits?' These people say five or ten things about him. What is to be gained by doing this. The dispute goes before the Court and then they get him adjudged mad. Some thing like this has now begun to happen here. To give authority into people's hands is the best principle of administration. No one disputes this; because the same thing is going on in the country of those officials who are here. When they go there they have to advocate the same principle. Therefore no one says that this historical principle is bad. Then what is bad? They distinctly say that the Indians are not to-day fit for *Swarajya* (laughter), and some of us are like the cunning men in the story occurring in the Panchatantra. That story is as follows: A villager had come taking a sheep on his head. One man said to him 'There is a she goat on your head.' A second said 'There is a dog on your head.' A third one said quite a third thing. The villager threw away the sheep. The men took it away. Our condition is like that. The story relates to human nature. There are among us people who are just like them. Why are we not fit? Because fitness has not been created in us. We have not done it, our parents have not done it. We have not got such powers. But the Government has given you some powers in the Council. Sinha and Chaubal are in the Council. In the Executive Councils of other places also there are selected people. When these people were selected for appointment, did any one ever say, "We are not fit, do not give us the post." No one said it. (Cheers). What then is the use of saying so to our meeting? I should concede these people were speaking true, if, when the bureaucracy actually confers some great powers on them, they stand up and say "We do not want them, we are not fit for them,—the Brahmins alone must come and perform Shraddha at our house, we cannot perform it." I think that those men who say things because such and such a person would like or would not like and bring forward excuses for that purpose, exhibit their own nature (cheers.) Why are we not fit? Have we no nose, no eyes, no ears, no intellect? Can we not write? Have we not read books? Can we not ride a horse? Why are we not fit? As a Jew in one of Shakespeare's dramas asked, I ask you what have we not? You have not discharged your work. If it is not given at all, when are you to discharge it? (Cheers.) Has it ever happened that we did not do work when it was given? No one did say, we are unfit, do not appoint us. You appoint them. 'You get work done by them' and afterwards it is also announced in a Government Resolution. 'He has done his duty and so on.' If we go further we may ask 'You bring from England quite a new man of 21 years. What can he do? Has he any experience at all? He comes all at once and straight away becomes Assistant Collector, and becomes the superior of a Mamlatdar though the later be 60 years old. What is the comparison? (cheers). Is 60 years' experience of no value? A man of 21 years comes and begins to teach you. Generally he makes this Mamlatdar of 60 years stand before him. He does not give him even a chair for sitting, and this poor man stands before him with joined hands because he has to get Rs. 150, 200, or 400 (cheers). How then is the Saheb to acquire experience, how is he to become fit, and how is the work to go on? Has any one thought about this? Had it been true that the people of India are not fit for *swarajya* and that they would not be able to keep their kingdom in good order, then Hindus and Muhammadans would never have governed kingdoms in this country in ancient times. Formerly there were our kingdoms in this country. There were administrators. The proof of this is that before the advent of the English Government, in this country there was at least some order, there was no disorder everywhere, any man did not kill another. Since there existed such order, how can it be said that the people are not fit for self-rule. To-day science has made progress, knowledge has increased, and experience has accumulated in one place. We must have more liberty than before, and we must have become fitter. On the contrary it is said we are not fit. Whatever might have been the case in former times, this allegation is utterly false now. Better say, we shall not give you. What I say is, don't apply the words 'not fit' to us. At least we shall know that we are not really to be given. We shall get it. But why do we not get it? It is indirectly said that we are not fit. They say it is to teach us that they have come here. This is admitted. But how long will you teach us? We ask (Laughter.) For one generation, two generations or three generations! Is there any end to this?...Set some limit. You came to teach us. When we appoint a teacher at home for a boy we ask him within how many days he would teach him-whether in 10, 20 or 25 days, within two months, within four months. But if the study which should take six months for the boy to finish, would, he were to say contrary to our expectation, take one year, we tell him you are useless, go, we shall appoint another teacher (cheers). This applies to all people alike. Our officers have control over the people's education and it is their duty to improve them: this duty points one way, their attempts point another way. They say that whatever attempts they make it is impossible for the people to become fit for work.........We say our people are men like you, as wise as you. You take them in service, get work done by them. Your strictness is proverbial. What is going on in the *Khalsa* territory? There is no obstruction in the management. Is it obstructed in Mysore? Who are doing the work? The king of Mysore is a Hindu, the minister is a Hindu, the subjects are Hindus, the lower officers are Hindus. They carry on the administration of such a large kingdom as Mysore, but it is said that the people of the two districts beyond Mysore cannot carry it on in that manner. (Laughter, cheers). There are six districts in the Mysore territory, hence, it is like saying that six are fit and eight are not fit. There is fitness in us beyond any doubt (cheers). You may then, we say, for some reason admit it or not. Well. What authority is there for thinking that we possess fitness? I pointed to a Native State. I tell you another thing. Keep yourself aloof for 10 years and see whether it can be done or not (cheers, laughter). If it cannot be done take us under your control after ten years (cheers.) You are free to do so. This too, is not to be done.........There is no *swarajya*. There is no *swarajya.* What does it mean? What do we ask for? Do we say Drive away the English Government? But I ask what is it to the Emperor? Does the Emperor lose anything whether the administration is carried on by a civil servant or by our Belvi Saheb? (Cheers.) The rule still remains. The Emperor still remains. The difference would be that the white servant who was with him would be replaced by a black servant (cheers). From whom then does this opposition come? This opposition comes from those people who are in power. It does not come from the Emperor. From the Emperor's point of view there is neither anarchy nor want of loyalty, nor sedition in this. What does *rajadroha* (sedition) mean? Hatred of the king. Does 'King' mean a police sepoy? (Laughter) I said some time back that this distinction must first be made. Otherwise, if to-morrow you say 'remove the police sepoy' it would constitute sedition. Such is the belief of police sepoys (laughter). In the same manner, go a little further and you will see that the demand made by us is right, proper, just and in conformity with human nature. Other nations have done what we are doing. It has not been done only in our country. *Swarajya, swarajya*—what does it mean? Not that you do not want the English rule. There is the mistake at the root. Some one has some object in perpetuating it. It is served out by men whose interest lies in deceiving you. Do not care for it at all.

"If you think that you are men like other men, that is enough. When our objectors go to England their intellect and they are put to the test there. Therein we stand higher. What then is trotted out? They say your intellect may be good, but you do not possess character, courage and other qualities. Their character, I admit for a ghatka (24 minutes) the absence of that particular character. But it does not follow that we cannot acquire it (laughter). How can such character be developed in men whose life is spent in service and in service alone? Can it be said of any person—He worked as a clerk for 25 years, wrote on the cover the Saheb's orders, obtained the Saheb's signature thereon and thus he acquired the necessary character after 25 years.--Even if some truth is presumed in such a statement yet he will at first find it difficult to do responsible work. This is not denied. But when the system under which such men are, has disappeared, it cannot be said that men would not become fit in the next generation. Hence in my opinion we are fit for *Swarajya*. I shall now briefly tell you what we wish to obtain and what we should demand and then conclude my speech.

"You know what Indian administration is. It must be noted that it is carried on in accordance with a particular law. Its rules are fixed. What are the powers of the Secretary of State? What are the powers of the Governor-General? They define.

There are three great parts of the system. The Secretary of State is in England. The Governor-General is at Delhi in India. Under him there is a Governor for every Presidency. For the present let us omit those under him. But the main system is of the above triple character. Let us begin to consider each. Who appoints the Secretary of State? Not we. This is a heritage from the Company's government. When there was the East India Company's rule in this country, all matters were carried on in the interests of trade. The whole attention was directed towards the question how might the Company's shareholders obtain considerable profit; the Company's Directors were in the place of the present Secretary of State. You might say that it was a contract given for governing the entire kingdom. You know for instance under the Peshwa's rule Mamlatdar's offices were given away under a contract. This Indian administration was, as it were, according to the then law of Government, a trade carried on by the East India Company. They were to derive from it as much profit as possible. The Company's Directors were to be in England. The attention of the administration was directed to the fact that profit was to be given to the Directors, *i.e.*, shareholders. A letter used to come to the Governor-General here to this effect :—'So much profit must be paid to us this year. Realise it and send it to us.' This was the administration. The people's good was not considered under it. It was the story of the milk-man and his cows. If the cows did not yield sufficient milk, he says fill the pot with water. The administration of India was carried on like that. Subsequently it appeared after discussion that this administration was not good. And when Queen Victoria—you may say the Parliament —took the administration into their own hands, they did not approve of this trading system. Therefore they took it into their hands. This was alright. However the system of administration was modelled on the policy which was in existence when the administration was assumed (by the Parliament) and under which the Directors were masters in England and their servants were masters here. The State Secretary has come in the place of the Directors. The Governor-General has come in the place of their Governor. Thus what was done? The Sovereign—the Parliament—took the administration into their hands, but the establishment of employees which then existed has remained just as before. This happened in 1858 after the Mutiny. From that time to this the administration of India has been carried on in accordance with rules and arrangements formed as a heritage of the Company's policy. If the power had really to go to the sovereign this modelling after the policy of the Company should have disappeared. He is the King and we are his subjects. It is his duty to rule for the good of the subjects. And an arrangement should have been made in accordance with the rules—lawful—that may be included in that duty. But the arrangement was made thus—the Directors disappeared, the Secretary of State stepped into their shoes as the final authority. Who is to decide how much money is to be spent in India and what taxes are to be imposed? The State Secretary. Such powers are not placed in the Governor-General's hands. He is the chief officer. The Governors are under him. They are servants. There are other servants under them. And the entire administration must be carried on with the consent of and in consultation with and with the advice of this State Secretary? Such is the present policy. What has happened gradually? It has continued but a commercial policy. Though the rule went into the hands of the Queen's Government, and though they issued a great proclamation, the policy of the administration is not on the lines of that proclamation. It is in accordance with the trading Company's policy, the administration of the Kingdom is in accordance with the Company's policy. So the proclamation has had no effect. (Laughter, cheers.) Such was the arrangement. At the time our people did not know it. I believe, that if education had spread as much as it is now, the people would have contended that since the Queen had taken the reins of Government into her own hands, the administration of the kingdom should, as regards the sovereign and the subjects, be for the good of the subjects. Our people would then have told that the arrangement made by the Company was simply for its own benefit, and that a change must be made in that policy—in that arrangement. Such contention did come. The people have now contended for many years. To put the matter very briefly, Mr. Dadabhai Naoroji (cheers), who is one of those living persons who clearly saw and pointed out the defects, began this work. How did he begin? He said, What is the difference between the Company's system and this system? We do not see any in it. The rules are all made in accordance with the Company's policy. Are the people likely to derive any benefit from them? Then came the Legislative councils. They were such that the Governor-General was to appoint them. Originally the members were not to be elected by the people. Gradually your men became members of the Municipality and of the Legislative Council. Still the final keys are in the hands of the authorities. Discussion may be held in the Legislative Council. They say 'You have full liberty to hold a discussion. You may hold a discussion about spending the money in this country. But we shall decide whether it should be so spent or not. Exert yourself mentally and vocally as much as you can, we have no objection to it. Be awake throughout the night, prepare your speeches. Instead of printing them in a newspaper, we shall publish them in the Bombay (Government) Gazette.' This is the result. Nothing is hereby gained. Hope is held out no doubt. There is a *slokh* (stanza) in the *Mahabharat* which says hope 'should be made dependent upon time.' Our friends say 'Rights are to be given to you when you become fit. We do not wish to remain in India. When you become fit, we shall give the bundle into your possession and go to England by the next English steamer' (cheers). Very well. A time limit should be laid down. 'We shall give in two years. 'We shall give in ten years.' It did come afterwards. Time should be coupled with obstacles. Ten years were mentioned. These days passed and were very wearisome. 'We are obliged to make them fifteen' was the next. Hope and time should be coupled with an obstacle. The obstacle came. 'You yourselves must have brought it' was the retort. We did not bring it. We were awaiting good time. Excuse should be coupled with it. The excuse came. How did it come ? It is an excuse, only nothing can be said about it. Some cause should be shown. This is a sort of policy. When you do not mean to give, you cannot do otherwise. This policy does not find a place in the modern works on morality and politics. Only, the old tradition has continued. Thus this bureaucracy has been cajoling us. For the last 5 or 50 years the State Secretary and the Governor-General too have been cajoling us in this manner, have kept us afloat. As soon as you proceed to make some noise, it is said there were five members, to-morrow we shall make them six. What do we benefit by raising the number from five to six ? One of our men has merely to waste his time there for nothing for a while (Cheers.) There is no more advantage than that. If you object to six they say we make them eight. We raise 10 to 12, if necessary. (Laughter and cheers.) The people are already convinced that this matter cannot be disposed of in this manner. Whatever rights you may give, give them to us absolutely, however great you may keep your own powers. Take for instance, the management of the Educational Department. Most of the subordinate servants are from among us only. There is a Saheb at the head. Why is he kept there? With a view to restrain their mouths and the scope of their intellect. Even if 20 years' service be put in by the next subordinate, work cannot be done without the Saheb. That poor man actually begins to say so. It is such men that are prepared. I shall present to you two points of view. When a gardener is asked to prepare a garden just here, beyond this place, he wants flower pots. When big forests are to be prepared under the Forest Department, pots are not required. Bags of seeds are brought and emptied. Trees grow everywhere to any extent. Some of them grow small, some big. The present arrangement is that of the gardener. Owing to this arrangement the trees amongst us do not grow. Nay, care is taken that are planted in pots look pretty, so that flowers can be reached and plucked by the hand. We are educated in such a way that such pretty plants may grow. In such a manner is our man treated and made to work. And then after 25 or 30 years are past, he begins to say 'I am really not fit for this work.' We do not want this system. We want the English Government. We want to remain under the sway of this rule. But we do not want the State Secretary who has been created a son-in-law (cheers). We want at least *our men*, men elected by us, in his council. This is the first reform that must be made. In like manner the decision as to who is to expend India's revenues, how much money is to be collected and how many taxes are to be imposed should rest in our hands. (Cheers). We say, there must not be those taxes. They say how can the expenditure be met? That, we will see afterwards. We know this much. Expenditure is to be proportionate to the money we have and that again has to be raised according to the expenditure undergone. We understand this. We will later see what arrangement should be made. The second principle of Home Rule is that these powers should be in the people's hands, in the hands of good men, *viz.*, in the hands of men elected by the people. At present a great war is going on in Europe. The Emperor does not decide how much money has to be spent on the war. Mr. Asquith decides it. If there is a complaint against the work done by Mr. Asquith, it goes before Parliament, and if Mr. Asquith has committed a mistake, he has to tender his resignation. Will it be sedition if he has to tender his resignation? There-is the difference in the arrangement, there is the difference in the organization, there is the difference in the system. And we are asking for a change to such a system. 'The rule will fall, the rule will go away'—these thoughts are utterly foreign to us, they do not come within our limits, our reach, our view. And we do not also wish it. I again say, if the nation is to get happiness, if the thousands of complaints that have arisen to-day are to be removed, then first of all, change this system of administration. There is a saying in Marathi, "Why did the horse become restive? Why did the betel-leaves rot? Why did the bread get burnt? There is one answer. 'For want of turning' the leaves ought to have been turned, the bread ought to have been turned. Had the horse been turned, it would not have become restive." The root cause is here. Complaints about forests, complaints about Abkari, complaints about Kulkarni Vatans have arisen because authority is not in our hands. To state it in slightly changed words—because we have not *swarajya* (cheers). That we should have *swarajya* for us is at the root of our demand, we need not then dance to anybody's tune. However, this thing may happen even in *swarajya*. I do not deny it. When we have deficiency of money, and powers are placed in our hands, we may increase the tax; we increase it altogether voluntarily. Otherwise, whence is the expenditure to be met? But as it will be increased voluntarily, it will not oppress our minds.

Here is the right door. We are passing through it. When we are passing through it learned aliens may tell us that we should not pass through it but take another door. We cannot change. If others come and obstruct we must give them a push and make our way. The very same is the case with Swarajya. The obstruction comes from the Bureaucracy. We do not want such obstruction. The demand for *Swarajya* is such that it has nothing to do with sedition. It has nothing to say against the invisible Government. All domestic concerns should be managed by yourselves and by doing so what will happen is that in the first place your minds will remain in peace. Whatever you have to do you will do with the thought that you are doing it for your good. Nay, you will also reduce the expenditure. I do not think that in any Native State a Collector does get a pay of twenty five hundred rupees. If there is any place in the world in which a man doing the work of a Collector gets the highest pay, it is India (cheers). To give 2,500 rupees as pay to a Collector, would, in terms of the former rule, have been like giving an annual *Jahagir* of Rs. 30,000. Have we ever given in our Swarajya such a Jahagir of Rs. 30,000? Rs. 30,000 is not a small amount. There are reasons however now for it. What reason is given? Some reason or other can always be given. This man has to send Rs. 2,500 to England for his children, etc. For your welfare he has come from a cold climate to a hot climate risking his health

Must he not then be paid? The I.C.S. have laboured so much, made such self-sacrifice, and suffered so many hardships, and you would not pay them money? It appears to be right at first sight. But now the principal question is, who asked them to come here from there? (Cheers). We did not call them. They do such work as they may be fit to do. We do possess as much fitness as they have, but we shall be able to do the work on less pay. Men can be had. Then why give so much pay to them? We don't need it. We feel that we do not get to-day money for education. The excuse of 'no funds' which is brought forward in connection with the execution of works of public utility will then disappear. Business will go on unobstructed just as at present. In the beginning it may not be so efficient. Perhaps it may be less by an anna in the rupee. Still the satisfactory thought that the business has been carried on by the people, is of greater value. In this direction good management is to be asked for in administration. The present law must be amended. It is to be brought about through Parliament. We will not ask for it from others. We have not to get this demand complied with by petitioning France. The Allies may be there, we have not to petition them. The petition is to be made to the English people, to the English Parliament. The present state of things is to be placed before them. We have to do whatever may be required for this. If you carry on such an effort for 5 or 25 years, you will never fail to obtain its fruit. Moreover, such a time has now arrived. On account of the war effort must be made as will increase the value of India, India's bravery, India's courage, and India's stability. If the fact that the nation itself is making this effort' comes to the notice of the Government, then there is hope of our demand soon proving fruitful. I have, therefore, purposely brought this subject before you. The subject is being discussed elsewhere also. The League which we have established for this purpose is such that I myself or some one else will have occasion to place the subject before the people at every place, if not to-day some days afterwards, for carrying on this work. Let this subject be always discussed by you. Always think about it, get its usefulness explained, and carefully consider how much of loyalty and how much of disloyalty is in it. This is all I have to tell you on the present occasion. Though what I have to say be much more than this, still I have told you its substance in a brief manner. If the consideration of this be begun among you, be begun in Maharashtra, be begun in India, then some day or other this work will succeed, and even if the matter lies in God's hands still this is necessary. I admit that it does not lie in our hands. But the effect of action (*karma*) cannot fail to take its place in this world. The effect of action may not be obtained so soon as

I say, may not be obtained before my eyes, perhaps I may not be benefited by it. But this action must have its fruit (cheers). According to the law of action, when a certain action is done, another results from it, and a third one results out of that. Such succession goes on. Time will be required, there will be delay. But do we ask at all that we should have *moksha* before our eyes ? Again do we ask for it with the thought that we should have it in the hands of a certain person ? Only just a little ago a Resolution was passed in our conference that the parties of Moderates and Nationalists are not wanted. That is to say, it is the same to us to whomsoever *swarajya* is given. There is no objection even if powers be given to your sepoy to-morrow. You may say, how will the sepoy exercise such a great power ? The sepoy is to die some day or other and then we will see (cheers.) We want rights. We want a certain sort of arrangement giving happiness. We will get it. Our children will get it. Make the effort that is to be made. Be ready to do this work with the thought that it belongs to you. I am sure that by the grace of God your next generation will not fail to obtain the fruit of this work, though it may not be obtained in your life-time (cheers).

HOME RULE SPEECH AT AHMEDNAGAR

31st May, 1916

GENTLEMEN,—Before saying a few words to you it is my first duty to thank you very much. It is my first duty to thank you for the honour you have done me and for the address you have presented to me. Whatever the motive with which you have conferred the honour upon me may be, the few words, which I have now to tell you, relate to my own work. Perhaps this may appear strange to you. You have called me here and I make a statement about my own work before you, that would be a sort of impropriety. Even if you should think that Mr. Tilak came here and talked to people of his own things I say I do not hesitate at all since what I have to tell you is of as great an advantage to you as it is to me. Controversies and discussions about the state of our country have taken place in various ways and at various places. What is beneficial to the people in general? Many things are beneficial. Religion, which relates to the other world, is beneficial. Similarly, morality too is beneficial. Provision for one's maintenance is beneficial. Our trade should expand, the population should increase, there should be plenty and that plenty should safely fall into our hands—all these things are desired by men. But it is not possible to discuss all these things in the short time allowed to me. I will, therefore, say a few words to you about such of the above things as are important and are considered important by thousands of people and about a subject which is now discussed on all sides. This subject is *swarajya* (Cheers.) What concerns our homes we do with authority in our homes. If I desire to do such and such a thing, if it be merely a private one, I have not to ask any one about it nor to take anybody's permission nor is it necessary to consult any one else. That is not the case in public matters to-day. As is our own good, just so is the good of all people. If we turn to consider how people would begin to live well and how they would attain a condition of progressive improvement we shall see that, we are handicapped in consequence of want of authority in our hands. If a railway is to be constructed from one place to another, that is not under our control. As for trade, I might talk much about giving encouragement to such and such an industry but it is not wholly in our power to acquire knowledge of that industry at the place where it is carried on, to lessen the trade of those people in this country, and increase our own trade. Wherever we turn it is the same state that we see. We cannot stop the sale of liquor. There are also some things which are not wanted by us or by our Government, but the course of the general administration is such that it is not in our power to make any change,—the slightest change,—in it. We have till now made many complaints and Government have heard them ; but what is the root of all the complaints ? What things come in the way of improving our condition as we desire and what is our difficulty ?—this has been considered for about 50 years past, and many wise people have, after due consideration discovered one cause and that is that our people have no authority in their hands. In public matters, different people have different opinions. Some say, 'Do you not possess authority? Do not drink liquor, and all is done.' The advice is sweet indeed, but stopping all the people from drinking liquor cannot be done by mere advice. This requires some authority. He who has not got that authority in his hands cannot do that work. And if it had been possible to do the work by mere advice, then we would not have wanted a king. Government has come into existence for giving effect to the things desired by a large number of people. And as that Government is not in our hands, if anything is desired by thousands of you but not by those who control the administration, that can never be accomplished. I had come here on a former occasion. What about the famine administration of the time ? When Government came to know that the weavers sustained great loss during famine no doubt some steps were taken about it. We have lost our trade. We have become mere commission agents. The business of commission agency used to be carried on formerly; it is not that commission agency did not exist before, nor that it does not exist now. The difference is that while at that time you were the commission agents of our trade, you have now become the commission agents of the businessmen of England. You buy cotton here, and send it to England and when the cloth made from it in England, arrives, you buy it on commission and sell it to us. The business of commission agency has remained, but what has happened in it is that the profit which this country derived from it, is lost to us and goes to the English. The men and the business are the same. Owing to a change in the ruling power, we cannot do certain things. Such has become the condition that certain things as would be beneficial to the country cannot be carried out. At first we thought that even though the administration was 'alien' it could be prevailed upon to hear. Since the English administration is as a matter of fact 'alien,' and there is no sedition in calling it so, there would be no sedition whatever nor any other offence in calling alien those things which are alien. What is the result of alienness. The difference between aliens and us is that the aliens' point of view is alien, their thoughts are alien, and their general conduct is such that their minds are not inclined to particularly benefit those people to whom they are aliens. The Muhammedan kings who ruled here at Ahmednagar (I don't call Muhammedans aliens) came to and lived in this country and at least desired that local industries should thrive. The religion may be different. The children of him who wishes to live in India, also wish to live in India. Let them remain. Those are not aliens who desire to do good to those children, to that man, and other inhabitants of India. By alien I do not mean alien in religion. He who does what is beneficial to the people of this country, be he a Muhammedan or an Englishman, is not alien. 'Alienness' has to do with interests. Alienness is certainly not concerned with white or black skin. Alienness is not concerned with religion. Alienness is not concerned with trade or profession. I do not consider him an alien who wishes to make an arrangement whereby that country in which he has to live, his children have to live and his future generations have to live, may see good days and be benefited. He may not perhaps go with me to the same temple to pray to God, perhaps there may be no intermarriage and interdining between him and me. All these are minor questions. But, if a man is exerting himself for the good of India, and takes measures in that direction, I do not consider him an alien. If any body has charged this administration with being alien, he has done so in the above sense. At first I thought that there was nothing particular in this. The Peshwa's rule passed away and the Muhammedan rule passed away. The country came into the possession of the English. The king's duty is to do all those things whereby the nation may become eminent, be benefited, rise, and become the equal of other nations. That king who does this duty is not alien. He is to be considered alien, who does not do this duty, but looks only to his own benefit, to the benefit of his own race, and to the benefit of his original country.........At first hundreds of questions arose. Agricultural assessment increased, the Forest Department was organised in a particular manner, the Abkari Department was organised in a particular manner,—about all these things we have been constantly complaining to the Government for the past 20 or 25 years. But no arrangements about the different departments, the different professions, the different trades and the different industries, were made to accord. This is the chief question of the past 50 years. While looking out for a cause we at first believed that when we informed the administration of it, it would at once proceed to do as we desire. The Administration is alien. It does not know the facts. When 5 or 10 of our prominent men assemble and represent, the administration will understand. It being alien it cannot otherwise understand. As soon as it is informed of facts it is so generous minded and wise that it will listen to what you have to say and redress the grievances. Such was our belief. But the policy of the Bureaucracy during the last 50 years has removed this belief. However much you may clamour, however much you may agitate, whatever the number of grounds you may show, its sight is so affected as not to see the figures drawn from its own reports and set before it. Its own arguments and its own grounds do not meet with its own approval. If we urge any further it sticks only to what may be adverse to our statement. Some may say there is nothing to wonder at in this. Whoever were your rulers those kingdoms have been broken up and now the rule of the English has been established. Of course those people do just what is beneficial to them. Why then do you complain about them? This is sure to happen.' Such is the opinion of several people. 'Your outcry only causes pain to the Government and in a manner disturbs its mind. So do not raise this outcry. Accept quietly what it may give. Accept gladly, what little it may give and thank it.' Such is the opinion of several others. I do not approve of this opinion. My opinion is that whatever be the Government whether British or any other, it has, as Government, a sort of duty to perform. Government has a sort of religious duty to perform; a sort of responsibility lies on its shoulders. I say that when a Government evades this responsibility it is no Government at all. Government possesses authority. All the power possessed by Government may be acquired by it by fighting or may be conferred upon it by the people. ....Even if it is acquired by conquest still Government has a duty to perform. As we have a duty, so those who are called Government have also a duty. They must do certain things. The

Government has already admitted certain duties. Does not Government do such works as constructing roads, establishing post offices and telegraphs? It does. If to-morrow some one were to say 'If Government does not construct roads, it is its pleasure. It may construct them if it likes, but not, if it does not like,' then all of you who are assembled here would find fault with him saying, 'If these things are not to be done by Government, why do we pay taxes? If the Government will not utilise for the people's conveniences taxes levied from us, it has no authority to take any taxes whatever from us. Government take these for our benefit.' When persons argue that the Government is good, what do they point to? The question is always asked, 'This our Government has constructed roads, made railways, established telegraphs and post offices—are not these conveniences made for you? Why do you then raise an outcry against Government?' I do not say that these things have not been done, but that those that have been done are not sufficient. These things have been done, done well and have been done better by the British Government than they would have been done by the former Government—this is an honour to them. But should we not ask it to do those things which it does not do? That is not a real Government which considers itself insulted when told of those things which have not been done and a desire to do which is not apparent, which does not direct its attention to them though urged in many ways, and which thinks that we should not urge things to it. What then is meant by a real Government? This must be considered a little. There is a vast difference between the present system and the old system. At present an effort is being made to create a sort of erroneous conception. Neither the Collector nor the Civilians arriving here who are called the bureaucracy in English, are Government. A police sepoy is not Government. It does not constitute any sedition whatever to say, 'Do something if it can be done, while maintaining the British rule which is over our country, without harm being done to that rule and without weakening it.' We want the rule of the English which is over us. But we do not want these intervening middlemen. The grain belongs to the master, the provisions belong to the master. But only remove the intervening middlemen's aching belly, and confer these powers upon the people so that they may duly look to their domestic affairs. We ask for *swarajya* of this kind. This *swarajya* does not mean that the English Government should be removed, the Emperor's rule should be removed and the rule of some one of our Native States should be established in its place. The meaning of *swarajya* is that explained by Mr. Khaparde at Belgaum, *viz.*, we want to remove the priests of the deity. The deities are to be retained. These priests are not wanted. We say, appoint other priests from amongst us. These intervening Collectors, Commissioners and other people are not wanted, who at present exercise rule over us? The Emperor does not come and exercise it. He is in England. If facts were communicated to him, he would wish that good should be done to you. Is good done to us? We do now want these priests (cheers). These people are clever. We say that no priest is wanted. They say, 'We have passed examinations. We do much.' That is all true. But their attention is directed more to the remuneration belonging to the priest. Hence this priestly office should remain in our hands. The position of the Badwas of Pandharpur and these people is the same (cheers). Will there be any loss to the Emperor if the said priestly office does not remain in the hands of the bureaucracy who are endeavouring to retain? There will be none. Some may say that the English people belong to the Emperor's race. We have become the Emperor's subjects. He does not make any difference between the English subjects and the black subjects. He does not wish to make it. The meaning of the word *swarajya* is Municipal Local Self-Government. But even that is a farce. It is not sufficient. When an order comes from the Collector, you have to obey it. He (Collector) has power to call the President and tell him to do such and such a thing. If the President does not do it, the Collector has power to remove him. Then where is *swarajya*? (cheers). The meaning of *swarajya* as stated above is retention of our Emperor and the rule of the English people, and the full possession by the people of the authority to manage the remaining affairs. This is the definition of *swarajya*. What we ask for is not that the authority of the English should be lessened, nor that the English Government should go away and the German Government should come in its place. On the contrary, the present war has proved and the whole world has seen that it is not our wish that the German Government should come here. Nay, in order that the rule of this Government should remain here permanently, thousands of our people are to-day sacrificing their lives in the most distant and cold climes (hear, hear, cheers). If in order that this rule may remain and that this rule should not go away and the rule of the German people should not come in its place, we pay money—be it according to our means—though we are not as wealthy as the English. What then is left of the charge......... According to our ability, our fighting men are going there and sacrificing their lives and in this way exerting themselves. France, Germany and other nations are commending and applauding them (cheers, hear, hear). By shedding our blood we have proved our desire that our loyalty to the English Government should be of this intense kind (hear, hear, and cheers). I do not think that any man can adduce stronger evidence than this in his favour. Thus to-day it is an undoubted fact that we want here the rule of the English alone and accordingly we are exerting ourselves. When such is the state of things, why should not these intervening people who have been appointed be removed and why should we not get the rights possessed by the people in other places within the British Empire? We are not inferior to them in point of bravery and education, we possess ability. Such being the case, why should we not get the rights? Why should the Emperor make a distinction between his black and white subjects? Who has given such advice to the Emperor? The peculiar feature of this British constitution is that the Emperor acts on the advice of the people. Why should the ministers give him such advice? At present those who possess power, *i.e.*, the bureaucracy, are white. When a black man joins them he too becomes like them. Under the present system, if a native on his arrival from England after passing examinations be appointed to be Collector, he becomes just like them. Note then that I am not speaking only about the whites. We do not want this system. What does it matter if a man or two of ours is exalted to the Bureaucracy. He cannot do anything in particular. Therefore this system must be done away with. We would not be satisfied by the appointment of one or two persons. Let us pass on. Who introduced the system? The Emperor did not introduce it. The Queen's proclamation as promulgated declares one policy and the present system is quite its opposite. At present it is not at all in our hands to bring about our own good. Were we to think that encouragement should be given to swadeshi goods by imposing duty on certain imported foreign goods, that is not in our hands. Were we to think of starting such and such industries required in this country or of importing paid teachers from foreign countries, that is not in our hands. What a trifling matter this is after all! It is necessary that all people should know reading and writing. Whether a man be a Muhammadan or of any other religion or of any caste, he ought to know a little of reading and writing. This is now acknowledged by all people throughout the world. There is now no doubt about this. By reading and writing a man derives at least some benefit. No one requires to be told of this anew. Then why is not that achieved here? Because there is no money. Who gives this excuse? The bureaucracy. Their pay is Rs. 2,500 and if they want a raising to 3,000 then there is money. Think of exchange compensation. When the price of the rupee fell, six crores of rupees were brought out by Government on account of exchange. At that time money was found. Unless you have authority in your hands this state of affairs cannot be got over. There is no money for education, but there is money to pay a salary of Rs. 2,500 to the Collector. However clearly we may explain this aspect it cannot carry conviction. The present bureaucracy cannot consider this matter from the point of view from which we would consider it if authority were to come into our hands.

No doubt we have been told that money should be spent on education. When people begin to know how to read and write the number of offences committed falls by thousands, they carry on their dealings well; they understand what is of advantage and what is of disadvantage to them. When people become fit in this manner an officer on Rs. 2,500 will not be necessary to govern them. One on Rs. 500 will do and we shall be able to spend Rs. 2,000 on education. In no other country are there so highly paid officers at present The Viceroy who comes to govern India gets Rs. 20,000 a month while the Prime Minister of England gets Rs. 5,000. He who has to live in England and manage the affairs of the whole Empire gets Rs. 5,000, while he who carries on the administration of India here gets Rs. 20,000. Why so? There is no answer to this. This is so because the latter is managed at the cost of others (cheers). This is India. Go and eat. If any shop belonging to other people is made over to you for management, you will naturally pay the employee a salary of Rs. 100 if he belongs to your community or caste even when you are prepared to pay him a pay of Rs. 50 only in your own shop. In this way the present arrangement is being carried on. We are not at all benefited by this arrangement. It is not the case that these things have come to our notice for the first time. It is 50 years since the things came to our notice. When the National Congress was held at Calcutta in 1906, Mr.

Dadabhai Naoroji (cheers) stated this distinctly. He gave it as his 50 years' experience that for counteracting this present irregularity and the sort of injustice that is taking place in India, there is no other remedy than that the power should pass into the people's hands. and rest in the hands of the people. He called it Self-Government. We must decide upon the arrangement as regards what is to be done in our homes, what is to be done in our villages, what is to be done in our presidency and what is to be done in our country. If we decide about this, it will be done at a small cost, it will be done well, and our decision as regards in what matter we should expend more money, and in what matter less will be more beneficial to the people. The bureaucracy say that we do not possess knowledge as if they alone possess it. Their first look out is to see how their pay will be secure. When money comes into the treasury the expense on account of their pay must be first defrayed. Their military expenditure must be first defrayed. They must be first fully provided for. If money remains after this, it is to be applied to education. They do not say that education is not wanted. Education is not a bad thing in their eye. But the people are to be educated and their other conveniences are, if possible, to be looked to after all the above expenditure is defrayed. This is to be thought of afterwards. Now we shall first see whether we could manage things or not if power were to come into our hands. If we think that more pay is demanded of us then we reduce it and tell them that they will have to do the work for the country. If all things can be considered in this manner, we shall have in our hands the opportunity of bringing about those things which it is desirable to bring about. This is mere speculation. Where is your difficulty? There is a common saying in Marathi: A certain man asked three questions. Why does the horse become restive, why did betel leaves rot—the story occurs in the third book it was there formerly, I do not know whether it is there now.—He gave a single answer to two or three such questions, which is, 'owing to not turning.' Similarly why is not the consumption of liquor reduced in our presidency, why are the people subjected to zulum in forests, why is money not available for education? —All these questions have one answer, and it is this: Because you have no power in your hands (cheers) and so long as this power will not come into your hands, so long there will also be no dawn of your good fortune. Whoever may be the Emperor we speak not anything about him. But we must do those things which relate to business, trade, religion and society. Unless the power of doing those things comes partially into our hands—in the end it must come fully—unless it comes fully into our hands, it is impossible for us to see a time of plenty, the dawn of good fortune, advantage or prosperity. Water cannot be drunk with others' mouths. We ourselves have to drink it. The present arrangement makes us drink with others' mouths. We ourselves must draw our water—the water of our well—and drink it. If that well belongs to Government a tax of a rupee per month may, if necessary, be paid. But we want power. There are no means of salvation for us unless we have it in our possession. This principle of politics is almost settled—proved—from the point of view of history, morality and social science. Now you may ask why it is told you so late that power should come into your hands or the time of its coming into your hands is approaching. I have to say a few words about this. Up till now the generality of people in England thought of deriving as much profit from India as possible and that India was a sort of burden to them. The people in England used to think that the 30 crores of people in India would overthrow their rule some time or other, that they should be disarmed and that they must be kept in slavery and under control as much as possible. But that condition is now changed. Owing to the war which is now going on in Europe, it has begun to be thought that unless all the many parts of the British Empire unite together, that Empire would not attain as much strength as it should. It has so happened now that a consciousness has been awakened in England that they stand in need of help from other countries called colonies belonging to them—Australia, Canada, and New Zealand, which are inhabited by Sahebs. If you take advantage of this awakened consciousness, you too have this opportunity of acquiring some rights. No one asks you to obtain these rights by the use of the sword. To-day the nation's mind has undergone a change. India can give some help to England. If India be happy England too will acquire a sort of glory, a sort of strength and a sort of greatness. This consciousness has been awakened in England. If no advantage is taken of this awakened consciousness at this time, such an opportunity will not occur again. The bureaucracy considers this to be bad. Who will be the loser in this? Not the Emperor, but the bureaucracy. They, therefore, consider this thing to be bad, and they are now telling us that we are not fit for *swarajya* and that, therefore, they have come here. As if there was no *swarajya* anywhere in India when they were not here. We all were barbarians and ready to cut each other's throats. There was no system of administration under the Peshwa's regime. There was no system of administration under Muhammadan regime. We were not able to carry on State administration, we were not able to construct roads. We did not know how the people might be happy. Nana Phadnavis was a fool, Malik Amber was a fool, Akbar and Aurangzeb were fools. Therefore these people have come here for our good and we are still children (laughter). Let us admit for a moment also that we are children. When are we to become grown up? In law when one attains his 21st year one is considered to be grown up. Though these people have ruled over us for 50 years we have not been able to grow. What then did they do for 50 years? If the people of India were children whose duty was it to educate them? It was their duty. They were the rulers. I go so far as to say that they have not done this duty —hence not only are we children, but they are unfit to rule (cheers). It is better that those people who could not improve the condition of their subjects during 50 years should give up their power and make it over to others. If there be a manager of your shop and if he performed the duty of *munim* for 50 years, but there was only loss continuously for 50 years what would you tell him? 'Sir, give up your place and go away. We shall look to our own management.' Another may be of a lower grade. Though he may be less clever he will at least know that in managing a shop there should at least be no loss. This at least he must know. What those people tell us, *viz.*, that we have not become fit, proceeds from selfishness. If what they say be true, it is in a way disgraceful to them. They are being proved to be unfit. And if it be false, they are selfish. We can draw no other conclusion from this than the above. What is meant by 'we are unfit?' What is the matter with us? Our municipal management is tolerated. If some one comes from England after passing an examination and becomes a Collector that is tolerated. He discharges his duties and Government commend him. But when the rights of *swarajya* are to be given to the people, to tell all people—crores of people—plainly that they are unfit is to make an exhibition of one's own unfitness (cheers). Besides this objections of many other sorts are taken against *swarajya*. In the first place, I have already said that they unhesitatingly decide that the whole nation is unfit. If we say, hold an examination' no examination too is held. Unfit, unfit—what does it mean? Set your men to work and set our men also to work. See whether they do or do not work properly. No opportunity to work is given and yet we are called unfit. Are even those, who have been given an opportunity, found unfit? There are members in the Legislative Council, are they unfit? Have they ever called themselves unfit? Have you ever called them unfit? No. What does then unfit mean? You don't mean to give. In order to say there is no butter-milk, why circumlocute and say to-day being Sunday, there is no buttermilk-such is the shuffling that is going on now. I want to ask you whether you-without permitting that shuffling-are prepared or not to make a resolute demand. If you are not prepared to ask, if you do not make urgent solicitation about this,—if you throw away the present opportunity, such an opportunity will not come again for 100 years. Therefore, you must be prepared. I know that if after being prepared we spoke a little forcibly, some police sepoy may say 'O you.' This is not unlikely. But it must be put up with. There is no help for it. We have no power in our hands. We cannot say to the police sepoy, you are a fool, go back.' He obeys to Police Inspector's order. But I can tell you that if you people of all castes and religions, become united and at this time make this demand of Government resolutely, unitedly press it earnestly, be prepared to bear any expense that may be necessary for this, and proclaim not only to the Government but to the whole world that unless your demand be granted you would not be satisfied nor remain contented,—if you possess so much resoluteness I am sure that by the grace of God you will not fail to have the demand granted to you as a fruit of your resoluteness. Whether in religion or in politics, resoluteness is required and that resoluteness of mind does not come without courage. It will not do to say 'How may it be?' Whether good or evil may result we want this very thing. We will ask for this very thing. For this we will collect money and undergo any expenditure or exertions that may be necessary and we will not stop this agitation till this our demand is satisfied. If this work is not completed within our lifetime, our children also will keep up this same agitation. When there is such devotion for this work, only then will it be fruitful. Without devotion, no fruit is obtained from God, from King, in this world or in the next world. If you do not possess this devotion, no fruit will be obtained though strenuous exertions be made in this manner. First, devotion is required. Both rich and poor must possess devotion. The poor must help in their own way, the rich must help in their own way. Those who possess intelligence must help by means of intelligence. Every man must bear this thing constantly in mind. If you do not bear this thing constantly in mind, if you do not prepare yourself to make exertions then it will be sheer folly to blame others for failure. Perhaps the word folly may not be to your taste. I have used it in the heat of speaking. But my firm belief is that we have not yet begun to make efforts as strenuously,, as earnestly and as devotedly, as we shoald do. If a Saheb were to ask whether there would be confusion or not if powers were given to us, we say yes, yes. We have no men. The men are not prepared! And then we laugh at the Saheb in our house. No we must laugh there in his presence (cheers) (laughter.) It will not do to laugh in our house. The reply must be given just to his face. We must be prepared to maintain what we consider to be true and proclaim it to the people, to the officers, and even to the Emperor. On the day on which you will be ready to do this—particularly in days after the war is over—the administration shall have to be changed in some respects at least. If the administration here continue as at present, England cannot hold authority among European nations. At present England is the most powerful of all. The English Government is the most powerful, but to keep it so, change must necessarily be made in the present administration. As a matter of fact they say, 'make that change' by all means. But India does not say that the change should be made! Some defect can always be found. I stood up to-day; another will stand up to-morrow and say 'your good does not lie in what I have said. The arrangement which exists at present is itself good. There is the benign Government. The bureaucracy is wise. Therefore if you act in accordance with their principles that would be well.' The question does not concern only our traders; nor intelligent people; nor people of any religion such as Musalmans, etc. It is not the case that it applies only to one class, only to Muhammadan merchants. The thing which I am urging is not for Musalmans, for Hindus, nor for traders. It applies to all. There is only one medicine for all people. That medicine is power; take it into your possession; when it comes into your possession, if there be any disputes between you and us, we would be able to settle them. After the power has come into our hands there would be much time to settle them. If there be any difference of opinion in religious beliefs, that too we will remove. We want power for this. We want power to settle disputes. It is not wanted for increasing them. Aliens do not know as much as we do what we have to do for our country. Their point of view is different. British Government being maintained at the head, one and the same Emperor will rule over India as he does over the British Empire. But introduce here an arrangement similar to that in other Colonies. There, in those Colonies, the people have got in their own hands all the power, the right of ownership, and the power to make laws. That does not affect the Emperor. There is no attempt to overthrow the British Government. Really it is an attempt to make the British rule more pleasing to the people. Certain people may lose means of maintenance, that may happen. We do not think that the Emperor has reserved India for those people. The present system has come into existence for some reason or other. It must go. The Emperor ought to give powers into the hands of the people, and without making any distinction between India and British subjects, between the white and the black subjects. As they are the Emperor's subjects, so are we too the subjects. We must become as happy as they. The thing which some wise, learned and thoughtful people have now decided to the key of all these, is *swarajya*. The time for it has now arrived. I have explained to you the meaning of it. I have told you how the time has come. All factors there may be, but your resoluteness is the final thing. Without it the opportunity which has come will be lost. Though the change, of which I speak, be in contemplation, you will not get it. There must be resoluteness on your part. Fortunately agitation of this kind has now begun. Recently we established at Belgaum an institution to work for *swarajya.* An institution has been established in Madras. This subject is already before the Congress and it will dispose it of one way or the other. The several provinces will make their arrangements and render help. You must show this much courage; that if some one, the Collector, Commissioner, etc.—were to ask 'what do you want?' you answer 'We want power, there must be power in our hands.' Government servants should be considered to be people's servants. Do not think that when in future power comes into your hands, you are not to entertain the European as a servant. If he can work well, we shall keep him, and we shall pay him what we may think proper. But he must be our servant, not we his servants. If we entertain this desire and make efforts for it, then our ideal is capable of accomplishment. Give the help that may be required. Be prepared to render such assistance as may be required to those who may come to speak to us in connection with this. And when you are thus prepared—people of different places, not only of Bombay, Poona, Nagar, but also of Bengal, Madras, etc., if people of all places be prepared this thing is feasible. To accomplish it, to accomplish it soon, begin to work for it.

May India enjoy quick, the fruit of such work.

SECOND HOME RULE SPEECH AT AHMEDNAGAR

[*On being requested by Mr. Chaukar, Mr. Tilak delivered the following lecture amidst cheers and shouts of Tilak Maharajki jai in the old cloth market at Nagar, on the* 1*st June*, 1916.]

I had thought that I would probably not have to deliver another lecture after the one delivered here yesterday. On that occasion I placed before you the few thoughts that commonly occur about *swarajya*. However this subject is such that, not only one, but even ten lectures on it may not suffice. Therefore to-day I speak again about two more matters relating to *swarajya* which were not dealt with yesterday, to make it clearer, better understood, and to render the people's ideas about it more distinct. My general opinion is that all reforms we want are reforms relating to *swarajya*. You may perhaps know the story about the old woman. It is to the following effect: That old woman in the story, after the deity had been propitiated, considered what she should ask, and prayed for the following boon: The deity should give her such a boon that she would actually see her grandsons dining in dishes of gold, that is to say, she should remain alive till that time, that she should have a son, that he should earn wealth, etc., etc. In this small boon the whole object was included. Similar is the case with *swarajya.* If we do not get *swarajya,* there will be no industrial progress, if we do not get *swarajya* there will be no possibility of having any kind of education useful to the nation, either primary or higher. If we do get *swarajya,* it is not merely to advance female education or secure industrial reform or social reform. All these are parts of *swarajya.* Power is wanted first. Where there is power there is wisdom. Wisdom is not separate from power. If it be, it becomes useless. In no nation this proposition is required to be made particularly clear. But it is required to be explained in a particular manner to our people. The reason of this is that there is no *swarajya* in our country. Some people raise this objection against our party : Why do you not effect social reform ? This is said not by us but by those who do not mean to give rights of *swarajya* to us, but wish to transfer the train of our agitation from one track to another. There are many people who have effected social reform amongst themselves. Social reform is thoroughly introduced in Burma. There is one religion. There the people are prepared for anything. Their children marry any one they like. But that country is wholly immersed in a state of dependence. There is no spirit of nationality in respect of anything there. Then, what is wanted ? We are one nation. We have a duty to perform in this world. We must get the rights which belong to man by nature. We want freedom. We must have in our hands the right of carrying on our affairs. If you do not get these things, no reform would be fruitful to you. That is the root of all reforms. No power, no wisdom. Mere book learning is useless. Do you believe that the people who have come to rule over us are superiors to us in intelligence and learning ? Such is not my own belief. We can show as much learning, as much courage, as much ability as they. Perhaps they may not be apparent now, but they are in us. There are conjunctions in history as well as in astronomy. When the Muhammadan rule was declining, the Marathas had only recently risen. Afterwards, the English having set foot in India, the whole power has passed into their possession, and their power is the cause of the admiration which we feel for them and the pride—be it true or false—which we feel for their ability. And when even a small portion at least of this power comes into your hands, then your wisdom will be of use. Many things are now wanted by us. Our industries must be improved. But why are they stopped ? Who stopped them ? If we begin to look out for the cause of this, it will appear that we did not stop this industrial reform, we did not stop this economic reform. In that nation in which there is a way and there is liberty to rise and to show one's ability, good qualities flourish. You may possess wisdom. When you assist some great officer and he commends you, then only you think that you possess ability. This is a sort of feeble-mindedness—want of spirit—and it has enveloped the whole nation. You say 'I cannot do it.' You never did it, no one gave you *sanad*: even before it you make an outcry that you cannot do such and such a thing. You say so and advocate some other path. In my opinion it is a great misfortune that, in our Maharashtra at least, some people should bring forward this excuse and stand in the way of the agitation which is carried on for the acquisition of the rights of *swarajya*. Have we not achieved anything? Think of this, Maharashtra certainly possesses a quality that can be utilised for the nation. But at the present time we do not get an opportunity of making use of that quality, and our mind does not turn to other things, such as female education or this or that simply because that opportunity is not given to us (cheers). If any one else sees any danger in this he may do it, but my mind cannot be convinced, has not been convinced, nor do I think that it will be convinced during the few years that are left (cheers). It is vain to speak of other subjects. At present our people are not endowed with heroism, courage and learning, when our women are educated their generation will become of that sort, but even that is to arise from our own seed (cheers). If any one has such a belief (as the above) that is wrong. I do not say that female education is not wanted but when they tell us to turn to it, in order to stop this agitation on this side then we say: this is a remedy to kill the nation. If you do not possess strength, if you have no pluck to acquire anything, it is quite foolish to take an educated wife and say that the issue begotten of her would be of the above sort and that those our sons would make some exertions in order to discharge the obligation under which they would be to us (cheers). You must stand on your own legs. You must bring about these things. And you must first bring about the chief of those things. The experience of those who have made exertions for the past fifty years is that this *swarajya* is the key to all things. And if this does not come into your hands, then you say 'We shall effect this reform after making exertions for minor reforms.' If you mean to effect it thus do so, I have no objection to it. But that will not be helpful to this *swarajya*, is not helpful to this course. And I am to speak again to-day on the same subject on which I spoke yesterday in accordance with the same opinion. Yesterday I told you what *swarajya* means. By *swarajya* it is not meant that the English should be driven away. It does not matter whoever may be the king. We have nothing to do with the king. When we get our rights, that is sufficient. And whoever might be the king over us those rights can be obtained. There is a king in England. But have the English people rights or not? The King of England is himself our Emperor. Hence, if, while his kingly position is maintained in England, the English people obtain rights of freedom, then what difficulty is there in our obtaining the rights of British citizenship, the same King continuing to be Emperor in India ? No difficulty of any sort remains. This dark imputation which is made, *viz.*, that the agitation about Home Rule—*swarajya*—is seditious and in the belief of which as sedition a security of 2,000 rupees was taken from Mrs. Annie Besant the other day—this imputation, this accusation, does not come from the Emperor or from the subjects, but from the intervening granary-keepers (cheers). The duty which you have to do is to agitate that this administration must be changed. The King need not be changed. Unless the system —the arrangement—according to which the present administration is carried on is changed, every man in India will become more and more effeminate. The duty which we have to perform is to stop that. Some people say, what does it matter if there is slavery ? Do they not give us to eat ? They do not starve any one to death. Even the beast and the birds get to eat. To get to eat is not the aim of man. To feed the family is not the end of man. 'Even a crow lives and eats offerings.' A crow maintains itself. I do not consider it manliness merely to maintain oneself and fill the belly, to obey the commands of the administration accepting posts which may be kept open within the limits laid down by it and to maintain oneself according to its direction. This docile nature is common to beasts and men. If there is required the quality of manhood in man, then we should see whether there is any scope open for our intellect, our ability, our courage and boldness. Such scope is not open in India. Therefore, if we have any duty to perform then the first duty is, take a portion of this authority into your possession, it does not matter if you take a little portion of it; as the President (Mr. N. C. Kelkar, President of the Nagar District Conference) has said briefly, if we do not entertain the hope of being free to act in matters of spending our own money, deciding according to our own understanding according to the consent of five or ten men as to what purpose the tax which we pay is to be applied, then, according to the law of nature this kind of hope or thought which is in the minds of men will gradually lessen and to that extent we shall more and more descend to the level of beasts. *Swarajya*, *swarajya*, what does it mean? And what will be the effect of it? Does *swarajya* mean that one Collector is removed and yours has come? There is no objection to say, remove such and such a man and make such and such an arrangement in such and such a place. Perhaps, a white man when paid will be a servant of us too; If he be good we shall also keep him. The question is not at all about individuals. The question is about the nation. The chief question is whether a certain nation is to be treated like beasts or whether considering the people in the nation to be men, their sentiment, their desire for liberty is to be given the right direction and they are to be brought and placed in the rank of civilized nations. If the matter be considered from such a standpoint, then there is no other way to accomplish this than *swarajya*, than the possession of authority. When the authority once comes into our hands then we shall be able to do thousands of things. A great attempt was made at Poona to close a liquor shop of Ghoda,—which may be bringing a revenue of a thousand or two to Government. But it is not under our control to close it. Why is so much correspondence required to decide that a liquor shop should be started at a certain place or should not be started at all? I think that the annual profit of the shop may not be equal to the price of the paper that may have been used in connection with the business (laughter, hear, hear.) This business which goes on under the present system should be put a stop to, this high-handedness should be ended and the authority should come into our hands By the authority coming into our hands the hereditary qualities which we possess will be heightened. We shall find a way to make a use of those qualities in some way or other. That is *Swarajya*. *Swarajya* is nothing else What if it be to a small extent? It does not trouble you. It does not trouble you as much as it should. If it be said, one sits at home, does some business or other, gets some money, maintains his children,—this much will suffice, wherefore should there now be the movement for *swarajya*? The only answer to this is the idea in respect to the nation, *viz.*, that there is in this world something more than ourselves, that there is one more duty of bringing about the good of a greater number than yourself—this duty you have begun to forget. There was a time when in this country, among the succession of great men in the Maharashtra there were able men who were awake to ideals. But unfortunately this characteristic has not survived. If another man begins to do our work, we say alright, when the work is done, that is sufficient. But the sense of discrimination where to say aye and where not has left us. The English poeple carry on our administration, we are sitting idle. Take cattle for example. If there be any dirt in the cattleshed the keeper sweeps it away, looks to sanitation, feeds the cattle and gives them water at the proper time,—have the cattle put the question that the management should come into their hands? (Laughter). The difference between men and cattle is no more. The Collector of Nagar looks to sanitation, tells what should be done if a disease comes, makes arrangement if a famine comes, takes measures that no calamity may befall you. Your condition has become that of a parrot kept in a cage; such a condition is not wanted; I tell you why. We are not envious, they are doing our work. Owing to the existing arrangement all the good qualities possessed by us are gradually disappearing. In order that those qualities may not disappear, we must be at liberty to do what they now do; we need not go in search of fresher work to do. We are not to leave alone what they do and do any other work we may not like. What they do we have to do. We want the same power to be in our hands. There is only one objection to this. It is very bad indeed that such an objection should arise at all. A story was published in the *Kesari*: Rabindranath Tagore has given in his autobiography a poem to this effect about a parrot kept in a cage. It narrates in full a conversation between a parrot kept in a cage and a free parrot. The free parrot said to the parrot in the cage: "There is such fun outside; one can roam so much, go anywhere one likes, can eat at any time one likes. Have you got such joy?' The parrot kept in the cage replied: "Sir, what you say is true. But where can this golden perch be obtained after going?" Some urge an objection like this if *swarajya* be got, how are we to manage it? None yet to give, none yet to take. Your anxiety is if *swarajya* be got how are we to manage it? We are not fit. If the said parrot went out, how was he to get the cage and the perch to sit on, etc? We have reached just the same condition. This condition is not natural. It is artificial. Just as that sentiment arose in that parrot's mind owing to his being confined in a cage for many years so also the above sentiment arose in our mind owing to the above powers having passed out of our hands. This is not our original natural sentiment—the natural human sentiment. As that is not the parrot's natural sentiment, just so this is not the natural sentiment of our nation. This must be borne in mind at first. We become fit to do the work that falls to us. We are the descendents of those people who were fit in this manner, and if we be their true descendants, the same qualities must become manifest in us when we have that opportunity. And we must make exertions for it with the confidence that they will become manifest. This is what I say (cheers.) If heredity has any value, recognise it, otherwise at least give up calling yourselves the grandsons,—great-grandsons—of such and such a person. There are now many *sardars* in our country. They say that their grandfathers were *sardars* and that they also have inherited the qualities of their grandfather's blood. But in order to save the vatan acquired by them (the grandfathers,) they serve Sahebs in any manner they choose; well I say, they began to do so because they are *sardars*. But why should you or we, who have nothing to obtain, run after them? A sort of shadow has thus been thrown over the nation and we have to get out of it. This is an eclipse. When the moon is eclipsed, alms are given for its becoming free. You are not prepared to spend even a pie to put an end to the eclipse which has overtaken you, nor are you prepared to move from it. When the moon was eclipsed the Brahmans of ancient times used at least to make *jap* (repeating passages from Vedas, etc.). Do you make any *jap* at least ? Are you making exertions for this ? Are you prepared to pay two pice to any one for this ? No, nothing. Our objectors raise this objection. If powers be given to the Hindus, what are the Muhammadans to do ? If the rights of *swarajya* be given to the Hindus, the Muhammadans would not get them. As if we cannot afterwards duly consult our Muhammadan brethren and come to a settlement. If powers came into our hands we would exercise *zulum* over the Muhammedans, and if the powers pass into their hands they would exercise *zulum* over the Hindus ! These men come to tell you these things on people's behalf. Who are they ? Why do they tell you ? To delude you. This must be remembered. These civil servants are far more clever than you. They want to keep power in their hands. This case is like that of the story of the three rogues.

When you make a demand in political matters you are told 'you are effeminate.' The Muhammadans are opposed to you. So will they say. If the Muhammadans say that they have no objection, they point their finger at a third thing. In this manner this trickery is practised. Be not deceived by this trickery. I do not say to any of you that you should do unlawful things in order to acquire these rights. There is a lawful way. But that lawful way is such that you must not listen to others at all. You must be prepared to say resolutely that you want what is yours. So long as you do not make a resolution in your mind, as soon as some police officer comes and asks you, 'Well, had you gone to Mr. Tilak's lecture?' You answer, 'Yes, I went towards the end of it, sat at a distance, and could not hear the whole.' You cannot deny, as the police officer has seen you. Why is there such a fear in your mind? What is there to fear in saying that you want *swarajya*? It is here that the difficulty arises. When subsequently asked by the people who had attended the lecture you tell the truth. But when asked by the Police you say, 'I did not hear it well, two or four were talking, what could be done?' Well, my opinion is not like his. Such shuffling will not do in this matter. No goddess is propitiated by shuffling. That goddess knows what is in your mind, and of all these knowing goddesses, the goddess of Liberty is most particular on this point. Ask what you want and they will give it. Perhaps they may say 'no' once or twice. How many times will they say 'no'? They must be convinced that there is no shuffling in this matter. They must be convinced. There is no other course. Effort must be made. It is the business of every goddess to frighten you until it appears that there is some stuff in you. If we look into our *yoga* shastra it appears that goddesses have to be won over. They begin to frighten us. If we succeed all goes well. If, without yielding to fear we do our work resolutely, the goddesses of the *yoga* shastra become propitiated. This admits of proof, this is the rule. Even in political matters there is no other rule—no other way. We want *swarajya*, we shall secure it and we shall not give up our exertions without getting it,—unless there be so firm a confidence in yourselves this cannot be obtained at all. Fear will remain behind, the Police will remain behind, the C.I.D. and the Collector will remain behind, in the end *swarajya* will be obtained. You must not be afraid of others blustering and bawling. Nay, you must expect this as a definite consequence. There is a saying in English ' How can a light be seen without going through darkness ? To rise in the morning, the sun has to go through darkness, I tell you the belief of the common people, and not a proposition of science. Without going through darkness, light cannot be obtained. Without getting out of the reach of these blasts of hot air, troubles and others blustering and bawling, liberty cannot be obtained. Resolution is wanted. I told you what is *swarajya*. Efforts for it must be begun as strenuously as possible. By the grace of God, the world's condition is at present undergoing a change. To speak in the language of faith, God is ready to render help. But though God be ready, you are not ready (laughter). God is quiet. Do you expect a gift from heaven ? None will send you. Even God does not send. And if He sends, it will be of no use. For when you are afraid, what already exists may afterwards disappear. If this gift is given, how is it to be used ? If there be any place of God, you will send it back to his house. You will send it if it can be sent by post (laughter). However if there is a rise of the real sentiment, after authority of the sort which forms part of the national rights, of which I have spoken, comes into your hands, what will take place? What will be the effect upon the nation? This I am going to tell you to-day. I have told you what is *swarajya*. My friend, Mr. Kelkar, has already told you that *swarajya* does not mean that our authority is to be established here by driving away the English. Some people will have to be driven away. *Swarajya* is not driving away the King and taking his authority into one's hands. It means taking into the hand the subjects' rights. Consider carefully if England derives any benefit by keeping this one nation a slave. It will be seen from the condition of the whole of the world to-day that England will have some day or other to give liberty to the provinces and countries forming parts of the Empire under its control. This must take place some day. It must take place. But if you do not do anything then it may not take place. Keeping awake the whole night, you fall asleep when the thief enters. That will be your condition. The time is coming. Perhaps the nature of the change occurring in the world—in other nations—will by the grace of God prove favourable to you. But if the time be favourable, it will be of use if you are awake. Otherwise once you sleep, you will sleep on. What will it avail even if we get the right of *swarajya*? I will briefly give you a picture of what will happen. What happened during Peshwa's time? We must examine history a little for it. At the time of the Peshwas the administration of Maharastra was going on well. Elphinstone was the Saheb who brought about the fall of this rule of the Peshwas, and who became the Commissioner after its fall. That Saheb is witness to what I say. Though the city of Poona was such a big one, there took place no dacoities in it at night. The consumption of liquor was *nil*. It was altogether prohibited. The original system of *jamabandi* which was once settled by Nana Farnavis, was itself copied afterwards. Nay, the science as to how accounts are to be kept took its rise among us under the Peshwa's rule and those very accounts are now kept. We knew how to administer provinces. The C. I. D. of Nana Farnavis was so very excellent that information as to what a certain *sardar* spoke to a certain man at the time of dining used to be sent to him (cheers). The following incident is said to have happened at one time. The Bombay Government had sent ammunition to the Resident in a palanquin by way of the Khopoli Ghat. An order was issued from the Poona *Dafter* that the palanquin which might come on such and such a date should be stopped on the Ghat. It had the information that ammunition was to come in a palanquin. Afterwards the Resident complained "Why is our palanquin stopped?" Thereupon he received a reply from Nana Farnavis, "You yourself think about it. We have attached the palanquin and will not let it go. The King must needs be informed what has taken place and at what place. We have done it." So he was told. The C. I. D. is wanted. Who says no? If the King has no information he will not be able to carry on the administration. We have no complaint against the C. I. D. Our complaint is about its method of working (cheers, hear). That method is not under our control. He who has to carry on the administration, must have all departments. Police is wanted, C. I. D. is wanted. The Revenue Department is wanted. The Judicial Department is wanted. All departments are wanted. Where then is the difficulty? There is difficulty in one matter. All the departments must be under the control of the people—our control. The difficulty lies only in this. Several people have formed the opinion that the English are the most civilized, we too must civilize ourselves. Who does not want civilization? All reforms are wanted. During Nana Farnavis' time letters had to be sent: now the C. I. D. will send a wire. Means have become available. The administration is to be carried on by making use of all these. But the whole of this system of administration existed at the time of the Peshwa's rule. Consider what has taken place now after the break-up of that system. When the Peshwa's rule passed away Nagar, Satara, Poona, which were in the possession of the Peshwa himself, came into the possession of the English. The lieutenants of the Peshwa at that time were great generals. Gaekwar, Holkar and Scindia were the chief among the *jahasirdars* and *sardars* who commanded the army. These three survived as all others soon came under the English Government and the Peshwa's rule was overthrown. This is the history of 1818. What is the condition of these three to-day? What is the condition of the Baroda Sarkar? What is the condition of Holkar? What is the condition of the Scindia Sarkar? And what is the condition of the territory or the districts adjoining Poona? Think about this. These districts having gone into the possession of the English Government, the whole of their administration gradually passed into the hands of a bureaucracy. The policy of this bureaucracy is not to listen at all to the people. First the Governor, then the Commissioner, then the Collector, the Collector's subordinate the Assistant Collector, Mamlatdar, Aval Karkun, Fouzdar, Police sepoy—such is the arrangement of the whole of the bureaucracy from first to last. What is to be done for the people is to be done by them. The Government above issues orders in respect of anything which it may think beneficial to the people, and accordingly steps are taken below. At first this arrangement was thought very good. The disorder under Baji Rao's rule was put an end to. They said they were safe now. They saw the ghee but not the rod (laughter). It began to be seen gradually afterwards. All authority went under the control of this bureaucracy. People got education. They began to make use of railways. A telegram can be sent if some one is to be informed whether I am coming to Nagar or not. Education was revived. All these benefits were got. But all authority are in the hands of the bureaucracy. It had passed into their hands to some extent at the time of the Company. And it passed wholly into their hands by the Government of India Act passed in 1858. It is 58 years now since that Act was passed. What has happened during these 58 years? The officials became powerful, and possessed of authority. The people's authority became less to such an extent that it was said we do not want the Kulkarni, we want all servants. Whatever hereditary rights we might have possessed they too have gone. This did not strike us when the Inam Commission was appointed. That cannot be helped. They said Vinchurkar was a *jahagirdar* at that time. He was the master of the army. Some one was an officer of an army of 10,000 while some other was the officer of an army of 15,000. They were told, 'You have to supply an army of 15,000, while you have to be paid 15 lakhs of rupees of which you have to spend 14 lakhs. Then, take one lakh of rupees.' They consented. The amount can be enjoyed sitting at home, what more was wanted? This a great principle. Nobody said at that time, 'We lost our right to keep an army, to fight for Government ;' nobody thought so. It was thought that the administration was good as it gave enough to eat sitting idle at home. What more is required ? We have been reduced to this condition owing to this state of things. In 50 or 60 years all the powers of this province have passed into the possession of the European bureaucracy. You should not understand from this that I call the European bureaucracy bad. They are very much learned. These posts are given to the best students from England. Their abilities are greater. But even if all this be admitted still it is a fact they have to undergo great wear and tear while working for us and the climate of England being cold and that of this country hot, larger pay has to be given to them. They come for our good, will you say 'no' to them ? (laughter). All things are admitted by us. I do not also deny that they may perhaps be working a little more than we. I only say, when we are ready to do the work, when it is our work, why give it to others ? Nor do I say that they do it badly. Our minds have begun to grow weak owing to restrictions being placed on our work and against our interests. Our enthusiasm has begun to become less. Effeminacy is increasing. Therefore, we do not want this. I do not say that they are not wanted because they are not educated. They are good. They are merchants. Will you not get for your shop some agent more clever than yourself ? There may be such men but will you give your shop into the hands of such an agent and stand aside, taking such money as he will give? This is indeed a question in business. It is a question in any matter. Such is the management of this province. What became of Baroda? Look at the history of Baroda. The history of Baroda is all there written. And what could be done there by degrees was not done here by degrees. The *gadi* of the Maharaja of Baroda had to be perpetuated. That was a matter of regular succession. That is a part of history. Formerly Baroda used to be managed or supervised from Poona and the rest was done by the Kings of Baroda. It might have been done by other kings. Therefore, if you become ready now by receiving education here you go to Baroda and ask for service there. There are men educated in Poona and Bombay who are District Magistrates, Munsiffs, Subhas and Diwans there. There are Naib Diwans and High Court Judges. These people are working there. They work there without complaint being heard about them. Then where is the objection to the same being done here? If men from the districts of Poona and Satara go and conduct the administration of Baroda, what objection is there for them to carry on the very same administration in the same way in this our province? There can be none. The nation being divided into two parts, one part—the Marathi nation—went into the possession of the English on account of some historical reason, and one remained in the possession of the native Chiefs. One part proves that the people of this nation are fit to do work. In the other part the authorities say that they are unfit and we too dance to their tune and begin to talk like them. There are two standards, two sides. Then, what is it that is wanted when one talks of *swarajya*? Where is the objection to make the very same arrangement with regard to Poona and Satara as exists in Baroda? The authority of the English Government will remain. It is over Baroda also. The Chief of Baroda is not an independent king. When the Peshwas ruled at Poona Baroda was subject to them. Had the State of Poona remained, they too would have been able to manage it. Satara and Nagar could have been managed by them. The same management exists in the Nizam's territory. *Swarajya* means this much ; Give those rights which Native States have and which the Baroda and Scindia 'Sarkar have. to Poona and Satara after forming them into a State of the Central Division. One difference must, however, be made in this. Now a hereditary chief will not do for us. We shall have to elect our own President. This is the only difference. It is a historical puzzle or inconsistency, that the province which was the capital of the Marathas should not be given the arrangement which exists in Native States, while those provinces which were dependent on that province should have it. There is no reason for this. Why should we not become like them? I have told you that the Gaekwar and Scindia have sent money and armies to Europe for the war. If these districts had been in our possession, we too would have done the same. This thing has nothing to do with the question whether the British Government will go or will remain. The only difference lies in the continuance or the disappearance of the authority of the bureaucracy, the foreign bureaucracy. This is the difference in the arrangements. There is no difference as the sovereign authority, which is at the root. I think Mr. Lawrence had formerly suggested that in view of the *swarajya* agitation going on, India should be divided into separate Native States, that some experts should be kept there, and only the powers with regard to making treaties with foreign powers and the management of the army and the navy should be kept in their hands so that the English rule may not be in danger. I do not say that they should not retain these powers. In the arrangement of *swarajya* these will be the higher questions of Imperial politics. England should freely retain in her hands the questions as to what kind of relation should subsist between India and other nations, whether war should be made for a certain thing or not, and what policy should be followed when relations with foreign nations arise. Those who want *swarajya* do not wish to interfere with these things. What we want is that just as we are to-day managing our own affairs in Native States, we want authority to do the same with regard to ourselves. We shall expend on items of our own choice the revenue which we get from taxes, we shall spend it on education, if there is less revenue from liquor we shall decide what other taxes should be imposed in lieu thereof and arrange accordingly; we shall manage all affairs, others shall not interfere in them. The people of India do not go to any other nation. Why do they not? See if you want to, whether they join France or Germany. One must be able to understand from the present state of things that if Indians are prepared to have connection with any particular country that country is England (cheers). We will not be benefitted by England going away and Germany coming in her place. We do not want the thing. Even if the matter be viewed from another practical point of view, England is here for 100 years, while Germany will be a newcomer, and its energy will be fresh and hunger unsatisfied. How will that help us? What is now is all right. A new king is not wanted. But give into our possession a portion of the powers by the loss of which we have become mere orphans. It is not I alone that am saying this. Mr. Lawrence has said so. He writes that if hereafter improvement is to be effected in India after the war, if Government intends to effect some new arrangement with regard to the people then India should be divided into different parts. The question of language did not enter his head, but we shall add that idea. Form one separate State each of Marathi, Telugu and

Kanarese provinces. The question of vernaculars also comes into this question of *swarajya*. There is no question which is not dependent upon *swarajya*, Had there been general liberty, there would have been a Gujarati University, a Marathi University, an Agricultural University. But to do that does not lie in our hands. Is the question whether education should be given through vernaculars such a big one, that there should arise differences with regard to it? Our voice is nowhere. Do the English educate their people through the French language? Do Germans do it through the English language? So many examples are before our eyes, why should we write articles, columns upon columns upon the subject? Why does that which so many people practise not take place now? Because we have no authority. You have not got the authority to determine what should be taught to your children. So many of you send your children to school, but do not consider what will become of them. In short, there is no question at present which is not dependent on 'swarajya'—on authority Ranade and others have up till now made efforts with regard to the Fergusson College and the University. But who is to be prevailed upon? The administrators! They know what arrangement obtains in their own country. Why should the same not be here? For imparting English education to all, the English language has to be taught for seven or eight years. Eight years is not a small part of life. Such a state-of things exists nowhere else. This arrangement does not exist in any civilized country. If in spite of this your attention is not drawn towards *swarajya* then be sure that there is something wrong with your vision (cheers). Whatever you have to say, whatever prayer you have to make to Government, let that prayer be for giving authority, and not for anything else. We want those powers which are the leading ones under this rule. I have already told you that wherever we go our path is ultimately obstructed. The question of education is an ordinary one. There must be schools in each village. Whence is the money to be brought by us? We pay taxes to Government. Do we pay them for nothing? Let us have the system prevalent in England for imparting education. There is money in the treasury; it is utilised, it is paid for other purposes; but it is not expended on those things which are necessary for us. Therefore, what I told you a little while ago is necessary. India is a big country. Divide it if you want according to languages. Separate the Marathi-speaking part and the Gujarati-speaking part. But how are the Hindus and the Mussalmans to be taught in them? I am going to speak about this also. In Canada the population consists of Frenchmen and Englishmen. If English statesmen could settle the question there, would they not be able to settle how Hindus and Muhammadans should conduct themselves here? Thus these are excuses for not giving us powers. This you must realise well. If India be divided into different States in the manner, there may be separate States. The province of Bengal may be one. Instead of appointing over it a Chief from this side, I say, a European Governor may be appointed for some years. What used to happen in Canada before president elected by the people was secured? A Governor used to go from England to Australia. He was obliged to work in the Council as he was told. Here, it is the contrary. If you want anything, a resolution is to be brought before the Council, much preparation is to be made, figures are to be collected, our representative does not get even a pice. The other members of the Council are paid. He has to work for nothing, and at last the resolution is rejected. Though it be passed, Government cannot be forced to give effect to it. It is a childish thing. He who does not feel this possesses proportionately less patriotism (cheers.) This is like setting us to fight by throwing grains of boiled rice, without giving anything to us, without giving any power to us. If any further rights can be obtained from this in future, if any power will come into our hands, if this be given to us as a step towards the above, then it has a value, otherwise it has no value. What does happen? Good and well-educated men are set to fight for two or four ghatkas. Hence, bear in mind what will result from *swarajya* and what we ask. In asking for *swarajya* we ask that in the end there should be such States throughout India, that at first Englishmen coming from England and at last presidents elected by the people should be appointed in these States, and that a separate Council should be formed for disposing of questions relating to the whole nation. Just as there is an arrangement in Europe, America and the United States, and just as there are different small States and there is a Congress to unite them together so the Government of India should keep in their hands similar powers of the Imperial Council. There are at present seven or eight different provinces; make them twenty if you like and make such an arrangement in respect of those provinces as will give facilities to the people, meet with their approval and place power in their hands. This itself is what is meant by the demand for *swarajya.* The demand for *swarajya* does not mean that the Emperor should be removed. Perhaps, for this arrangement you may have to bring English officers in some places. This is admitted. But those officers will be ours, will be of the people, will remain servants of the people, will not remain our masters. The intelligence of our people will not alone suffice to bring about the reforms which are to be effected in India. We shall have to bring men from England or America, but those men will be responsible to us. They will not be irresponsible. Hence from one point of view, it cannot be said at all that this agitation is against Europeans. To whom would they be responsible?

To themselves or to us, so long as the responsibility is not to us, so long as their responsibility has not come under our power, it will continue to be just what it is. Till then, our efforts in all directions will be vain, till then, in whatever other matter we may move, it will be ineffectual, and the desired object will not be accomplished. As long as a nation is not free to bring about its own good, as long as a nation has no power to make an arrangement to bring about a certain thing which it may desire, so long I do not think, your belly will be filled if you are fed by others. Now the people know, some people are convinced that the people's good cannot be effected by what is called 'despotic rule in English. Hence, my object is to tell you that you should make efforts. If my words fall short of expressing it, that is my defect not a defect in the idea, which is faultless. All these things, their different natures, cannot be placed before you in a single lecture. As regards this idea of states about which I spoke, there are many questions, *viz.*, what arrangements should there be in them? What right should there be in them? And what amendment should be made in the India Act of 1858 about consolidation? And though I may deliver not only one but four or ten lectures, they would not be sufficient to deal with those questions. Our principle is one—about this alone I have to speak in this lecture. Those of you who are competent, by virtue of intelligence, wealth or in some other manner, to consider these things, will spontaneously know that these things are wanted. Why ask, 'Will this be obtained? Will this be obtained?' To acquire it or not lies in other hands. I do not understand this question at all. You are making so much exertion. No matter if it be not obtained. As for making exertions, it is in our hands. We need not consider whether we shall get it or not. Exert yourself. The work which you do will not fail to produce some result or other. Have firm belief in yourself. Have not men obtained freedom in other kingdoms? Had goddesses descended from above in other nations? I tell you plainly that if you have no courage you cannot obtain anything. If there be courage, if it be not obtained to-day, it will be obtained to-morrow, it will be obtained after 10 or 20 years. But you must make efforts for it. The principle of your religion is this, 'You are only to work, you are not even to look to the fruits.' Why is this said in the Gita? Is it for going to worship, for obtaining a *sher* of rice by reciting Puran? Great religions tell this very thing. The Western history tells this very thing. In spite of this, will you ask, 'What will become of us? How shall we fare?' 'As made of a ball of earth, etc.' There is a ball of earth. We have it to be called Vishnu. We have it to be called Shiva. And we impart so much importance to it that it is worshipped by the people. Lo! it is merely a ball of earth without any movement. When dropped on the ground it falls down with a thud. We can give a form to that ball by some act, exertion and ceremony. If a form of some sort cannot be given to an earthen ball, it must be said to be your fault. It is possible to give it a form. Now, these our bodies which are, unlike that earthen ball, endowed with life. How much better form can we give to ourselves. Do not make haste. Nothing will be gained by it (haste.) If you work resolutely, a different form can be given even to an earthen ball. This thing is told in the *shastras*. It is proved. It is proved by experience, proved by evidence, by history. If, in spite of this testimony placed before you, you are not convinced, if you are not satisfied, at least give up talking about the country attaining a flourishing condition afresh. Do not bother our heads. These things are capable of happening—must happen. There must be such faith. That faith brings about work. Where that faith does not exist nothing can be done, our Administrators do not give anything, they only say they would give—such a promise is not wanted. I do not say that what may be given should not be taken. Take what is given, ask for more, do not give up your demand. (Laughter.) We want so many rupees. You gave one hundred, we take one hundred. Why should we not? If even some out of hundred be not offered, what can you do? (Laughter.) We want one thousand. When we get a thousand rupees, we shall be satisfied. If 1/10 of a hundred be given we shall thank (laughter.)

Not that we shall not thank. This is human nature. If my paper falls down, I shall say 'thank you' when you give it to me. This is human feeling. I do not ask you to give up what you may get. But the humanness of man lies in securing those aspirations which are included in this very feeling. All other feelings must be treated as servants of that feeling, that exertion, that one goal. When this is done *swarajya* will be obtained. *Swarajya* is not a fruit ready at once to fall into the mouth from the sky. Nor is another man competent to put it into your mouth. It is hard work. And for it this beginning is made. The paper which my friend Tatya Saheb has now given into my hands is of such a sort. The work has been begun a little in India. Mrs. Annie Besant has established a Home Rule League at Madras. Here also we have established one. And in the same manner Home Rule Leagues will soon be established in Bengal or elsewhere. If, perhaps, the Congress will take up this question and itself establish a league, the other leagues will be merged into it. The same work is to be done. This work is one and you are to do it. This is a question of securing benefit. We have to obtain *swarajya*, I have told you what sort of *swarajya* is to be obtained. I told you what change it will hereafter produce in the present condition. The House of Lords have begun to dream such dreams. Lord Hardinge said that the Civilians will soon have to place in your hands the rights belonging to you. The people belonging to the party opposed to you in this matter have begun have had dreams (laughter). You alone say. 'We are unfit, we shall not take this.' Whence does this obstinacy arise? (Laughter.) What is the rationale of this? It is that they have begun to have such dreams. They think that some arrangement or other of this sort will have to be made. The work you have to do first is this: You must agitate in the whole country and convince every man that this alone is our goal. For this we have to work. Nay, we must settle what is it we want, what arrangement should there be—this demand must be settled. We must go to England and convince the people of it. And when this subject has to be discussed in Parliament this subject must be placed before it in a proper manner. That proper manner means that a bill to amend the existing India Act must be brought before Parliament. What we have to demand is this: Amend this Act for us. When the East India Company was abolished and the rule of the Queen's government came, this Act was amended *i.e.*, minor amendments were made in it. We want to have it amended in a certain manner. And this is wanted not merely for our good but for the good of the Empire. To make such a demand is a part of our work. This work must be done with the help and acquiescence of all. There must be left no difference of opinion about this. The moderates and the Nationalists have one and the same goal, and the same demand is to be made and one and the same result is to be obtained. For doing this work which is to be carried on by entertaining this sentiment, a separate institution called the Home Rule League is established. Subjects are placed before the Congress. But as the Congress is to assemble once a year, once an opportunity is gone, we have to wait till the next year. But we have to do work throughout the year. This is admitted by the Congress. With this object we have established this League. Not very great exertion is required. Recognize this goal. We have a right to demand the fulfilment of this goal. The demand for money made to-day is only this: Every man should pay one rupee per annum. The admission fee is Rs. 2. But if this is not to be paid, pay at least one rupee. If one *lakh* out of thirty crores of people be not found willing to pay, then at least cease to prate about India. Do not tire our ears. I do not think that more than a year will be required for this agitation to become successful. The subscription for one year is fixed at Re. 1. It is not necessary to carry on the agitation for 10 or 20 years. The real time has come. Hence if you are not disposed to make the self-sacrifice of taking one rupee out of your pocket for this agitation then at least do not come to the lecture, so that it may not be necessary to talk so loudly. If you have to do anything it is only this. Those belonging to this institution are prepared to make the remaining arrangement. For this purpose many lectures like this will have to be delivered in various places. People will have to be got together. The matter will have to be explained to the people. If the police come to stop the proceedings, if it is not allowed here, we must go elsewhere and assemble. We must go there before the police go. We must persist. Do not think that this can be obtained easily and pleasantly. One rupee is nothing. There must be resolution of the mind. If any one comes to ask, you must plainly tell him: The goal we demand is lawful. We have become members and paid one rupee. We want *swarajya*. You must say this fearlessly. If you have not the courage to say this, that is a different thing. I trust that this thing will be considered good by the whole of India, perhaps by your descendants if not by you. Though you may not have the will, this must go on. If not you the people of the next generation will make efforts, but they will call you asses. If you mean to put up with this then I have no objection. My own conviction is that *swarajya* will be obtained. Bear in mind what work you have to do and what help you have to give. Perhaps there will be trouble from the police, this is not denied. If they ask, 'Well, have you become subscribers? Have you become members?' you must say, 'Yes, we have become.' Such is the law, nothing else will happen. If a prosecution be instituted, the pleaders in this institution will conduct the defence without taking any fee (laughter). If a rupee be paid for this work that would not be sedition. More than this (*i.e.* Paying

Re. 1 and becoming a member) you have not to do. This League undertakes to do the remaining work. Strange that the people of Maharastra should remain idle at such a time! We want all, whether they be Muhammadans, Hindus or Marwaris. Among these there are none who are not wanted; in this there is no distinction of caste or religion. This work is to be done for India. I have already stated on a former occasion at a certain place. that there is a practice amongst you traders that you keep one anna in the rupee out of profits for cow protection. Such is your habit. I ask, 'Why should not the traders give to us a pice or half pice in the anna for this object also?' India is a great cow, not a small one. That cow has given you birth. You are maintaining yourselves on that cow's industry, on her fruitfulness, drinking her milk. You forget that cow, but sit on seeing the accounts, one anna, one anna is seen debited in her name. For cow protection. For what is the anna taken out? For giving fodder to the cow, for rescuing her from the hands of the butcher. We are dying here to-day without work. But does the idea ever occur to you that this is a cow for you? That idea never occurs to you. This is a work for the protection of religion and for the protection of cows. This is the work of the nation and of political progress. This work is of religion, of progress. I ask you to take into consideration all this and to assist us as much as lies in your power. I have already said we do not ask for more than one rupee per man. He who has the ability should obtain the merit of protecting the cow by paying this one rupee at least once to this institution. This is a great work. If sons of the cow will not care about this then you shall have to be called bullocks, as the sons of the cows are called (laughter). You shall have to be given that name which is commonly applied to cow's sons. I have told you these things. This institution has been started. Work has commenced. If perils overtake it we are prepared to bear them. They must be borne. It will not do at all to sit idle All will be able to support themselves. Therefore assist in this manner this undertaking. Then God will not abandon you : such is my conviction. These things will be achieved by the grace of God. But we must work. There is a very old principle that God helps them who help themselves. The principle occurs in the Rigveda. God becomes incarnate. When? When you take complaints to him and pray to him. God does not become incarnate for nothing. God does not become incarnate for idle people. He becomes incarnate for industrious people. Therefore begin work. This is not the occasion to tell all the people to-day what sort of amendment is to be effected in the law. It is difficult to discuss every such thing at such a large meeting. Hence put together the few general things which I told you now and those which I told you yesterday and set about to work. And at last having prayed to God to make your efforts successful I conclude my speech (cheers).

SELF-GOVERNMENT

[In supporting the resolution on Self-Government, at the 31st Indian National Congress of 1916, held at Lucknow, Mr. Bal Gangadhar Tilak, said]:—

Mr. President, brother delegates, ladies and gentlemen.—I thank you sincerely for the reception that you have given me on this platform; but let me tell you that I am not fool enough to think that this reception is given to me personally. It is given, if I rightly understand, for those principles for which I have been fighting. (*Hear, hear*). The resolution which I wish to support embodies all these principles. It is the resolution on self-government. It is that for which we have been fighting—the Congress has been fighting for the last 30 years. The first note of it was heard ten years ago on the banks of the Hooghly and it was sounded by the Grand Old Man of India—that Parsi Patriot of Bombay, Dadabhai Naoroji. (*Applause.*) Since that note was sounded a difference of opinion arose. Some said that that note ought to be carried on and ought to be followed by detailed scheme at once, and that it should be taken up and made to resound all over India as soon as possible. There was another party amongst us that said that it could not be done so soon and that the tune of that note required to be a little lowered. That was the cause of dissension ten years ago. But I am glad to say that I have lived these ten years to see that we reunite on this platform and that we are going to put forward our voices and shoulders together to push on this scheme of self-government. We have lived—there is a further thing—not only have we lived to see these differences closed, but to see the differences of the Hindus and Mahomedans closed as well. So we are united in every way in the United Provinces and we have found that luck in Lucknow. (*Laughter*). I consider this the most auspicious day, the most auspicious in the most auspicious session of the 31st Indian National Congress. And there are only one or two points on which I wish to address you.

It has been said, gentlemen, by some that we Hindus have yielded too much to our Mahomedan brethren. I am sure I represent the sense of the Hindu community all over India when I say that we could not have yielded too much. I would not care if the rights of self-government are granted to the Mahomedan community only. (*Hear, hear*). I would not care if they are granted to the Rajputs. I would not care if they are granted to the lower and the lowest classes of the Hindu population provided the British Government considers them more fit than the educated classes of India for exercising those rights. I would not care if those rights are granted to any section of the Indian community. The fight then will be between them and the other sections of the community and not as at present a triangular fight. We have to get these rights from a powerful Bureaucracy, an unwilling Bureaucracy, naturally unwilling because the Bureaucracy now feels that these rights, these privileges, this authority, will pass out of their hands. I would feel the same if I were in that position and I am not going to blame the Bureaucracy for entertaining that natural feeling. But whatever the character of that feeling may be it is a feeling which we have to combat against; it is a feeling that is not conducive to the growth of self-government in this country. We have to fight against that feeling. When we have to fight against a third party—it is a very important thing that we stand on this platform united, united in race, united in religion, united as regards all different shades of political creed. That is the most important event of the day.

Let us glance. As I said, ten years ago when Dadabhai Naoroji declared that Swaraj should be our goal its name was Swaraj. Later on it came to be known as self-government or constitutional reform; and we Nationalists style it Home Rule. It is all the same, in three different names. It is said that as there is objection raised that Swaraj has a bad odour in India and Home Rule has a bad odour in England we ought to call it constitutional reform. I don't care to call it by any name. I don't care for any name. If you style it as A. B. C. reform scheme or X. Y. Z. reform scheme I shall be equally content; I don't mind for the name, but I believe we have. But I believe you have hardly realised the importance, hardly realized the importance and character of that scheme of reform. Let me tell you that it is far more liberal than the Irish Home Rule Bill and then you can understand what possibilities it carries with it. It will not be complete Home Rule but more than a beginning of it. It may not be complete self-government but it is far better than local self-government. (*Laughter.*) It may not be Swaraj in the widest sense of the word but it is far better than Swadeshi and boycott. It is in fact a synthesis of all the Congress resolutions passed during the last 30 years,—a synthesis that will help us on to proceed, to work in a definite, in a certain responsible manner. We cannot now afford to spend our energy on all 30 resolutions—Public Service resolutions, Arms Act and sundry others. All that is included in this one resolution of self-government and I would ask every one of you to try to carry out this one resolution with all effort, might, and enthusiasm, and everything that you can command. Your intelligence, your money, your enthusiasm, all that you can command, must now be devoted for carrying out this scheme of reform. Don't think it is an easy task. Nothing can be gained by passing a resolution on this platform. Nothing can be gained by simple union of the two races, Hindus and Mahomedans and the two parties, Moderates and Nationalists. The union is intended to create a certain power and energy amongst us and unless that energy and power are exercised to the utmost you cannot hope to succeed. So great are the obstacles in your way. In short you must now be prepared to fight out your scheme. I don't care if the sessions of the Congress are not held any longer. I think it has done its work as a deliberative body. The next part is executive and I hope I shall be able to place before you later the executive part of the scheme. It is only the deliberative part that has been placed before you. Remember what has been done. It is not the time for speaking. When Swaraj was declared as our goal it was questioned whether it was legal and the Calcutta High Court has declared that it was. Then it was said that Swaraj was legal but it must be expressed in such words as do not amount to a criticism of the Bureaucracy. That too has been judicially decided. You can criticize, you can make any criticism in order to further your object, in order to justify your demand, perfectly within the bounds of law. So the goal has been declared legal. Here you have a specific scheme of Swaraj passed by United India. All the thorns in our way have been removed. It will be your fault if you now do not obtain what is described in the scheme. Remember that. But I will tell you it is a very serious responsibility. Don't shirk it. Work. I say the days of wonders are gone. You cannot now feed hundreds of people on a few crumbs of bread as Jesus did. The attainment of your object cannot be achieved by a wonder from heaven. You have to do it. These are days of work, incessant labour, and I hope that with the help of Providence you will find that energy, that enthusiasm and those resources which are required for carrying out this scheme within the next two years to come. If not by the end of 1917, when I expect the war will be closed, during at least 1918 we shall meet at some place in India, where we shall be able to raise up the banner of self-rule. (*Loud applause*).

HOME RULE CONFERENCE

FIRST MEETING AT LUCKNOW

[*A large meeting of the Home Rulers was held on the evening of Saturday, 30th December,* 1916 *at the pandal of the Theosophical Convention near Aminabad High School, Lucknow, when Lok. Bal Gangadhar Tilak addressed as follows* :]—

I did not come here to deliver an address; nor did I think that I would be asked to speak. But the subject is so fascinating and one cannot resist the temptation of saying at least a few words. The Lucknow Sessions has become the most important Sessions of the Congress. The President of the Congress said that it was *the* Indian National Congress. Two things have taken place. Hindus and Muslims have been brought together. There is a feeling among the Hindus that too much has been given. I think the objection is not national. As a Hindu I have certainly no objection to making this concession. When a case is difficult, the client goes to his Vakil and promises to pay one half of the property to him if he wins the case. The same is the thing here. We cannot rise from our present intolerable condition without the aid of Muslims. So in order to gain the desired end there is no objection to giving a percentage, a greater percentage, to the Muslims. Their responsibility becomes greater, the greater the percentage of representation you give to them. They will be doubly bound to work for you and with you, with a zeal and enthusiasm greater than ever. The fight at present is a triangular fight. You have to wrest the whole Self-Government from out of the hands of a powerful bureaucracy. This body has already commenced to work in order to retain power in its own hands. It is but natural. You would do the same thing yourself if you were in possession. Possession is nine points of law. Bureaucracy is in possession of power and why should it part with it? Rights cannot be obtained by yearly resolutions. There are difficulties in the way of carrying out these resolutions, but these difficulties must strengthen us in our beliefs and in our actions.

GOOD DONE BY BUREAUCRACY.

Bureaucracy too have done some good in our country. They have tried to clear India of the jungle that was there. But further on, after clearing the jungle, there is one thing they do. They do not want to sow in the ground thus cleared. We want to utilise it for agriculture. India has united into one mass under this bureaucracy, now it is expected to rise on the call of duty. The next point naturally arises. We now want liberty. Similarly, we educate our children and expect them to take our position later on in life. So is the case with Englishmen. They have united us, they have educated us and they must expect us to take the position we are fit for. History and reason are against the difficulties created by the bureaucracy and we must triumph in the end. The only thing that comes in our way is that we are not yet prepared. No shillyshallying will do. Be prepared to say that you are a Home Ruler. Say that you must have it and I dare say when you are ready you will get it. There is nothing anarchical in this demand. Are you prepared to work for it?

Home Rule is an extensive subject. A strong resolution has been passed by the Congress and now the education of the masses lies in your hands. Home Rule is the synthesis of all Congress resolutions Home Rule is the only remedy. Insist on your rights. India is your own house. Is it not? (*Cries of Yes*). Then why not manage it yourself? (*Cheers*). Our domestic affairs must be in our own hands. We do not want separation from England.

VEDANTA'S SUPPORT

There is a saying in our Vedanta, meaning that if a man tries he can become God himself. If that is so, do you mean to say that you cannot become bureaucrats if you want to? It is very obvious. Have firm faith in the brighter prospects of humanity or, as they are called, in laws of evolution. Then, I believe, by that faith you will be able to realise your object within a year or two (*Cheers*).

HOME RULE

[*Under the presidency of Mr. Nana Saheb Data, a public meeting was held at Akola, on January 5, 1917, when Bal Gangadhar Tilak spoke on Home Rule as follows*]: —

It was about 8 years ago that I had occasion to speak to you and I well remember what I said then when concluding my address. "Surat split" had occurred 2 years before, and I said, that the split was not due to divergence in ideals, but to differences of opinion as to the method of work which was to be followed to gain the one common ideal of Swaraj which was held up before the eyes of the Nation by the Grand Old Man of India, Dadabhai Naoroji, in his Presidential speech, as the President of the Indian National Congress. The difference being one of method and not of ideal it would surely be forgotten as time rolled on, and the keenness of it would be lessened every year till we met again on a common platform. The events since the last Congress have proved my prophecy. The ideal of Home Rule has passed through trials and ordeals, and stands to-day perfectly vindicated as both loyal and practical. It is now conclusively proved that the gain of the one is the gain of both, and in India's Self-Government lies the future stability and safety of the British Empire. Since Home Rule became an ideal, vindicated in Courts of law as legal and loyal, it had to be proved by arguments that India stood in immediate need of it, that India should demand it, that the demand was justified by defects in the method of the working of the existing mode of Government which could not be remedied except by Self-Government and that it was also proved that we were fit for receiving and handling the right of Swaraj when they came to us. In justifying Swaraj and pointing out the defects of the present system of Government one had to use hard arguments and a language which—taking the subject-matter into consideration—could not be soft. And in certain quarters this again was resented. Our opponents said: "Ask for your Home Rule as much as you like but you must not criticise the bureaucracy; that creates discontent." This was asking us to achieve an impossibility. It was as if you asked a man to eat a fruit without biting it. To ask you to do so is only another way of preventing you from eating the fruit. How could the demand for Home Rule be justified without showing that there were defects in the present mode of working of the Government which were incurable without Home Rule for India? And how could those defects be shown except by irrefutable arguments which hit hard? Luckily this question has been solved by the Bombay High Court for us now, and it is pronounced that criticising the visible machinery of the Government is not sedition, that an angry word, a hard expression, and an indiscreet phrase might have been employed without meaning the least harm. Thus we know that the ideal of Home Rule is legitimate and just, and criticism of the existing mode of Government is not illegal, but the great question is yet undecided and the question is

WHAT IS MEANT BY HOME RULE?

That is the third stage in the history of Home Rule. I am glad to tell you the last Congress has given a satisfactory answer to this question. It is not a solution which one party puts forward; it is not a solution which one community advances It is a solution unanimously accepted by Hindus, Mussalmans, Moderates, and Nationalists alike. It means Representative Government, Government over which the people will have control. I shall tell you also

WHAT IT DOES NOT MEAN.

It does not mean shaping as under the connection between England and India; it does not mean disclaiming the suzerain power of the King-Emperor. On the contrary it affirms and strengthens both. We need the protection of England even as a matter of pure self-interest. This is the key-note to which the song of Home Rule must be tuned; you must not forget this nor must you forget that it is the connection with England and the education she gave, that has given rise to the ambitions that fill your hearts to-day.

Self-Government, as I told you, means Representative Government in which the wishes of the people will be respected and acted upon and not disregarded as now, in the interests of a small minority of Civil Servants. Let there be a Viceroy and let him be an Englishman if you like, but let him act according to the advice of the representatives of the people. Let our money be spent upon us and with our consent. Let public servants be really servants of the public and not their masters as they at present are. The question as to how many members will sit in this Council is immaterial. The material question is, will the greater majority of them represent the Indian public or not, and will they be able to dictate the policy of the Government or not? This then is what Home Rule really means.

LONG AND WEARY PATH

Now, I need hardly tell you that a long and weary path lies before you. You must tread it with courage and steadily. It is a difficult thing to gain and therefore worth gaining. Great things cannot be easily gained and things easily gained are not great. In the *Gita* Lord Shri Krishna says that among the 5 causes that lead to success "Daiwa" is one. Daiwa is the chance that God gives you and leaves you to profit by it or not. Daiwa is something that human effort cannot control but which comes just at the time which is most opportune and it is entirely our fault if we do not know how to take advantage of it, and knowing it, fail to take advantage of it. You have now Daiwa in your favour. You must press your claims now. This is the time. If you fail to make an advance, the world will march ahead and you will be left behind like the grass that grows by the road side, like the mile-stone that ever stands there.

PROFIT BY THE OPPORTUNITY

Everybody in the world is trying to profit by the opportunity. The colonies are proclaiming aloud their claims. They are making their own schemes ready and pressing their claims on England. A great reform, a great re-arrangement is inevitable after this War and the Colonies are thrusting their hands in the management of the Empire. They have their claim on the fact of having helped the British Empire in this War. Have we not done it equally if not better? If the Colonies succeed in their effort we will be brought under their heels and they will trample on our liberties. In order to justify their schemes they have sent their men in India to collect evidence in support of what they say and their messengers are already at work. None will be more unlucky and unfortunate than yourselves if you lag behind at this critical moment. You have the ideal of Swaraj, you have the legal methods to work for it, and you know what the ideal means. The Almighty helps you in His inscrutable Divine ways by offering a unique opportunity. Now it is for you to say whether you will answer by vigorous efforts or sit silent and let the opportunity slip through your fingers. By allowing this golden opportunity to escape, you are incurring the just blame of those that will be born hereafter. Your daughters and sons will be ashamed of you and future generations will curse you. Take courage therefore and work now. Strike the iron whilst it is hot and yours shall be the glory of success.

HOME RULE CONFERENCE

[At a very well-attended meeting of the citizens of Cawnpore, on January 1, 1917, *Mr. Tilak spoke on Home Rule for India as follows]*.—

GENTLEMEN,—It is extremely unfortunate that I am not addressing you in your mother-tongue Hindi which claims to be the *lingua franca* of India. I am sorry for it the more when I see the large crowd that has assembled here to welcome me on this occasion. I am sorry because I am one of those who hold that Hindi should be the *lingua franca* of India in future. But unfortunately not being able to speak in Hindi I have thought it fit to address you in English on this occasion, a few words which relate to a subject in which all of us were engaged at Lucknow. Gentlemen, you must have all probably heard that the Lucknow Congress was a memorable Congress, a momentous step being taken therein as regards Home Rule. You will be able to learn that after 30 years of deliberation we have at last come to the conclusion that nothing will save us except Home Rule. As I have said in the Congress it is a synthesis of all the resolutions hitherto passed by the Congress during the last 30 years. Whatever side you may look at the question from, you will be convinced that the freedom which Home Rule implies is necessary for the regeneration of this country. Everything in the moral, material or intellectual sphere of this nation depends upon the freedom which at present we are deprived of. You cannot do anything which in your opinion is calculated to raise your status to that of a civilized nation according to the modern standard. It has been pointed out by more eloquent speakers than myself and men who are entitled to your respect and veneration far more than I am. I say it has been pointed out to me several times that unless we get a part of the freedom for which we are trying, for a part of the power which rests in the hands of the bureaucracy at present, it is impossible for us to attain that position to which we are entitled as a birthright. If you see what is your position at present, if you look around, you will see that you are crippled in every respect. Whether you take the question of industry, whether you take the question of education, or any other question, everywhere there is a stumbling block in your way, so that you have not the power to carry out what you wish. We must be prepared to face this one important question before we can hope to make any progress—progress that is worth the name. Many of the objections to the attainment of Home Rule have already been answered in the Congress and out of the Congress. I would only take one or two of them because I am afraid that speaking in English I shall not be understood by this large audience and secondly because the time at our command is very short. You, who are assembled here to listen to me and to do honour to me will, I think, agree that in honouring me you are honouring the cause of Home Rule. The very fact of your presence here to hear a speaker who has devoted some time to this question shows that you are all interested in that important question. They say that there is no public opinion in India in favour of Home Rule. This is a proposition which if our opponents were here will find contradicted by the presence of you all. I do not think that you have come here to respect my person but I think you have come here to respect the cause of Home Rule: and a very large gathering like this is a splendid refutation of the objection that we are not prepared for Home Rule, that we are unable to exercise influence over the masses in this country, that we can take no interest in it and that it will take several decades of years if not hundreds of years according to our opponents to render us fit for Home Rule. This meeting is in itself, as I said, a refutation of the charges that are brought against us. Another objection that is raised is that we, Hindus never enjoyed Home Rule. Nothing can be more incorrect, more erroneous and false, I may say, than a statement like this. Many of you in Northern India enjoyed Home Rule in ancient days. The Hindu polity which is included in the King's duties in the Manusmriti text lays down a kind of social organization which is known as Chatur Varna. Many of you now believe that Chatur Varna consists merely of different castes that divide us at present. No one thinks of the duties belonging to these castes. A Kshattriya will not take food with the Brahmin and a Brahmin will not take food with a Vaishya and a Vaishya will not take food with a Shudra. It was not so, let me point out, in the days of Manu and Bhagvatgita. Bhagvatgita expressly states that this division was not by birth but by the quality and by the profession which were necessary to maintain the whole society in those days. The Kshattriyas defended the dominion and defended the people against foreign aggression and against internal interruptions. Where are those? The whole of that class is gone off and their duties devolve upon the British who have taken charge of the duties of Kshattriyas. Take again commerce. You think this is a commerical town. There are many labourers but you find that the country is exploited for the benefit not of India but of other nations. Raw products are exported and refined products are brought in to the sacrifice of several industries for which India was famous in ancient times. See the Vaishya class—that too is now being dominated by the British people or British merchants. Take the Brahmins. I am a Brahmin. We boasted that we were the intellectual heads of the community—we were the brain in fact—but that brain is now rendered so dull that we have but to import into this country foreign philosophy at the cost of our ancient learning in every department of life. What I consider is that Chatur Varna divides the whole society into so many departments of life and in every one of these departments you have been a loser every year, every decade. I want you now to recognize this fact and to try for gaining the position which we occupied in our own societies. We have been deprived of volunteering, we have been deprived of the right to the higher grades in service. The men remain, but the duties are gone and all your feeling at present is that I am a Kshattriya and you are a Brahmin and that he is a Sudra. All have lost their titles. I am not partial to one or the other. I want you to realise the fact that although you may claim the blood of Kshattriya, although you may claim the blood of a Brahmin, you do not claim that polity, those qualifications which the Sudras are enjoying which should have been yours at this moment. Now one aspect of Home Rule is to encourage you to acquire the freedom which you enjoyed in these various departments of life and to come up to that standard by the co-operation of and under the sovereignty of the British rule. This result is not to be achieved by any unlawful and unconstitutional means, but I am sure by a desire and interest to raise your status to achieve this goal by means of the sympathy of the British people and by remaining a permanent part of the Empire. But this part is of two kinds. In a household, servants form part of a household and children form part of a household. We want to occupy the part of children and not of servants—not a dead part but an equal part in that greatest Empire which the world has seen. We are quite willing to remain a part but not a dead part which will be a burden to the Empire but a living member, and a living member is expected to develop all the qualities which you find in the department of social life. It is with this view, gentlemen, that the Home Rule agitation has been started to make you masters in your house and not servants. This is the real sense of that situation which every one is bound morally and intellectually to attain. Home Rule is nothing else, but to be masters of your houses. Have you ever thought of such a simple question 'what am I in my house—am I a dependent or am I master ?' And if India is your house I want to ask you, gentlemen, whether there can be any ground or reason to tell you that you ought to be masters so far as your domestic affairs are concerned. When an Englishman has been deprived of his rights he will not be content unless he gets back his rights. Why should you lag behind, why should you not in the name of religion, in the name of polity, in the name of that polity, which was cultivated in the past to the largest extent the history of the world has yet produced—in the name of that philosophy that is religious, I appeal to you to awaken to your position and do your level best for the attainment of your birth-right

—I mean the right of managing your own affairs in your own home. If you do not do it who will do it for you ? Do not be hypnotised. You are fit for it, only you have not seen it. You can get your object by your own efforts, by your own action, and this is the self-realization that I want you to feel. If you once realise that you are the master of your domestic affairs as other men are, as in the colonies and as men in the other parts are, I daresay nothing can stand between you and your object to attain it. It all depends upon your efforts. In Lucknow and Cawnpore you will find better men very soon addressing you on this subject, and if I can prepare the ground for the noble workers that are to come here hereafter, I shall not have spoken in vain to-day. It is a thing which you must look to now. Give up apathy. You are as good men as members of any other community in the world. You have hands and feet and you know what has been said in one of Shakespeare's dramas. We are certainly better than Japanese and yet Japan has attained what you seem hopeless to attain and are indifferent to aspire to get. Your fault lies not in the want of capacity or want of means but your fault lies in the want of the will. You have not cultivated that will which you ought to have done. Will is everything. Will power makes it as strong as you can and the material world round you cannot drive you from attaining the object which you will attain. You must make up that will and if that will is made up by every community there is a proverb in my part that the divine power resides in five persons. Instead of 5 let me now change that 5 into 500 millions; and if you realise the fact that you have a certain object to get that, you must attain to a particular stage to which you are entitled as birth-right. You must say that this will so strengthened, cannot resist the forces that are arrayed against you. It is the will you have not been thinking over. You do not devote to it one moment of your life, one moment during the day. A Brahmin is, for instance, enjoined in the Shastras to perform his prayers once in the morning and once in the evening. What is that prayer? It is the cultivation of the will. Now let your prayer be, 'I will try to have my birth-right.' Have that prayer every morning and evening. Do not forget it during all the work or business that you do during the day. If there be temptations in your way repeat that prayer in the morning and evening. Prayer has such a power as to surmount all obstacles; that is the effect of prayer. It is no use praying merely for nothing. God does not want prayer for himself. God does not need it. God does not want any praise from you—it is all useless. Realise that fact. What is the good of praying without any object. God has created you, God knows how to conduct his own creation. Do you mean to say that by your praying you cannot change the course of events of *karma*? Do pray morning and evening for Home Rule and I daresay that within a year or two you can attain your object.

Thanking you for your reception I close my remarks on the subject; and if any of you have not understood me because I have spoken in English then some one of the gentlemen on the platform will undertake to repeat that for you, and I ask your pardon not to have been able to address you in your own words.

HOME RULE

[*An address enclosed in a silver casket specially ordered from Bombay was presented to Mr. Tilak, at Yeotmal and in reply, Mr. Tilak spoke as follows*] :—

Mr. President, brothers and sisters,—I thank you very much for the presentation of an address to me and for the hospitable reception, you have been kind enough to accord to me. But let me tell you, I have not come here to receive these marks of honour and I never expected them. I have come here to do something and if possible to ask you to do it, and that something is the work to be done in connection with the attainment of "Swaraj" or "Home Rule." It does not require high intellectual gifts to understand the meaning of "Swaraj." It is a simple Sanskrit word, meaning nothing more or less than the power to rule our homes, and hence it is called in short "Home Rule." It is your birth-right to govern your own house or home; nobody else can claim to do it, unless you are a minor or a lunatic. The power of the Court of Wards ceases as soon as "Malik" attains majority or becomes non-lunatic. The agent or the Court, to which the power was transferred, is in duty bound to transfer the same power back to the "Malik" or the real owner: If the Court or the agent will not do it, he must bring forth evidence to justify his action. We tell the Government that we are no longer minors, nor are we lunatics, and we are able and competent to look after our affairs, our "home" and we will rule the "home;" we have got a right to say that we want this agent or that and we will guide the "Home policy." This demand for "Home Rule" is not a new one. The Congress and the other older and younger institutions in the country have been demanding it. Nor is the idea novel or new to us. The Village Panchayats, the Councils of Pandits or Elders to advise and guide the King or Emperor and such other kindred institutions were in existence for long. The King was not the final authority in matter of law; the king himself used to consult wise men of high spiritual and moral development, sages well versed in Shruti and Smriti, and then decide the point. King Dushyanta actually did it, when he had to accept Shakuntala and her son. The words *swarajyam*, *vairagyam*, were actually seen in the Shastras. Of course, the word "Swaraj" or "Home Rule" has got a limited meaning to-day. "The Swaraj" of to-day is within the Empire and not independent of it. There have been lots of misrepresentation during the last ten years by our opponents and persecutions and prosecutions were the consequences. Now the meaning of "Swaraj" has been definitely defined by the Congress at Lucknow; there is now no room left for doubts and misrepresentations. This "Swaraj" or Self-Government as embodied in the Congress resolution should be now openly owned and preached by every one. There is no sedition in it; the High Courts do not find any sedition in it. Our way is now quite clear; the difficulties have been removed. Every one of us, whether a Hindu or a Muhammadan, a moderate or nationalist, should start with this clear conception of "Swaraj" and fearlessly preach it, with all the enthusiasm he can command. Our opponents say we are not fit; but that is not true. Every one who is an adult and not a lunatic is fit to manage his house. We may commit mistakes in the beginning; but who is so perfect as to be beyond human failings? Even great men err. We want the right to commit mistakes also; we will commit mistakes and ourselves rectify them; even the great Avatars commit mistakes. The Government does not lay down any standard of fitness, if they will lay down any we will try to attain that standard. Government are not at all definite: those who ask us to be first fit and then demand Swaraj have no mind to give it to us at all. It is as good as to ask a boy to learn swimming and then to go into the river. The second clause of the resolution in Self-Government passed at Lucknow, demands "Swaraj" at an early date. Our opponents advise us not to embarrass the Government at this time; furthermore they want us to believe that this is not the time to make the demand. My reply is that this is exactly the time when our demands should be put forth in a definite manner. The colonials are doing the same thing at this time and why should we not do it? The policy of the Imperial Government is going to be changed, and important changes are expected in the constitution and if we will not awake at this time to guard our interests, who else will do it for us? We ought not to sleep at this time; we must work for attaining our goal.

It appears God is helping us, for this time the present circumstances are not the results of our actions or efforts; and so I say the time is favourable to us. When God has come to help us, shall we not exert ourselves? Remember, if we lose this opportunity, we may not get another for a century or so; the colonials have seen this and they are demanding a voice in the Imperial affairs at this very time. Our demand is comparatively moderate. We simply demand a right to govern ourselves. In the year 1906, Dadabhai Naoroji proclaimed from the Congress platform this "Swaraj" as our ultimate goal. Till then separate demands were made in separate departments; till then we tried to catch the small hairs on the head: but now we say we want to catch the hair tufts so that we will be reinstated in our position which is ours by birth; so you see that your demand is clear and emphatic, made by persons of different opinions after much discussion about it at Lucknow. We have also seen that this is the most proper time to make that demand; and we must work and work incessantly. You ought not to shirk for fear of difficulties and dangers and pitfalls. They are bound to come and why should they not come?

Our Vedanta says that there is little happiness and much of evil and misery in the world. The world is such, it cannot be helped. I foresee dangers in the way and the signs of these dangers are not wanting; recently Lord Sydenham, the late Governor of Bombay, has asked the Government in the *Nineteenth Century* to proclaim once for all that they do not intend to give any more reforms to the Indians; let the Government declare, he says, "thus far and no further." He expects by this move to shut permanently the mouths of the Indians. I wonder what he means. How can a proclamation of this nature shut our mouths? It is a pity that Lord Sydenham should betray so much ignorance of human nature; most of the white-skinned papers are raising the same cry; perhaps this may be an indication of the future policy of the Government.

Whatever that be, one thing is certain, that the work before us is not easy. Tremendous sacrifices will be necessary; nay, we shall have to tide over it; there are two ways of dying, one constitutional and the other unconstitutional. As our fight is going to be constitutional and legal, our death also must, as of necessity, be constitutional and legal. We have not to use any violence. Nay, we condemn the unconstitutional way of doing. As our fight must be constitutional it must be courageous also. We ought to tell Government courageously and without the least fear what we want. Let Government know that the whole Nation wants Home Rule, as defined by the Congress. Let there be no shirking, or wavering or shaking. I said that it was our "right" to have Home Rule but that is a historical and a European way of putting it; I go further and say that it is our "Dharma"; you cannot separate Home Rule from us, as you cannot separate the quality of "heat" from fire; both are inseparably bound up; let your ideas be clear; let your motives be honest; let your efforts be strictly constitutional and I am sure your efforts are bound to be crowned with success; never despair, be bold and fearless and be sure that God is with you. Remember "God helps those who help themselves."

GITA RAHASYA

[*The following is the summary of the speech of Mr. Tilak re : Gita Rahasya,* delivered at Amraoti, in* 1917] :—

Let me begin by telling you what induced me to take up the study of *Bhagavad Gita.* When I was quite a boy, I was often told by my elders that strictly religious and really philosophic life was incompatible with the hum-drum life of every day. If one was ambitious enough to try to attain Moksha, the highest goal a person could attain, then he must divest himself of all earthly desires and renounce this world. One could not serve two masters, the world and God. I understood this to mean that if one would lead a life which was the life worth living, according to the religion in which I was born, then the sooner the world was given up the better. This set me thinking. The question that I formulated for myself to be solved was : Does my religion want me to give up this world and renounce it before I attempt to, or in order to be able to, attain the perfection of manhood? In my boyhood I was also told that *Bhagavad Gita* was universally acknowledged to be a book containing all the principles and philosophy of the Hindu religion, and I thought if this be so I should find an answer in this book to my query ; and thus began my study of the *Bhagavad Gita*. I approached the book with a mind prepossessed by no previous ideas about any philosophy, and had no theory of my own for which I sought any support in the *Gita*. A person whose mind is prepossessed by certain ideas reads the book with a prejudiced mind, for instance, when a Christian reads it he does not want to know what the *Gita* says but wants to find out if there are any principles in the *Gita* which he has already met within Bible, and if so the conclusion he rushes to it that the *Gita* was copied from the Bible. I have dealt with this topic in my book *Gita Rahasya* and I need hardly say much about it here, but what I want to emphasise is this, that when you want to read and understand a book, especially a great work like the *Gita*—you must approach it with an unprejudiced and unprepossessed mind. To do this, I know, is one of the most difficult things. Those who profess to do it may have a lurking thought or prejudice in their minds which vitiates the reading of the book to some extent. However I am describing to you the frame of mind one must get into if one wants to get at the truth and however difficult it be, it has to be done. The next thing one has to do is to take into consideration the time and the circumstances in which the book was written and the purpose for which the book was written. In short the book must not be read devoid of its context. This is especially true about a book like *Bhagavad Gita*. Various commentators have put as many interpretations on the book, and surely the writer or composer could not have written or composed the book for so many interpretations being put on it. He must have but one meaning and one purpose running through the book, and that I have tried to find out. I believe I have succeeded in it, because having no theory of mine for which I sought any support from the book so universally respected, I had no reason to twist the text to suit my theory. There has not been a commentator of the *Gita* who did not advocate a pet theory of his own and has not tried to support the same by showing that the *Bhagavad Gita* lent him support. The conclusion I have come to is that the *Gita* advocates the performance of action in this world even after the actor has achieved the highest union with the Supreme Deity by Gnana (knowledge) or Bhakti (Devotion). This action must be done to keep the world going by the right path of evolution which the Creator has destined the world to follow. In order that the action may not bind the actor it must be done with the aim of helping his purpose, and without any attachment to the coming result. This I hold is the lesson of the *Gita*. Gnanayoga there is, yes. Bhaktiyoga there is, yes. Who says not? But they are both subservient to the Karmayoga preached in the *Gita*. If the *Gita* was preached to desponding Arjuna to make him ready for the fight —for the action—how can it be said that the ultimate lesson of the great book is Bhakti or Gnana alone ? In fact there is blending of all these Yogas in the *Gita* and as the air is not Oxygen or Hydrogen, or any other gas alone but a composition of all these in a certain proportion so in the *Gita* all these Yogas are blended into one.

I differ from almost all the commentators when I say that the *Gita* enjoins action even after the perfection in Gnana and Bhakti is attained and the Deity is reached through these mediums. Now there is a fundamental unity underlying the Logos (Ishvara), man, and world. The world is in existence because the Logos has willed it so. It is His Will that holds it together. Man strives to gain union with God ; and when this union is achieved the individual Will merges in the mighty Universal Will. When this is achieved will the individual say : " I shall do no action, and I shall not help the world "—the world which is because the Will with which he has sought union has willed it to be so ? It does not stand to reason. It is not I who say so ; the *Gita* says so. Shri Krishna himself says that there is nothing in all the three worlds that He need acquire, and *still* he acts. He acts because if He did not, the world's Will be ruined. If man seeks unity with the Deity, he must necessarily seek unity with the interests of the world also, and work for it. If he does not, then the unity is not perfect, because there is union between two elements out of the 3 (man and Deity) and the third (the world) is left out. I have thus solved the question for myself and I hold that serving the world, and thus serving His Will, is the surest way of Salvation, and this way can be followed by remaining *in* the world and not going away from it.

THE RIGHTS OF THE POOR RAIYAT

[*The people of Chikodi from the Bombay Province gave an entertainment to Lok. Tilak, when he made the following speech*]:—

I do not quite understand what you mean by entertaining me "on behalf of the poor raiyats." I am myself a poor man like you and I have no great privilege whatsoever. I earn my livelihood by doing some business as you do. I do not see any difference between what is done on behalf of the rich and what is done on behalf of the poor. I have long been thinking as to what the grievances of the raiyats are, what difficulties are ahead of them, what help they require, and what things are necessary to be done. I have been doing this as a poor raiyat myself and on that account not only do I feel sympathy for you but I feel proud that I am one of you.

My heart aches for *our* present condition and such important questions as (1) what must we do to improve our present condition, (2) what are the duties of the Government, etc., rise before us for consideration. The Government is the Ruler of the poor raiyat, and, therefore, it is not that, as a poor raiyat, I have no rights over Government. The Government is not for the rich; it is for the poor. The poor raiyat cannot protect himself and when one section tyrannises over another, it is the duty of the Government to protect the oppressed. Every man must exercise his rights over the Government, place his grievances before them and see that they are redressed. If the Government will not listen, he must compel their attention. The rich are not to be given the benefit of what is taxed from the poor. During the present times, it is the rich who ought to be taxed more. If the Government does not enquire if the raiyat—the poor raiyat—is happy or not they must be made to do so and that is why we want our own people in posts of authority. All cannot be in posts of authority, and so those who carry on the government must be elected by us. The question is whether the present Government is of this kind. There arise also other questions like the one, whether our industries are prospering. The solution of all such problems depends upon authority as the very foundation of all things. This has now been accepted by all.

I stand here to-day to ask you to help the Government on the occasion of this War. But do not fail to place your grievances before them when you help them in the collection of the War Fund. Give money, but throw on the Government the responsibility of listening to your grievances. In no other country could be tolerated the statement that money should be given first and the grievances might be heard sometime later on. Money payments and your demands must go hand in hand.

We say that millions of people should go to War. But when Bombay alone is supplying 800 young men, the Government needs only 1,000, from the whole Presidency including Berar. Purchase War debentures, but look to them as the little deeds of Home Rule. To ask for money, to ask for help and not to give any privileges, is something strange. The King does not say that you should give money but that you should not make any demand for your rights. It is not sympathetic to say: "Give money now, and when afterwards everything is calm and quiet, we shall consider things." The Government must be taught that money is obtained when hearts are won over. The small and the great, the rich and the poor, every one should think of his rights, make up his own mind, give help and secure rights. Even a child knows that the country is in a very poor condition. Remember how difficult it is found to raise 150 crores of rupees. Only a hundred years ago, our enemies carried away crores and crores of rupees at each plundering expedition from our country, and now in this very country, with all our desire to help, we find it difficult to collect the amount necessary for the War Fund. Does this not clearly show to what poor condition our country has gone? There is only one way of getting out of this difficulty, and that is the obtaining of Home Rule. Home Rule means that my affairs shall be carried on in accordance with my opinion. The Collectors are very clever people but they would do ten times the good they are doing now, if they will act as servants of the people. The people will have control over the authorities when the pay and the posts will be in their hands. The original servants have begun to consider themselves as the masters to-day. They must remain servants. If the money is ours, it must be expended according to our opinions. No one says that white people should be driven away. The help that we give in raising the War Loan is certainly not with a view that the Germans should rule over us. We want the Imperial Rule and we wish to make progress with the help of the English. There is no sedition or anything against law in this. The servants, who have begun to think that they are the rulers, must remain as servants. Give up your lives for the Government, help them, but never forget that Home Rule is your ideal and that your good is only in that. The advice of to-day is that you should help, but not silently. Do not put mere purses into the box but attach to them, a slip that it is the earnest money for getting Home Rule. If the Government promises Home Rule, we will get for them 300 crores of rupees, instead of 150 crores which they need.

Do not be afraid of speaking out things, which are plain in themselves. There might be some trouble, but nothing can be had without any trouble. Home Rule is not going to be dropped into your hands from the sky.

One who suffers might groan, but we cannot help

it. You must, therefore, work in earnest. It is our good fortune that the people in England are willing at present to listen to us. The Congress has passed the Home Rule resolution, the Hindus and the Muhammadans are united, the extremists and the moderates have made up their differences—this is the time for work. I speak all this more to the poor. I have not much faith in the rich. Our experience in collecting money for the Paisa Fund is that the poor put their hands into their pockets more willingly and promptly than the rich. I speak to you as I am a poor man myself. Home Rule is such an ideal that if we once get it, all our desires will be fulfilled. If we work earnestly and hard, there are signs that we will get Home Rule within about 2 or 3 years after the War is over. Let us stop quarrelling among ourselves, let us not listen to those who talk against Home Rule, make up your minds and have a firm resolve, do not stop working, be perfectly loyal, work in such a way that the people in England will come to your side, and then God will surely fulfil all your desires. God helps those to suceed who work earnestly.

HOME RULE

[*Speaking on the Home Rule resolution, at the Naisk Conference*, 1917, *Lok. Tilak said*]:—

I am young in spirit though old in body. I do not wish to lose this privilege of youth. To deny the growing capacity to my thinking power is to admit that I have no right to speak on this resolution. Whatever I am going to speak to-day is eternally young. The body might grow old, decrepit and it might perish, but the soul is immortal. Similarly, if there might be an apparent lull in our Home Rule activities, the freedom of the spirit behind it is eternal and indestructible, and it will secure liberty for us. The Soul means Parameshwar and the mind will not get peace till it gets identified with Him. If one body is worn out the soul will take another: so assures the Gita. This philosophy is quite old. Freedom is my birthright. So long as it is awake within me, I am not old. No weapon can cut this spirit, no fire can burn it, no water can wet it, no wind can dry it. I say further that no C. I. D. can burn it. I declare the same principle to the Superintendent of Police who is sitting before me, to the Collector who had been invited to attend this meeting and to the Government shorthand writer who is busy taking down notes of our speeches. This principle will not disappear even if it seems to be killed. We ask for Home Rule and we must get it. The Science which ends in Home Rule is the Science of Politics and not the one which ends in slavery. The Science of Politics is the "Vedas" of the country. You have a soul and I only want to wake it up. I want to tear off the blind that has been let down by ignorant, designing and selfish people. The Science of Politics consists of two parts. The first is Divine and the second is Demonic. The slavery of a Nation comes into the latter part. There cannot be a moral justification for the Demonic part of the Science of Politics. A Nation which might justify this is guilty of sin in the sight of God. Some people have the courage to declare what is harmful to them and some have not that courage. The political and religious teaching consists in giving the knowledge of this principle. Religious and political teachings are not separate, though they appear to be so on account of foreign rule. All philosophies are included in the Science of Politics.

Who does not know the meaning of Home Rule? Who does not want it? Would you like it, if I enter your house and take possession of your cooking department? I must have the right to manage the affairs in my own house. It is only lunatics and children who do not know how to manage their own affairs. The cardinal creed of the conferences is that a member must be above 21 years of age ; do you not, therefore, think that you want your own rights ? Not being lunatics or children you understand your own business, your own rights and, therefore, you know Home Rule. We are told we are not fit for Home Rule. A century has passed away and the British Rule has not made us fit for Home Rule ; now we will make our own efforts and fit ourselves for it. To offer irrelevant excuses, to hold out any temptation and to make other offers will be putting a stigma on the English policy. England is trying to protect the small state of Belgium with the help of India ; how can it then say that we should not have Home Rule ? Those who find fault with us are avaricious people. But there are people who find fault even with the All-Merciful God. We must work hard to save the soul of our Nation without caring for anything. The good of our country consists in guarding this our birthright. The Congress has passed this Home Rule resolution. The Provincial Conference is only a child of the Congress, which submits to mandates of its father. We will follow Shri Ramachandra in obeying the order of our father the Congress. We are determined to make efforts to get this resolution enforced even if the effort leads us to the desert, compels us to live incognito, makes us suffer any hardship and even if it finally brings us to death. Shri Ramachandra did it. Do not pass this resolution by merely clapping your hands, but by taking a solemn vow that you will work for it. We will work for it by every possible constitutional and law-abiding method to get Home Rule. Through the grace of God England has changed its mind towards us. We feel our efforts will not be without success. England proudly thought that a tiny nation might be able to protect the Empire by itself. This pride has gone down. England has now begun to feel that it must make changes in the constitution of the Empire. Lloyd George has openly confessed that England cannot go on without the help of India. All notions about a Nation of a thousand years old have to be changed. The English people have discovered that the wisdom of all their parties is not sufficient. The Indian soldiers have saved the lives of the British soldiers on the French battlefield and have showed their bravery. Those who once considered us as slaves have begun now to call us brothers. God has brought about all these changes. We must push our demands while the notion of this brotherhood is existing in the minds of the English. We must inform them that we, thirty crores of the Indian people, are ready to lay down our lives for the Empire ; and that while we are with them none shall dare cast an evil glance at the Empire.

KARMA YOGA AND SWARAJ

The Karma Yoga which I preach is not a new theory; neither was the discovery of the Law of Karma made as recently as to-day. The knowledge of the Law is so ancient that not even Shri Krishna was the great Teacher who first propounded it. It must be remembered that Karma Yoga has been our sacred heritage from times immemorial when we Indians were seated on the high pedestal of wealth and lore. Karma Yoga or to put it in another way, the law of duty is the combination of all that is best in spiritual science, in actual action and in an unselfish meditative life. Compliance with this universal Law leads to the realization of the most cherished ideals of Man. Swaraj is the natural consequence of diligent performance of duty. The Karma Yogin strives for Swaraj, and the Dnyanin or spiritualist yearns for it. What is then this Swaraj? It is a life centred in Self and dependent upon Self. There is Swaraj in this world as well as in the world hereafter. The Rishis who laid down the Law of Duty betook themselves to forests, because the people were already enjoying Swaraj or People's Dominion, which was administered and defended in the first instance by the Kshatriya kings. It is my conviction, it is my thesis, that Swaraj in the life to come cannot be the reward of a people who have not enjoyed it in this world. Such was the doctrine taught by our fore-fathers who never intended that the goal of life should be meditation alone. No one can expect Providence to protect one who sits with folded arms and throws his burden on others. God does not help the indolent. You must be doing all that you can to lift yourself up, and then only you may rely on the Almighty to help you. You should not, however, presume that you have to toil that you yourself might reap the fruit of your labours. That cannot always be the case. Let us then try our utmost and leave the generations to come to enjoy that fruit. Remember, it is not you who had planted the mango-trees the fruit whereof you have tasted. Let the advantage now go to our children and their descendants. It is only given to us to toil and work. And so, there ought to be no relaxation in our efforts, lest we incur the curse of those that come after us. Action alone must be our guiding principle, action disinterested and well-thought out. It does not matter who the Sovereign is. It is enough if we have full liberty to elevate ourselves in the best possible manner. This is called the immutable Dharma, and Karma Yoga is nothing but the method which leads to the attainment of Dharma or material and spiritual glory. We demand Swaraj, as it is the foundation and not the height of our future prosperity. Swaraj does not at all imply a denial of

British Sovereignty or British ægis. It means only that we Indians should be reckoned among the patriotic and self-respecting peoples of the Empire. We must refuse to be treated like the "dumb driven cattle." If poor Indians starve in famine days it is other people who take care of them. This is not an enviable position. It is neither creditable nor beneficial if other people have to do everything for us. God has declared His will. He has willed that Self can be exalted only through its own efforts. Everything lies in your hands. Karma Yoga does not look upon this world as nothing; it requires only that your motives should be untainted by selfish interest and passion. This is the true view of practical Vedanta the key to which is apt to be lost in sophistry.

In practical politics some futile objections are raised to oppose our desire for Swaraj. Illiteracy of the bulk of our people is one of such objections; but to my mind it ought not to be allowed to stand in our way. It would be sufficient for our purpose even if the illiterate in our country have only a vague conception of Swaraj, just as it all goes well with them if they have simply a hazy idea about God. Those who can efficiently manage their own affairs may be illiterate; but they are not therefore idiots. They are as intelligent as any educated man and if they could understand their village concerns they should not find any difficulty in grasping the principle of Swaraj. If illiteracy is not a disqualification in Civil Law there is no reason why it should not be so in Nature's Law also. The illiterate are our brethren ; they have the same rights and are actuated by the same aspiration. It is therefore our bounden duty to awaken the masses. Circumstances are changed, nay, they are favourable. The voice has gone forth 'Now or never.' Rectitude and constitutional agitation is alone what is expected of you. Turn not back, and confidently leave the ultimate issue to the benevolence of the Almighty.—(*Poona Sarvajanik Sabha Quarterly*).

HOME RULE

[The following is the text of the Speech delivered by Lok. Tilak, on 7th October, 1917, in the compound of the Home Rule League, Allahabad, under the presidency of Mrs. Annie Besant] :—

Every one knew what Home Rule meant. Home rule was nothing but to have the management of their home in their own hands. That was simplest definition that could be given of the word. There was absolutely nothing to say why they wanted Home Rule. It was their birthright. Some people had been managing their affairs for them now, and they wanted that that management should be transferred to their hands. They were entitled to that right and the burden of proving that they were not entitled to it lay on the other party. Home rule was not a new expression. It was an expression that had a definite meaning and it could not be misunderstood, though it was to the interest of some people to misunderstand it. All that they asked for was not a change in their rulers but administrators —he distinguished rulers from administrators. The theory inflicted on them was that the rulers of this country were the administrators who had been appointed or selected under the Government of India Act. His view was entirely different. Those were not the rulers in the strict sense of the word. They represented the King but they were not the King. The Indians also represented the King because they were his subjects just as much as those officers. So in the matter of representing the King the Indians and those officials stood on equal basis. What then was there more in the position of these officers which made them say that they were the real rulers? That was that certain powers had been given to them— they had not usurped those powers —under a statute of Parliament. If another statute of Parliament repealing that statute and giving the Indians those powers was passed the Indians would be what those officers were at present. That was Home Rule and nothing more. There would be no change in the Emperor, absolutely no change in the relations of India with England or in the relations of India with the Empire as a whole. What was there to complain of in this except that some men would lose their trade? If the power was transferred from one man to another the man to whom it was transferred would gain and the other would lose and if that other man would be angry it was natural. He did not think that any English politician would be deterred by such things for a moment from doing his duties.

Ten or fifteen years ago to talk of Home Rule was sedition and people were afraid, he himself was afraid, of talking about Home Rule. But now it was conceded both by the judiciary and the executive that Home Rule was a proper ambition for a dependency to entertain. Ten years of fighting was thus required to remove this prejudice against Home Rule, and now they could talk about it as a legitimate aspiration. The Viceroy, the Premier, the British nation and even the bureaucracy now agreed with them. Now what remained? They said that it was a very good ambition for a dependency; but there was time for it. They said that it would take centuries to attain it, and instances were cited of a number of colonies which attained self-Government in 50 or 60 years. His reply to it was this. The colonies, it was true, had attained self-Government in 50 or 60 years but Indians were being ruled for 100 years, and they had not yet attained self-Government. There must be a time-limit fixed by the bureaucracy. The bureaucracy said that it was not in sight at present. He would say that this was an entirely selfish argument. What was it that prevented them from attaining the goal within a few years after the war when the Empire would be reconstructed? At present India was nothing but a stone in the neck of the Empire. They knew on what principle the bureaucracy governed India for the last 100 years. They were a self-governing nation before. They knew how to organise an army, they knew how to dispense justice, they had laws, regulations, etc. All those had been swept away and now the bureaucracy said that they knew nothing about them. Who was responsible for that?

Not the Indians. When they came here their first care was—he gave credit to them for it—to reduce the disorders prevailing then. How was it done? Firstly by disarming them. Next all the principal posts in the administration were monopolised by them. Next there was a check to scientific progress, and industries gradually disappeared. But, they said, they restored peace. That was true but peace was not everything. It was an introductory condition to further development. They had restored peace, they had given railways, telegraphs and other things. All credit to the bureaucracy for these things, but he could not give credit to them for doing anything which would develop their national instinct. They had not done anything which would enable them to stand on their legs. The result was when in the name of the Empire they were asked to take up arms and fight the enemy they found that so few men volunteered. What was it that made them incapable of assisting the Empire to the extent that they wished to do? It was the system of administration followed by the bureaucracy. They had governed them in such a way that unless radical improvement was made in the system of administration the Empire would gain no material strength from this country. It was this thought that had actuated the best English statesmen to come forward and say that the system of administration in India must be revised after the war.

From the time of Mr. Dadabhai Naoroji up to now they had been crying that they had been deprived of the powers of administration and they should be restored to them. Now the British democracy had clearly seen that there was much force in their cry of reform and they were willing to hear their cry. Now the question was whether the bureaucracy should have a say or whether the Indians should have a say. There was a judge and he had given notice that he was coming here and would hear what the Indians would have to say. Therefore they must press their demand more strongly than their opponents. That was their duty at present. They had to convince him that all arguments used against them were due to prejudice. The great work before them at present was to educate the people to realize what Home Rule was. He would impress on them the supreme necessity of doing their best for getting Home Rule. They must wake up. If they made strenuous efforts then within a year or two they would realize, if not all, at least a part of their wishes. They did not want Home Rule at once; but they wanted a real beginning, and not a shadowy beginning. When Mr. Montagu came here he would speak to their leaders about their demand and he wanted that they should have the solid support of the country behind them. If that was done Mr. Montagu would carry their message to the British people and effectively support it with the authority of his office.

HOME RULE

[Under the presidency of the Honourable Pandit Madan Mohan Malaviya, Mr. Tilak delivered the following speech, in the compound of the Home Rule League, Allahabad, in October, 1917]:—

One objection raised against Home Rule was that if Home Rule was granted to them they would turn out British people from India. Indians did want English people, English institutions, English liberty and the Empire. But what they said was that the internal administration of India should be under Indian control. English people had it in England, they had it in the colonies and they had it everywhere and would claim it everywhere, and if it was not granted to them they would fight for it, and yet some denied to Indians that right. By whom was this bogey of expelling the English from India raised and for what purpose? That must be clearly understood. It was perhaps understood in this country but it was their business to see that the British people understood it in the right way. Those that held power in their hands at present imagined that Indians were not capable of governing themselves to the limited extent implied by the word Home Rule. They did not tell Indians when they would be able to govern themselves. They did not fix any time-limit. Once it used to be said that Asiatic nations were not fit for self-Government. That however was not said now. They now said that India was not now fit for self-Government. If Indians asked them why, they were told that they had not that thing before, they were deficient in education, there were numerous castes quarrelling among themselves, and only British administrators could hold the balance even between rival sections. As regards unfitness he had said something about it the previous day. But it required to be expanded. What was unfitness ? Did they mean to say that before the British came here there was no peaceful rule anywhere in India ? What was Akbar ? Was he a bad ruler ? No Englishman could say that. Let them go back to Hindu rule. There were empires of Asoka, Guptas, Rajputs, etc. No history could say that all these empires had managed their states without any system of administration. There were empires in India as big as the German empire and the Italian empire and they were governed peacefully. When peace reigned in the country under the Hindu, Buddhist and Mahomedan rules, what ground was there to say that the descendants of those people who had governed those empires were to-day unfit to exercise that right ? There was no disqualification, intellectual or physical which disabled them from taking part in the Government of any empire. They had shown their fitness in the past and were prepared to show it to-day if opportunities were granted to them. The charge of unfitness came only from those who held the monopoly of power in their hands. In every case of monopoly that argument was used. The East India Company used that argument. None of them present there whose ancestors had founded and administered empires would subscribe to the doctrine that Indians, whether Hindus or Moslems were incapable of governing themselves. The charge of incapacity was only brought forward by interested people, simply because their self-interest demanded that some argument must be advanced in their support. They were not given higher posts to show their capacity. They were only given subordinate posts. Without the aid of Indians in the subordinate departments it was impossible for the British people to carry on the administration; and so they were given all the subordinate posts. They had been fighting ever since the establishment of the Congress to break this monopoly and not without success. A few posts reserved for the civil service had been granted to them. A few appointments in the judicial department—High Court judgeships, etc.,—had been granted to them. What was the result? He had not seen any resolution of the Government saying that when any post of responsibility was given to Indians they had misused those opportunities, that they had failed to come up to the standard of efficiency required. On the contrary resolutions had been issued saying that Indians who had acted as members of executive councils had done their duty very well. If they went to the Indian States they would find that all higher posts were held by Indians. What did the British administration reports say about these States? They said that they were well administered. So the whole evidence that was possible for them to produce was in their favour. After barring them from these higher services and saying that they were not capable of governing was adding insult to injury. This kind of jugglery would not do. The British democracy would not tolerate it. If they simply pressed the right view on the British public, they would hear it now because they were in a mood to hear it. They had logic and experience on their side, but mere logic and truth would not succeed in this world unless backed up by persistent agitation and fixed determination to attain that truth. They must be determined to see that truth triumph and that triumph was what they meant to achieve. The Home Rule propaganda was intended for that purpose.

Another argument used against Home Rule was that there were certain British interests which would be endangered if Home Rule was given. Mr. Jinnah had told them the previous day that there were British interests not only in India but all over the world. Those British interests had been created, to speak in legal terminology, without their (Indian) consent. They had never been asked when those interests were created. Legally speaking they were not barred from agitating. They knew that those British interests would be safeguarded as far as justice and law were concerned. The law of the land would remain the same. The offices would remain the same. There would no doubt be a change but that change would be so far control was concerned. They wanted law. They could not do without law. To say that if Home Rule was granted to Indians there would be chaos was simple nonsense. They wanted law, they wanted all the departments, even the C. I. D. They wanted as much good rule as at present. They did not want to lapse into misrule. All that they wanted was to have those laws and rules and all those departments which administered those laws under their control. Only the previous day he read in the *Pioneer* the instance of Arrah riots and in mentioning the steps that had been taken to suppress that riot it appealed to Government to look to its duty, namely, that of governing people. Did they mean to say that they were going to tolerate riots under Home Rule? Certainly not. They wanted peace. They would frame such rules by which riots might be averted with the consent of the people, and not without their consent. As regards the question of employment, if the Europeans were prepared to serve they would employ them, if they were fit and if they would accept what they were paid. They did not want anybody to leave India. He knew that British capital was invested in railways; but they did not want to uproot the rails and send them away to England. They wanted the railways and he thought that railways could be better administered if more Indians were employed on them. There would be changes under Home Rule, but not changes for the worse; they would lead to more efficient and economical rule. Their demand was at once sober and constitutional. It remained to be seen whether the British democracy would grant those demands or not. What was at present required was a good statement of their case so that the British people who now felt inclined to make a change in the constitution of the Empire might perceive the case more fully than they had hitherto done. It was the interest of some people to have the case misrepresented, to create misunderstanding and create darkness. That ought not to be allowed to be done. In this connection he must say that Home Rule Leagues had done more work than the Congress Committees. It had been said that there was the Congress and they were opposing the Congress by supporting the Home Rule League. His answer was "No." The ideal and demand of the Home Rule League were the same as the ideal and demand of the Congress. It had been expressly stated from the Home Rule League platform. They did not go beyond the Congress demand. He might say the Home Rule League had been instrumental in bringing about that resolution passed by the Congress last year. So, there were no difference of ideas between the League and the Congress. Then, it was asked, where was the necessity for the Home Rule League? The work done by the Home Rule Leagues spoke for itself. These Leagues had been started to educate the people and make them understand what their goal should be. If this work had been done by the Congress he should at once have given up his membership of the Home Rule League. Some people wanted to work more vigorously than others. He thought every one was entitled to do that. They might form small leagues under any name. The object was the same. He wanted every one of them to work in their own way either by Leagues or by associations or individually under as many different names as they liked. Names did not matter so long as the idea was the same. The work must be done provincially and in the vernaculars of the provinces. The work of educating the people could only be carried on in this way. There was a time when the word Home Rule was looked upon with suspicion as suggesting Irish methods, and the Irish disturbances connected with the same. They could not find a thing which had no previous associations. They must not attach particular importance to particular words. The words were made for them and not they for the words. If they used the word Home Rule what was the objection to it provided they said in the beginning what they meant by it? That controversy was therefore out of place. The real dispute now was not about words. It was about educating the people and he knew that as they had begun to educate the people, the discontent among the official classes would increase, because they would see that eventually the demand would be forced on them. They should not care for that discontent. There was a time when it was held that they should work in such a way as to enlist the sympathy of the administrators in the land. Of course they did wish to enlist their sympathy, but if that sympathy could not be enlisted without lowering the tone of the educative work and without lessening their effort, he was not prepared to secure that sympathy. They were all agreed that they must have Home Rule for their goal. They must strive for it. The question was how to strive for it. Some wanted to proceed slowly, while others wanted to proceed fast. He did not think that this was a difference for which they should quarrel and give an opportunity to their opponents to use these differences against them. They should not talk of method. Every one might have his own method provided it was constitutional. He wanted each man to keep himself within the bounds of law and constitution. He made a distinction between law and constitution. So long as law-making was not in their hands laws which were repugnant to justice and morality would be sometimes passed. They could not obey them. Passive resistance was the means to an end but was not the goal in itself. Passive resistance meant that they had to balance the advantages and disadvantages arising from obeying a particular order and not obeying it. If in their balanced judgment they found that the advantages of disobeying it under particular circumstances were greater, the sense of morality would justify them in acting upon that conviction. This was a very complicated question, and not a question which could be discussed by a large gathering like that. They must leave the question to their leaders for their decision. They must clearly understand what passive resistance meant. It was a determination to achieve their goal at any sacrifice. If they wanted to reach their goal and if they were hindered by artificial and unjust legislation and by any unjust combination of circumstances it was their duty to fight it out. The Home Rule League wanted them to know this. If they did not want to use the words 'passive resistance' they might use the words 'at all sacrifices' but he would use both words in the sense in which he explained them. He did not preach unruliness or illegality, but he preached fixed determination to reach the goal at any sacrifice. Passive resistance, he said, was perfectly constitutional. Law and constitution were not the same. That was proved by history. So long as a particular law was not in conformity with justice and morality, and popular opinion according to the ethics of the 19th and 20th centuries, so long as a particular order was not consistent with all these principles it might be legal, but it was not constitutional. That was a distinction which he wished them to observe very clearly. They should not confound the words 'constitutionally' and 'legally.' He wanted them therefore to confine themselves to strictly constitutional means and he wanted to tell them at the same time that every law in the technical sense of the term was not constitutional. They should educate their people and see that the right political ideal was placed before them, and their sense of justice roused so that they might work hard for that ideal without flinching in any way from it, and with all the determination they could command.

In conclusion Mr. Tilak asked the people to join the Home Rule League in large numbers and do the work of educating the people. They must wake up, and do the work enthusiastically. If they would not do it, it would be a great misfortune to the country. They would not only be ruining themselves but they would be ruining the future generations who would curse them. They would have to do their duty to the country, to the future generations and above all to God. It was a duty which they owed to Providence which governed all nations. That Providence was favourably disposed towards them; and they should not let go the opportunity granted to them by Providence. He would impress on them the necessity of moving unitedly at present, irrespective of caste or creed, or jealousies fearlessly and boldly. If they did that he was confident that their efforts could be crowned with success in the course of a few years by the blessing of Providence. (Loud applause.)

THE NATIONAL DEMAND

[The following resolution on Self-Government was passed at the Calcutta Session of the National Congress in December, 1917.]

"This Congress expresses grateful satisfaction for the pronouncement made by His Majesty's Secretary of State for India on behalf of the Imperial Government that its object is the establishment of Responsible Government in India. This Congress strongly urges the necessity of the immediate enactment of a Parliamentary Statute providing for the establishment of Responsible Government in India, the full measure to be attained within a time limit, to be fixed in the Statute itself, at an early date. This Congress is emphatically of opinion that the Congress-League Scheme of Reforms ought to be introduced by the Statute as the first step in the process."

In supporting the above resolution, Mr. Tilak spoke as follows:—

I have not the eloquence of my friend Mr. Bannerji, nor of my friend Mr. Jinnah, nor the trumpet voice of Mr. Bepin Chandra Pal. Yet I have to do a duty, and I mean to place before you without any introduction a few facts in support of the resolution which has been so ably moved by the proposer, seconded by the Hon. Mr. Jinnah and certainly not amended but intended to be amended by my friend Mr. Bepin Chandra Pal. The resolution, as you all know, is about Self-Government or Home Rule for India. The first paragraph of it says: 'This Congress expresses grateful satisfaction for the pronouncement made by His Majesty's Secretary of State for India on behalf of the Imperial Government that its object is the establishment of Responsible Government in India.' The speaker who preceded me—I mean Mr. Bepin Chandra Pal—seems to think that it is not yet time to be grateful for the declaration of policy. To a certain extent I share in that view, but, at the same time, I cannot say that the wording of the resolution is not adequate. For gratitude, as you know, is defined by one of the best ethical writers of England to mean expectation of favours to come; and grateful satisfaction, translated in view of that definition, means satisfaction at the pronouncement attended with an expectation that the later stages of it will come in course of time as early as possible. That is how I interpret 'grateful satisfaction.' I am satisfied for the present that a thing that was not pronounced before has been declared now, and I hope, at the same time, nay expect, that it will be followed up by higher stages of development in time to come. All talk about further stages is out of place at present. What should be the first step is the point that I want you to understand. A very simple definition of Home Rule which any of you including a peasant can understand is that I should be in my own country what an Englishman feels to be in England and in the Colonies. The simplest definition is that, and that is the whole of it. All those bombastic phrases, such as 'partnership in the Empire,' 'terms of equality,' etc., mean that I want to be in my country not as outlander but as master in the same sense that an Englishman is a master in his own country and in the Colonies. That is complete Home Rule, and if any one is going to grant it to-morrow, I shall be very glad for its introduction, for it will be Indian Home Rule granted all at once, but I see that it cannot be done. Some compromise has to be made with those who are not in our favour and with some of our friends. The British power in India was introduced by a compromise, by a Charter. In fact, the first step in a province which you have not conquered is always with consent and compromise, and what the first step should be is explained in this resolution. All talk about future progress, about the establishment of Responsible Government in the Provinces and afterwards in the Central Government is a very good talk with which I fully sympathise but which I am not prepared to demand as the first step of the introduction of Home Rule in India. That is the difference between myself and Mr. Bepin Chandra Pal. He wants the whole hog at once. I say it should be granted to you by stages: demand the first step so that the introduction of the second step would be much more easy than it is at present. The Government in the pronouncement has used the words "Responsible Government," not Home Rule or Self-Government. Mr. Montagu in the declaration and the Government of India in their Proclamation have deliberately used the words "Responsible Government" unfortunately without defining it, because Responsible Government as naturally understood means Executive Government responsible to the Legislature. But in one place in Mr. Curtis's pamphlet I find that "Responsible Government" is defined to be one where the legislature is subject to the executive. You will see that it is quite necessary to define the words "Responsible Government;" otherwise words may be interpreted quite contrary to our intention and it may be said: "We promise you Responsible Government but a Government where the Legislature ought to be under the control of the Executive." And the more it is placed under the control of the Executive the more responsible it will become according to this. (Laughter.) I must state frankly here that this is not the kind of Responsible Government that we want. We understand by the words "Responsible Government," a Government where the Executive is entirely responsible to the Legislature, call it Parliament or by any other name, and that legislature should be wholly elected. That Responsible Government is what we want. When I say that the Executive should be under the control of Legislature, I go so far as to say that even Governors and Lieutenant-Governors must be elected by legislative bodies. That, however will be the final step. But in the present circumstances I shall be quite content, and so I think most of you will be content, if the first step that we demand is granted to you immediately, and Self-Government at an early date. And by 'early stages' I do not think that any sane man would understand to be anything which would be attained in fifty years, because a period extending to fifty years is not 'early.' Anything that exceeds the time of one generation is not 'early'. 'Early' means certainly in ordinary parlance ten or fifteen years. I should have liked that a definite number of years should have been introduced in this resolution. However, we do not lose much. I say that no sane man can understand 'early date' to mean other than ten or fifteen years. But some men thought that it would be rash to ask for Home Rule or Responsible Government in ten or fifteen years. It was dropped. Never mind. At any rate, the sense is there. I must draw your attention to the pronouncement made. What is it? It is that full Responsible Government or merely Responsible Government without any qualifications—that means the same thing—Responsible Government without any limiting qualifications will be granted to you in ten or fifteen years. That part of the answer given by Mr. Montagu we note with grateful satisfaction.

in the sense in which I have just explained it. There are certain other conditions. That pronouncement says that it will be granted to you by stages. We also agree to it. The third part of the declaration is that these stages would be determined by the Government of India. We do not agree to that. We want the stages to be determined by us and not at the sweet will of the Executive. Nor do we want any compromise about it but insist on definite stages and the time to be fixed in the Act itself so that the whole scheme may work automatically. There we differ from the wording of the declaration: however it is not said here in so many words but the second paragraph of the resolution demands it: it demands a Parliamentary Statute to be immediately passed definitely settling and fixing the time when the goal is to be reached, not leaving it to the Government of India to determine when and at what circumstances and in what stages they will grant full Responsible Government to us: definite time should be named in the statute which will be passed about the subject very soon. So, the second part of the resolution is practically a suggested modification of the declaration about which we have expressed our grateful satisfaction in the first part of the resolution. In the third paragraph of the resolution we stick to what was passed last year at Lucknow both by the Congress and the Muslim League. It has been said that that scheme is objectionable and that after a year's experience we should have modified it at this Congress. I hold a different view. I am glad that we all hold the same view. (A cry of 'no, no.') That will be determined when we take the votes. If we unanimously pass the resolution it may be that I shall be speaking for you when you pass the resolution without a dissentient voice. I hold that the Congress-League scheme is the minimum which might be granted to us to satisfy our aspirations at present and to make a decent beginning in the introduction of Home Rule in India. I tell you why. There have been a number of schemes suggested at various places in India by Congressmen and non-Congressmen, by Muslim League men and non-Muslim League men and by backward and forward classes as they call themselves and by other different communities, and all these representations have been sent up to the Secretary of State. What do you find if you analyse them? The majority of them say that they approve of the Congress-League scheme but they want something more, and if you take vote, you have all the votes for the Congress-League scheme and one vote for each scheme in the country. I say that that itself is an indication that the Congress League scheme is approved all over the country and we are not going to swerve from it an inch. It has been said that the Government is prepared to grant to you Responsible Government but that you do not ask for it because the Congress-League scheme does not make Executive removable at the pleasure of the Legislature; it cannot be technically said to be responsible. The pronouncement is that "Responsible Government" will be granted to you, that it should be granted to you by stages, so that the first stage also must have something of Responsible Government. I do not think that that argument is right. The Government meaning is that one stage will be Municipal and Local, the second stage is Provincial and the last stage is Central Government. That is not the meaning that I attached to it. I say that the Congress League scheme does not provide for the removal of the Executive at the will of the Legislature; true, but it gives you all the control over the Executive. We say that the Executive should be under the control of the Legislature and that four-fifths of the legislative body should be elected. What does it mean? It means that the Legislature which the Congress League scheme demands will not be fully responsible in the sense of being able to remove the Executive, but it can transfer the Executive. If the Executive will not obey the Legislature they may be transferred to some other post. Why should you ask that the Executive should be removed? Once the bureaucracy understand that they are responsible to the Legislative Councils, they are wise enough, intelligent enough to shape their future conduct accordingly: they are not fools. A beginning of the responsibility is made. The Executive are held responsible and they must take their orders from elected Legislative Councils. So, to say that the Congress-League scheme is not a beginning of Responsible Government is merely deceiving oneself and others by a use of words with which always wise and selfish men try to deceive the masses. The second objection urged against the Congress-League scheme is that it is better to begin from below, that it is better to build up from foundation, than to begin with the top, so that you must begin with your Municipality, gradually have District Boards under your control, then bring Provincial Governments under your control and then the Central Government. Even that argument is fallacious. The case may apply to the building of a new house where you cannot build the top without foundation, but the simile of a house does not apply to a political building, especially in the case of India. We in India are not children to be promoted from standard to standard until we pass our graduation either in Arts or in Law. We are full-grown people. We have had experience of governing Empires and Kingdoms in the past. (Cheers.) We fully know the art. Add to it that we have received western education which lays down certain principles of Government. We have learnt those principles and how to use those principles, having watched them so far in civilised countries. Are we not capable of carrying on the Government of India from to-morrow if the Government is given into our hands? (Loud cheers.) When we say that

Responsible Government should be granted to us by stages we cannot be meant to suppose that we should have training in Municipalities first, in District Boards afterwards, Provincial Legislative Councils next and then in the Supreme Legislative Council. There is no parallel between the two. The case of India is like that of an emasculated man who had lost or made to lose all his nervous power. In the case of a nervous disease, there is emasculation of the whole body and you have to begin the treatment with the brain and not with the toe. If you want to restore a man to health at once, you give tonic to the brain, the centre of all nervous system. So it is with India. If the present Government is unfit for the administration of the country in the best interests of the Empire, the best remedy is to give tonic to the brain and that is Simla or Delhi. Unless that centre is made sound soon you cannot expect that any local remedy applied to the different parts of the body—to the foot or hand or other parts of the body-would be of any avail. So the Congress-League provides that we must have certain powers in the Central Government. If it is not made removable, we must at least be placed on a footing of equality. Half the members of the Executive should be our representatives, *i.e.*, they should be elected by the people. Thus we must go on building from the top. We do not want to divide the political Government in this country into parts, horizontal or vertical. We want to treat the whole man, and we want such cure to be administered as will cure his brain first and power over the lower limbs will gradually be restored. Our scheme provides for that. To talk of Provincial Government when speaking of Imperial autonomy is to talk nonsense. We must have a share of the power in the Central Government. The control over the Municipalities remains with the Central Government, and you know how that power is being exercised and what actual independence you have in a Municipality. If you mean to have local Self-Government you must have power all through from top to bottom, *i.e.*, Responsible Government from top to bottom. In the Congress-League scheme it is provided that the Imperial Legislative Council should have four-fifths of its members elected and one-fifth nominated and that the Legislature should have control over the Executive. I admit that this is not Responsible Government but it is really the beginning of Responsible Government. Take the case of a minor whose estate is in charge of the Court of Wards. The minor having attained majority claims the estate from the Court of Wards. Suppose the defence of the Court of Wards is that they will transfer the power by parts, say the stables outside the house. What is the result ? When that is done, the Court of Wards will say " We shall then think at the later date of transferring the whole house to the man." That defence would not be good enough in a Court of Law ; any Judge will throw it away. The same is the case in the political struggle between the Bureaucracy and the Nation. Bureaucracy is the trustee of our interests. We have attained the age of majority; we claim our estate from Bureaucracy and men like Mr. Curtis are prepared to tell us: "Yes, we know that we shall have to transfer the whole power to you, but we shall see that it is transferred to you gradually when proper electorates are brought into existence, and that at some time in the course of a century or two when the preparations are complete or according to the Hindu time, some time in this Kali Yuga we shall transfer the power to you." That kind of defence ought not to be allowed for one moment. We are entitled to the possession of the whole house, and if we allow you to share our power with you in that house, it is a concession made for you in the hope that at you will soon clear out of it. You have managed the house so long; you have been living in the house; we will allow you to live in the house for a longer time, but eventually you must acknowledge that from to-day we are masters of the house; then alone there can be any compromise; otherwise, none. The first merit of the Congress scheme is that it asks for a transfer of power to the elective body in a Central Government itself. Without a share—an equal share—in the Central Government, it is hopeless to be able to govern the smaller portions of the Empire, such as Municipalities, Local Boards, etc., with any sense of

Responsible Government. You must banish from your mind the idea of building from the bottom. That is not the analogy applicable to our scheme. We consent to nothing less than what is embodied in the Congress-League scheme. We must have control over the Central Government. The Government of India is one body from the gods of Simla to the lowest police man in the village. If you want to grant our right, if you think that our claims are just, we must have a share at the top. All these arguments against our scheme are intended to deceive you and are advanced by people whose idea is to remain in possession of the house even though we have attained our majority and are entitled to the possession of the whole house. Mr. Bepin Chandra Pal admitted that we must have the whole Congress scheme *plus* something more. I want also that *plus* and not *minus*. But I claim the first term of this equation to begin with, the other terms will follow, and I shall be one with him when we fight for the second stage, and I ask him and entreat him to be one with me in fighting for the first. The second merit of our scheme is that it tries to build upon the existing foundation. It is not a new scheme requesting the Government to introduce any modification in the machinery of the government. The machinery has been in existence for hundred years or more. We want the Secretary of State, we want the Imperial Government, we want the Local Governments, we want the Municipality, we want the District Board, and we want also the Bureaucracy to stay in the land not to go out of it. We all want these, but we want certain transference of power, a decentralisation which will vest people with power, in every one of these institutions. We do not want to change the institutions. We do not say that India should be governed by a Crown Prince from England or that the administration should be transferred to any Native Chief. We say "Retain your administrative machinery as it is." Our question is not with machinery but with power. The Government of India is composed of Legislative and Executive. We want no changes in Governor, Governor-General and also Executive Councils but we want that the power that vests in the Executive should be transferred to the Legislature. We do not want to disturb the machinery. We do not want a new machinery to be introduced. What we want is that there are certain wheels in the machinery which have appropriated to themselves the power of regulating the machinery, and we want that power to be transferred to other wheels. It is no new scheme: it is a tried scheme, a tried machinery. All that is required is transfer of power from one part of the machinery to another. The Secretary of State should be deprived of the power of controlling the Government of India. The true Government of India should be in India. What next? The Bureaucracy also agrees with us that power should be transferred by the Secretary of

State to the present Government of India. We want it transferred to the Government of India and that the Executive should be under the control of the Legislature. At present about half the members are elected in the Legislative Council. What is the objection to electing a few more? All objection falls to the ground when you remember that when so many Imperial Council members are elected now and do their work often to the satisfaction of Government. All that we ask for in our scheme is to have a few more members of that kind and give them power to control the Executive. We are to build upon the existing foundation. The objection that our scheme is unworkable, untried and that it has never been tried in other countries is useless and harmful to our interests if the objection is put in a language which may deceive the unwary. The second objection was that if we have half the Executive elected and half the Executive nominated, there would be a deadlock. It is said that one-half of the Executive will be fighting against the other half and that the conflict would make the administration nugatory. I say no. Our scheme says that the Governor shall have the power of veto and he would decide which side is correct and the administration will not be hampered in any way at all. We have made provision for it, and that provision does not suit the Bureaucrats who are in power and they think that when power is shared like that they must act with greater respect to popular opinion. Lastly, I say that our scheme is better than any other scheme for another reason, and that reason is that no other scheme will be so compatiable with the wishes of the British Parliament as ours. Mr. Curtis and Sir Valentine Chirol have been forced—and I do not think quite willingly—to accept the pronouncement of the Government as the basis of future work. Government having declared the policy—those two gentlemen would have been very glad if the Government had not declared their policy—they have accepted that policy. But what are they trying to do with it? Given that proclamation, how much of it, in fact, what is the lowest proportion of it, that can be conceded to the people? They wish to draw the minimum length provided for in that proclamation. That is the problem before Mr. Curtis and Sir Valentine. Our problem is how long the line can be drawn. I must warn you not to accept any other scheme or to be carried away by it simply because the author of it professes to limit it. I therefore commend this resolution for your unanimous acceptance. (Loud and prolonged cheers.")

SHISHIR KUMAR GHOSE

[The sixth anniversary meeting to commemorate the ascension of Babu Shishir Kumar Ghose, was held at Manomohon Theatre, on January 3, 1918. Long before the appointed hour, the auditorium was filled to its utmost capacity, leaving not even standing room for anybody.]

The arrival of Lok. Tilak on the platform was signalised by repeated rounds of cheering the cries of Bandemataram which continued for some mintues.

Lokamanya Bal Gangadhar Tilak rose amidst loud cheers and said:—

Friends and Gentlemen,—We have all heard a number of incidents relating to the life of one whose memory we have come here to commemorate to-day. As for myself, I want to add only a few words to what has already been said. I must say first that I had the pleasure and honour of being personally acquainted with Shishir Babu. I have learnt many lessons sitting at his feet. I revered him as my father (Hear, hear,) and I venture again to say that he, in return, loved me as his son. I can call to mind many an interview that I had with him at the "Patrika" office some of which lasted for hours. I have distinct recollections of what he told me of his experiences as a journalist with tears in his eyes and sympathy in his words. I then requested him, I remember now, to put down those incidents, at least to leave notes in writing, so that they might serve the future historian of the country or even the writer of his life.

To me, Shishir Babu figures as the pioneer of journalists in this country. After the Mutiny when he was only 15 years of age, came the establishment of the British Bureaucracy in this country—it was a despotic rule and the country wanted a man who would cope with their devices—who would see the inner meaning of their devices-who was courageous enough to meet them bold and honest enough to expose them, and take defeat calmly and coolly in order to resuscitate for future strength. Such was Shishir Kumar Ghose. The "Patrika" is the manifestation of the spirit of which he was full—nobody may talk of the "Patrika" without being reminded of Shishir Kumar Ghose. At this time a man was required with a feeling heart to realise the position of the masses who were then governed by a despotic rule—one who must have sympathy with the people who were unjustly treated and did not know what to do but only looked up to heaven for help. The people were dumb. The bureaucracy had full power. The Mutiny had just been over and British Rule had been firmly established in the land. At such a time a man was required to steer the nationalship to a safe harbour constitutionally and legally—a man of courage, a man who could see through the actions of the bureaucracy—actions which were calculated to bear fruit in the distant future.

It is a very difficult task now to criticise the Government—it was more so in those days and not only biting sarcasm but great resourcefulness, great courage, great insight and large sympathy was required to make honest journalism a success in the land. Shishir Babu had these qualities in abundance. The authorities feared him. They could not raise their finger to crush him. You have just now heard the story of Sir Ashley Eden who wanted to strike at him but could not. What was it due to? It was not due to legal or any other protection—it was due to the character of the man which was his only protection. Sir Ashley feared not so much the writing of the man, but the character of the man who would persist in writing such things so long as the injustice was not removed.

In Shishir Kumar we had a man who would not care for honour or favour but would stand boldly by his guns until success was attained. (Hear, hear). Even a strong man at times is not able to do much —for strength is to be joined with prudence, prudence is to be coupled with foresight—both with courage and keenness of perception, which is granted only to a few people in the world. In Shishir Kumar all these qualities were combined. Such a man I had the honour and the pleasure of knowing.

Journalism—independent and free journalism—was not an easy task in those days—60 years ago, when many of you were charmed with Government Service. You looked upon such a man as rather eccentric—he might be independent, might be honest, but certainly not worldly. He had to calmly bear the reproaches of friends for having refused Government favours and other things that make life happy and easy. He stood alone and his conscience was his stand. He thought that he had a message to give to the world—he thought that he had a duty to do and he did it unflinchingly. That was the man who led Bengal in the last decades of the 19th century. I am glad to say that those traditions of the paper are being faithfully maintained to this day (cheers). I myself have something to do with journalism and when I take a survey of the papers that have been carried on for two generations with the same policy and with the same spirit—I can point to one paper and that is the "Amrita Bazar Patrika" (cheers). I had a talk on that subject with my friend Babu Motilal Ghose. I asked him how is it that he could copy his brother so exactly in language, style and sentiment and he told me that he had studied his brother and nothing else and hence he had been able to maintain the spirit of the paper.

These high ideals are out of the reach of the common people and the common people judge these men by their own standards, attribute to them motives which are foreign to them. Shishir Babu also had to face this and he did the work which can truly be called the work of an angel. He saw that the service of humanity was a stepping stone to the service of God. When he gave up, owing to physical feebleness, his work at the "Patrika" office, he devoted his time to the service of God with the same enthusiasm and fervour with which he did service to the people. Such was the man we have lost. I am sorry I am not an adept in character-sketching, but if I have given you certain prominent characteristics of his life, I think I have done enough. Such a man is rare to find. You have his life written; and from it you may know the story of his life but underneath all this do not fail to find out and properly value the man who had made journalism what it is in India.

I know with what enthusiasm and eagerness the "Patrika" was awaited in my province every week 40 years ago. I know how people were delighted to read his sarcasm, his pithy and critical notes written in his racy style, simple but at the same time effective. How people longed to see the paper on the day it was due by post, how people enjoyed it—I know it personally. (Hear, hear). You in Bengal cannot know what we felt and thought in the Maharastra. Strange stories circulated about these brothers in my province. People used to say that Shishir Babu was writing with one foot in jail and the other brother was waiting simply to see when the elder is sent to jail. There were stories like that and if they do not correspond with facts they at least illustrate the feeling and the reverence with which the paper was read in my part of the country. They show how the man was appreciated. They were really delighted to see his writings but very few had the courage to quote those remarks before others, they enjoyed them in secret.

I may further tell you that when we started our paper in vernacular, we tried to follow the editor of the " A. B. Patrika." This was the time when one had to teach the people how to criticise the bureaucracy and at the same time keep oneself safe, bodily at least if not pecuniarly. That was the idea fully developed by Shishir Kumar in those days of journalism. Bureaucracy is always anxi us to conciliate its critics not by mending its way but by offering bribes to them and the dignity of Shishir Kumar lay not so much in his writings as in the courage which he showed at a critical time, when favours were offered to him and he rejected them with contempt. Such a man he was.

Babu Shishir Kumar was a true political saint and I regret as much as you do that that kind of character is getting rare in these days, as it is bound to be by the demoralization of the despotic government. We thank God that we had such a man in the early years of journalism in India. He was a hero in the true sense of the word. He did not see his aspirations fulfilled. It might be fulfilled in a generation or two or more, but we cannot forget that it was he who laid the foundation. Such a man deserved to be respected not only during his life but for all time to come. I wish you to study his life—to look not to his failings but to his great achievements—to draw inspiration from him and follow in his footsteps as far as it is possible for you to do.

ALI BROTHERS

[The following is the speech of Mr. Tilak, in moving the resolution of the release of Ali Brothers, at the Calcutta Indian National Congress, in 1917] :—

Madam, Mother of Messrs. Mohomed Ali and Shaukat Ali, Fellow Delegates, Ladies and Gentlemen.—The mother of Messrs. Mohomed Ali and Shaukat Ali, the revered mother—the mother of the brave—is here, and it befits you all to hear in silence what is to be said in support of the resolution asking the Government to release the two interned detenues. I use that word deliberately because they have been suffering on suspicion for long from day to day and on grounds, which were discovered not at the time of this internment, but after they had been detained. The resolution runs this :—

That this Congress urges on the Government the immediate release of Messrs. Mohomed Ali and Shaukat Ali, who have remained incarcerated since October, 1914, *and are now kept interned because of religious scruples which they hold in common with the whole of Islam in India and elsewhere and which are not incompatible with loyalty to the King Emperor.*

Continuing the speaker said that they all knew why Mr. Mohomed Ali was interned under the

Defence of India Act in 1914. That Act was very elastic and invested the authorities with the complete power of despotism. If the Executive thought, without any further enquiry on the evidence of the C.I.D.—the evidence, he might say, manufactured evidence, manufactured according to their wishes, that there was a danger to the public tranquility or safety, without caring to divulge anything, they could intern a person. That was what happened in this case. Mohomed Ali was interned in 1914 apparently for publishing certain articles in the press, but the real cause was that he displeased the high authority. Though there was no convincing proof before the authorities they were interned. Both the Hindus and the Mahomedans requested Government to publish the grounds on which the Executive Government interned them. No response was made to their request and the public protest. Gradually Government climbed down and they were willing to let them off. Negotiations were going on, and the Hon. Raja Sahib of Mahmudabad and the Hon. Mr. Jinnah were both willing to assure Government that there was no danger in letting them off. Both those two Hon'ble gentlemen had the assurance of the whole of the Mohamedan community at their back. The whole of the Mohamedan community was prepared to stand guarantee for them. With it they might add the voice of the Hindu community. That meant that practically the whole of India was unanimous. But the C.I.D did not like their release. Sometime the C.I.D. tried to control the Executive Department. The speaker compared the C.I.D. with the "Rakshasa" who wanted to destroy his creator, "Lord Shiva." The C.I.D. were entrusted with the task of finding out evidence by which the detention of those two brothers could be supported. The C I.D. went to Chhindwara, had a talk with them and wanted to ascertain whether they would be loyal to the crown. It was not a new thing to them; they were loyal before. But there was a condition attached to it. The C.I.D. said that the two brothers owed allegiance to God above and the Executive god below. Mr. Mohomed Ali was prepared to be loyal to the King Emperor provided his religious scruples were observed. That statement was at once pounded upon by the C.I.D. and the Executive Government. Those two brothers were not detained for that. That fact was discovered after this detention and it was made the ground for detaining them further at Chhindwara (shame, shame). They detained the persons for some reason which did not justify them. Something subsequently cropped up and that was immediately laid hold of to justify their action. They then continued to detain them. "Religious scruple" could not be a ground for detaining a person. It was not a tenable ground. It was illusory, fallacious and unjust. The next step taken by Government was this. The C.I.D. discovered a letter supposed to have been written by the interned brothers. That letter brought out certain supposed connection between these two brothers and a religious Mahomedan gentleman of Delhi and it was alleged that they were in league with the King's enemies. Immediately it was got hold of, it was placed before the Viceroy. But Government, instead of asking these two brothers, who denied the charge, to explain, detained them further. If Government had reliable information on the point the two brothers would have been placed on trial on the information supplied by the C.I.D. This is a very solemn occasion. We are passing the resolution in the presence of their mother. Mind, mother's grief, and mother's care is something unprecedented. I am not going to compare it with anything else. But let me assure the mother on your behalf that the title to become a mother of a brave son so far exceeds in importance that I appeal to her to forgive and forget what Government has done and to take consolation in the fact that all of us have sympathy with her in her present position. I pray to God that we may have many more mothers like her in this country (hear, hear.) That is the only consolation I can offer in the present situation and I do so with your permission.

SWARAJYA

[*A great mass meeting was held on Sunday*, (15-11-17) *in the Conference Pandal, at Godhra, when Mr. Tilak, delivered a stirring address on Indian Home Rule. Mr. Gandhi presided*] :—

Mr. Tilak, who was accorded a tremendous ovation on rising to speak, apologised to them for the unavoidable necessity of his having to speak to them in Marathi. He then delivered his address on "Swarajya" and why they wanted it. He referred at the outset to the forces of opposition and reaction that had recently been brought into active play. An attempt was being made by these forces to create misunderstanding in the minds of ignorant Englishmen as to what they wanted in India. It was unfortunate that some of their own men should have allowed themselves to be led away by the campaign of calumny against the Home Rulers. Of course, it was explicable why the authorities were up in arms against the agitation for constitutional reform in India. They feared very naturally that, if the Indian demand were conceded, it would seriously interfere with the unfettered exercise of their power and authority to which they had been long used. Latterly, a body of retired Englishmen who had lost all touch with the rate of progress in India and who had otherwise done little or nothing to acquaint themselves about the real India had begun to pose themselves as the great "friends" of the Indian people and had been giving the world to understand that they were out for helping India to attain Nationhood. It was indeed very kind of them to be taking so much trouble for their sake. But it was somewhat curious that the Harrises and Sydenhams who in their day never did a good work to the Indian people should have now come forward, especially on the eve of Mr. Montagu's visit to this country.

He next referred to the internment of Mrs. Besant and the great humiliation that was in store for the Madras bureaucrats led by Lord Pentland.. It had irritated them considerably no doubt, and they lost their perspective in consequence. It had been forgotten that they did not want Lord Pentland to be removed but they wanted that Lord Pentland should act in consonance with their will. The Civil Servants too were afraid that, if "Swarajya" were given to the people, their power and authority (*Izzat* and *Ibrahat*) would be gone, and the Civil Servants were, therefore, opposed to it.

MEANING OF "SWARAJYA"

"Swarajya" meant only one thing, continued Mr. Tilak, and that thing was that the power should be vested in them (the people). It meant that, under it, the Sovereign Power would be strengthened and not Authority. The great claim of the bureaucracy was that it had made India "prosperous." He would fain concede it, but the facts were against it. During their 100 years' work in India, he wanted to know what the bureaucracy had done to train the people industrially and otherwise and make them self-helping and self-reliant. It was an open secret that the cotton duties, which had happily been done away with now, had been hitherto maintained in the interests of Lancashire cotton spinners. The authorities were naturally anxious to maintain power in their own hands and they had no quarrel with them for that. But that desire was unjustifiable the moment the lawful claimants demanded it back. It had been said that the English Government had given India peace and order; but that was all. The peace and order had been accompanied by no tangible results. During the time of the Peshwas, there were no elaborate commissariat arrangements and yet at a moment's notice hundreds of people were ready to render service to the State, and it was not said that the Peshwas had not maintained peace and order. As he had already remarked, it was the great secret of political Government by England that a so-called peace and order had been given without any tangible results. In this connection, he referred to Dadabhai's famous indictment of British Rule and paid a warm tribute of praise to the great work of the deceased patriot.

"A VIRTUAL SCRAP OF PAPER"

Referring to the Queen's Proclamation of 1858, he

pointed out now it had been treated by many of the bureaucrats, responsible as well as irresponsible, as no better than of antiquarian interest. To the ruler, colour made no difference in the treatment of his subjects, but men in authority were swayed by their own passions and prejudices and had nullified the great pledges given to them in the past. Dealing with the Morley-Minto Reforms, he observed that while there was some improvement over the past state of affairs. the progress was by no means satisfactory or even consistent with their actual needs. In the Legislative Councils, they were like witnesses in a Court of Law: they were mere lookers-on of the great drama of Government. They did not certainly want that kind of farce any more. What they wanted was real, effective control over the administration, both Legislative and Executive.

Mr. Tilak also referred to the recent Italian reverses and regretted that India was not in a position to support the Allied cause as well as they might have wished. India's military power had remained unexploited, and he doubted very much if it would have been so if the Government were "popular." As Mr. Lloyd George had said in his message to Lord Willingdon, what was wanted was that India's heart should be "touched." Until that was done, it was not possible to expect great help from India. After all, the Government had to remember that with this War, all the trouble would not automatically cease. As Mr. Bonar Law once remarked, there might be a second Punic war yet. The future was full "of perils and grave portents and it was statesmanship to be ready to face any eventualities."

THE ANGLO-INDIAN HUE AND CRY

The Anglo-Indians' hue and cry was not only ill-timed and ill-advised but was positively harmful to the lasting interests of the Empire. The people wanted Self-Government not only for their own benefit but for the sake of the Empire. In any struggle or crisis, a contented Self-Governing India was the greatest and surest asset of the Empire, and those who overlooked it were doing the greatest mischief to the Imperial cause. Apart from it the case for Self-Government was invincible. A strong wave of democracy was passing all the world over and even the British Government had hailed the Russian Revolution as the "first great triumph of the present War." Lord Sydenham's contention that they in India take advantage of Britain's troubles to agitate for Self-Government was false. They had already been agitating for Self-Government for over 30 years. All over the world Self-Government was on the anvil, and India alone could not be expected to sit still.

People were no longer prepared to put up with "stone-laying" governors and a civil service that spent public money as it pleased. They wanted to see that, after the War, the Government was thoroughly responsible to the people and carried on the administration according to their needs. Before resuming his seat, Mr. Tilak exhorted the audience to be bold and courageous and frankly tell the officials, if they were asked, that they wanted Home Rule. It was no crime to say that. The demand had been admitted to be fair, legitimate and constitutional by the highest judicial and executive authorities in the land, and lately His Majesty's Government had accepted it as the goal of British rule in India. Mr. Tilak resumed his seat amidst a fresh outburst of cheering after he had spoken for fully an hour.

SWARAJYA

[Under the auspices of the Amraoti Home Rule League, Mr. Tilak made the following speech, on February 13, 1917.]

Amidst shouts of cheering and applause Lokamanya Tilak rose to thank the public and various associations for doing him a great honour. He said that the fact that so many associations were doing him honour showed that all people had joined hands together for the great National work of Home Rule, or *Swarajya.* Hindus and Muhammadans, moderates and extremists had discarded their differences. They all wanted Home Rule, or *Swarajya.* Their demand was a united demand. The great Rakshasa in the path of union has disappeared. Minor ones, like the antagonisms of some non-Brahmana communities, were negligible. They in their own time would disappear after they had experienced the efforts of their suicidal tendencies. They had a definite plan and organisation of Self-Government settled at Lucknow by great men of all parties and creeds. Every one should ask with an open bold face for Home Rule and declare himself to be a thorough Home Ruler. The ideal of Home Rule for India was held legal. To preach it was not sedition. Great authorities in England

and in India had recognised it as the worthy aspiration of the Indians. The point at dispute was only time. Indians wanted it within two or three years, that is, at the conclusion of the War. If India were not to be raised to the status of a Self-Governing member within the Empire, they would be disappointed For the whole Empire to last long and to remain on a solid foundation, India must be granted Self-Government. War had given India an opportunity to show its loyalty to the British Throne, and its faith in the British connection. It had created confidence in the minds of the rulers about the ruled. It had changed the old "angle of vision" of British people. Even conservative people like Lord Islington had declared recently that something in the way of reform must be done for India. War had tested India's loyalty. If conservative men had changed to that extent, what must be the views of Liberals and Radicals in England. They must go to them, put their case before them and Home Rule would be had in two years. Colonies were trying to get a hand in the affairs of India, as the conspiracy of Mr. L. Curtis had showed. They must have Home Rule as soon as possible, to avoid any additional difficulties. The Almighty God had given them the opportunity to strive for. No one thought that Indian political aspirations would be so near realisation a few years ago. But unless they worked, they would not get Home Rule. Such opportunities did not come often. The whole of India must be converted into Home Rulers, so that the Government might know that not to grant Home Rule would be a permanent disappointment. They must say that they would not be satisfied with anything but Home Rule, which was their just and legitimate demand. They should strive for it and get it, their efforts should be sincere and continuous. The rulers would soon come round to their view and give them Home Rule.

POLITICAL CREED

I have, like other political workers, my own differences with the Government as regards certain measures, and to a certain extent even the system of internal administration. But it is absurd on that account to speak of my actions or my attitude as in any way hostile to His Majesty's Government. That has never been my wish or my object. I may state once for all that we are trying in India, as the Irish Home Rulers have been doing in Ireland, for a reform of the system of administration and not for the overthrow of Government and I have no hesitation in saying that the acts of violence which have been committed in the different parts of India are not only repugnant to me, but have, in my opinion, only unfortunately retarded, to a great extent, the pace of our political progress. Whether looked at from an individual or from a public point of view, they deserve, as I have said before on several occasions, to be equally condemned.

It has been well said that British Rule is conferring inestimable benefit on India not only by its civilized methods of administration, but also by bringing together the different nationalities and races of India so that a United Nation may grow out of it in course of time. I do not believe that if we had any other ruler except the liberty-loving British, they could have conceived and assisted us in developing such a National Ideal. Everyone who has the interests of India at heart is fully alive to this and similar advantages of the British Rule; and the present crisis is, in my opinion, a blessing in as much as it has universally evoked our united feelings and sentiments of loyalty to the British Throne.

MR. GOKHALE

[*Mr. Tilak, in moving the resolution on the death of Mr. Gokhale, at the 17th Provincial Bombay Conference, on 10th May, 1915, spoke as follows*] :—

He said that it was in a way a great misfortune that a day should come when he should have to propose the said resolution which he did. He felt sadness and sorrow more keenly than others, because he was in part responsible in introducing Mr. Gokhale into the field of politics, a field in which that zealous and sincere worker lost his life by over-work. People should not judge of his relations with Mr. Gokhale by what appeared on the outside. He had worked with Mr. Gokhale for eight years in the Fergusson College, and had known him in various capacities in his political career. No man could better know than he did Mr. Gokhale's qualities of head and heart—his zeal in the country's cause, his sincerity and singlemindeduess, his determination to take to the end the task he might take in hand. It was a misfortune of India that she could not boast of many such men. The loss of a man like Mr. Gokhale was irreparable but people must try their best to fill up the gap. He urged the audience not to simply rue the loss, but heroically determine to work as Mr. Gokhale did. Death awaited all; why not then work strenuously while life lasted? All men, he knew, could not be Gokhales; but surely all Indians were not women, with bangles on. Indeed he knew people who were almost the equals of Mr. Gokhale in abilities, but they unfortunately had not Mr. Gokhale's sincerity and single-minded devotion to the country's cause. The resolution he proposed rightly conveyed to the late Mr. Gokhale's bereaved family the condolences of the whole audience. That was to alleviate in a small measure, their sorrow which not, as all knew, tempered if shared with others. But that was not the chief reason why he had been there to propose the resolution. People must not simply be sad and cry; to do so, was to proclaim to the world their unmanliness. He would, therefore, urge his fellowmen to pass another resolution - a resolution which was to be made in the mind and, therefore, which was not expressed in so many words—to the effect that they would strive and to their best to fill up the lamentable void created by the death of Mr. Gokhale. He would not there, he said, speak of the actual lines upon which people should work, for the lines would differ according to individual capacities and temperaments, but the attitude of heart must be according to what he indicated.

This is not a time for cheers. This is a time for shedding tears. This is a time for expressing sorrow for the irreparable loss which we have sustained by the death of Mr. Gokhale. This diamond of India, this jewel of Maharashtra, this prince of workers, is taking eternal rest on the funeral ground. Look at him and try to emulate him. Mr. Gokhale has passed away from our midst after having satisfactorily performed his duty. Will any of you come forward to take his place? Like a triumphant hero he is passing away, after having made his name immortal. Not only none of you here assembled, but no other citizen in all India will be able to give a more satisfactory account in the other world of having done his duty to the Motherland. Up to this time very few have had the fortune of being able to render an account before God of having honestly done his true duty. I knew Mr. Gokhale from his youth. He was not an Inamdar. He was an ordinary and simple man in the beginning; he was not a Jaghirdar; he was not a chief. He was an ordinary man like all of us here. He rose to such eminence by sheer force of genius, ability and work. Mr. Gokhale is passing away from our midst but he has left behind him much to emulate. Every one of you ought to try to place his example before your eyes and to fill up the gap; and if you will try your best to emulate him in this way, he will feel glad, even in the next world.

SPEECH AT ATHANI

[The people of the Athani Taluka of the Belgaum district took advantage of Lok. Tilak's arrival there and presented him an address enclosed in a beautiful silver casket. Lok. Tilak, in the course of his reply, said] :—

On account of the Arms Act and similar measures of repression Indians have become foreigners in their own land. The Congress leaders moved heaven and earth for the last 30 years and at the end of that period they were given a toy of the Morley-Minto reforms to play with the administration. As a result of all this policy of distrust India has become a dead weight round the neck of England and if she is allowed to remain in this state any longer, not only she will be ruined, but she will ruin England also along with herself. English Statesmen have now begun to realise this and they have made up their minds to put a new life in the Indians by granting them self-government. This war is not the last. If another war becomes necessary and if India is to be able to fight for the Empire with all her might, she must first get Self-Government within the Empire to be able to do so. Government have now fully realised the necessity of granting it and at this juncture India must stand united and well-organised. Communal jealousies and caste rivalries are the weak points in our armour, but we must strengthen our position by sinking all differences amongst ourselves and make a united and firm demand. If every caste and community were to ask for separate electorate and separate representation then the administration would be a chaos. Religion has no place in modern polity. In His Highness the Gaikwar's State village communities have been established, but there separate representation has not been restored to. A representative must be judged by his merits and not by his caste or creed. Legislative Council is not an exhibition of the different castes and creeds in India. Communal representation would rake up old jealousies and would sap up the very foundations of unity in India. We would be divided by it and divided we will fall. This quarrel has not raised its head in other provinces and it is rather a misfortune that Maharashtra should find a fertile soil for it.

BOMBAY PROVINCIAL CONFERENCE

Freedom was the soul of the Home Rule movement. The divine instinct of Freedom never aged. Circumstances might affect its manifestation on the physical plane; the movements for freedom (the bodies) might be weakened and maimed for a time; but ultimately the soul—Freedom—must triumph. Freedom is the very life of the individual soul, which Vedanta declares to be not separate from God but identical with Him. Thus Freedom was a principle that could never perish. It might get darkened up by accumulations of moral and intellectual rust. Wherever and whenever Freedom was found thus darkened up, it was the duty of the leaders to set about removing the rust and making the people realise the glory of it. There were people who tried to thwart the Home Rule movement by intimidation, by the spreading of falsehoods and by other unworthier means. They were only helping to make the British administration 'blackened' (hateful) in the eyes of the people. The movement for Home Rule was being slandered in some quarters. But was not God Himself, the subject of slander with some of his children? Times were propitious for the achievement of our goal. For one thing, India's help was discovered to be indispensable. The old vanity that England could keep her Empire without the co-operation of India had vanished to the winds. This was of good augury. But this alone could not give us what we wanted. *We must work.* The more 'affirming' of Congress resolution on Self-Government could not go very far. To our 'we affirm' our Government might reply 'we hear'—and there the matter would rest, unless we went beyond affirming and felt to achieving. The pioneer deputation ought to have left India before now. Every day's delay was precious time irretrievably lost. *The present* was the time for putting forward gigantic efforts for the attainment of Home Rule—they might give it what name they pleased—in which lay the only solution of our infinite difficulties.

APPEAL TO VOLUNTEER

The Poona correspondent of the *Sandesh* sends the following report of the Poona meeting. The following is a very touching extract from Mr. Tilak's speech which he quotes in the beginning:

I shall give up the Home Rule movement if you do not come forward to defend your Home. If you want Home Rule be prepared to defend your Home. Had it not been for my age, I would have been the first to volunteer. You cannot reasonably say that the *ruling* will be done by you and the *fighting for* you—by Europeans or Japanese, in the matter of Home Defence. Show by your act that you are willing to take advantage of the opportunity offered to you by the Viceroy to enlist in an Indian Citizen Army. When you do this, your claim for having the commissioned ranks opened to you will acquire double weight.

SELF-GOVERNMENT

[A mass meeting to give a hearty send off to Mr. Tilak and other members of the Home Rule Deputation was held in Bombay on the 27th March 1918, *when Mr. Tilak, who on rising to speak was received with deafening cheers and loud cries of "Vande Mataram" said]:—*

I thank you all very sincerely for the honour done to me and my party, and for the good wishes for our success. The principle of self-determination lays down that every nation, every country, has to choose the sort of Government they shall have, and it should precede Self-Government. We are determined to have Self-Government in the near future—at an early date—and to have a substantial instalment to begin with. While the question of self-determination for the European Nations and the African colonies is discussed, India is excluded. President Wilson said that Ireland should have self-determination and our Prime Minister convened the Irish convention to draft a scheme of their own, but India without any such declaration, formed a scheme of its own. Mr. Montagu came to India and studied on the spot in consultation with the members of the Bureaucracy, who were primarily opposed to any sort of Self-Government in this country. He is to formulate a scheme and act as umpire and arrive at a settlement, a compromise between the two parties-the people and the Bureaucracy. We want Responsible Government which is agreed to by the Bureaucracy except in connection with the steps and time for establishing it. The chances of Mr. Montagu's scheme, I think, though I am an optimist, are not so bright, as many people imagine them to be. Our opponents are trying to impress upon the British people that if Self-Government is granted to India the Empire will go to ruin and that in the interests of the Empire India must continue to be governed in a despotic manner. A very keen campaign is undertaken by determined people to defeat our object. We have to fight two parties—the Cabinet who will have to be convinced and the Sydenhamites, who will have to be—(Mr. Jinnah suggested—"suppressed,") as our President suggests, suppressed. The way is not so smooth, as some believe. The question to be determined is whether if Mr. Montagu's scheme falls short, the leaders will accept the temptation held out and will be prepared to receive something shadowy, but looking substantial. Some of our leaders might advise, our Anglo-Indian friends and newspapers may. We are going to plead before the British Democracy the cause of Self-Government for India, taking our stand upon the Congress scheme. Stand by us not now but two months after, like men, resolute men, against anything less than the scheme. There should be no compromise in the matter. (Applause). If you accept any compromise, we shall be laughed at by the whole world. (Cries of No, No.) The bureaucracy may try to create a split amongst us. The bureaucracy may say that they have done enough and that given something we should be satisfied. I warn you, you will ruin your country if you accept any such compromise.

America did not enter the war simply because of German Kaiserdom to be substituted by Bureaucratic Kaiserdom. She did not go to help England simply because the latter was her mother country or to protect England, but to stop despotism in any part of the world. I want you to be careful, attentive and to act as men—resolute men and to stand by the resolution of the Congress and the Muslim League.

[*A Ladies' Meeting was held at China Bagh to bid good-bye and wish bon voyage to Mr. B. G. Tilak, Mr. G. S. Khaparde, Mr. B. C. Pal and others. A large number of ladies were present at the meeting, representative of the different communities. Mrs. Luxmibai Tricumdas presided and Mrs. Ramabai Morarji Kamdar, Mrs. Sushilabai Jayaker, Mrs. Ratanbai Pavri, Mrs. Maganbhen Manekbhen Mrs. Airabai Tata and Mrs. Godavaribai spoke in eulogistic terms of the services rendered by Mr. Tilak to the country. They hoped that he would return to India after accomplishing his work in England. Mr. Tilak in replying said*] :—

I thank you for wishing me God speed. I have also to thank you for the meeting you held in the year 1908 sympathising with me in my misfortunes, as I was unable to do so then. In all spheres of activities women are coming to the forefront and you have Mrs. Besant, a woman, who is your leader in all patriotic movements. It has been said by our enemies that men want Home Rule and women do not; one caste is for Home Rule and another against it, and so on, but this meeting is proof positive that they are wrong. This meeting is an encouragement to me, and I will carry your message to England.

THE RIGHT MOMENT

Time and tide wait for none; we will never get such an opportunity for which we have been waiting for so many years, and we must do our utmost to take the fullest advantage of it. We must make hay while the sun shines. The work of the ladies encouraging me in my difficult task is a good augury for the success of my work, and it will be of great help to me in England. We must carry the work, which had been handed down to us, by such patriots as Dadabhai Naoroji to a success. In all parts of the world, and particularly in India, women have always taken their proper share of the national work and I am not at all surprised that you have met here to wish me success in my endeavours. (Cheers.)

[*A large and crowded meeting was held at Dana Bunder, in honour of the Home Rule Deputation. Mr. Jamnadas Dwarkadas presided. Among those present were: Messrs. S. R. Bomanji, B. G. Horniman, Laxmidas Tairsee, Narayandas Purshotamdas, Khimji Hirji Kayani, Mavaji Govindji, Drs. Sathe, Velkar, Chandulal Desai, Mr. S. D.*

Navalkar, and many leading grain merchants. Mr. Jamnadas Dwarkadas rose amidst cheers and said]:—

This evening's occasion is specially a unique one, as we all have assembled on an occasion, the importance of which is even of a special and unique nature. We all have come together to honour, listen and show sympathy for and co-operation with the trusted delegates going to England to put our case for Home Rule before the British public in general; and the justice-loving, level-minded and truth-loving people in particular.

MR. TILAK'S GREAT SERVICE

The work of Mr. Tilak is unstinted from the beginning. He is the same, undaunted and courageous true son of mother Ind through thick and thin not caring for the frowns of the authorities. He takes to his national work, as if he is the only son born of Ind, specially to uplift her. He is grossly misunderstood and misrepresented and really suffers for the amelioration of our Motherland. His work is acknowledged even by his enemies. He is going to England with Mr. Bepin Chandra Pal, the Hon. Mr. Khaparde and Messrs. Kelkar and Karandikar as our delegates and champions to plead our case on behalf of our Motherland. He has the backing of the whole nation. We all hope and trust that God's blessings will be showering on him and he will come back with fresh laurels; and there will be the feather of Swarajya in his patriotic cap. We all pray God that he will have a speedy *bon voyage* and he may return to our Mother Country with double vigour and redoubtable energy. We are carried away by the same sentiments and emotion as when the great Rama left Ayodha and went to the forest in seclusion. The nation and his brothers felt for him in the same way we feel for Mr. Tilak. As Mr. Tilak is going to get Swarajya we wish him *bon voyage* and God speed in his work !

A POSITIVE SUCCESS

[*Mr. Tilak then rose to address amidst deafening cheers and said*] :—

I am ready to go through all the crucifying ordeals of sea-voyage at this critical and stirring times to secure Home Rule for myself, for my countrymen —the living and the coming generations. I assert that the whole country is at one on this point. A note of dissension is raised in some quarters by vested interests.

"MUST GIRD UP OUR LOINS"

We must gird up our loins to face it boldly. They have, it is said, collected nearly Rs. 30,000 to carry on the anti-Home Rule agitation. Lord Sydenham leads this party and is striving every nerve to spread his propaganda. We are here thirty-three crores and we must collect money accordingly for our cause. I am hopeful that India is sure to come out triumphant in the end. God made time and circumstances favourable to our cause. Death will come to any individual sooner or later. No one is free from it. Old age is the fittest age to undertake this kind of voyage.

POLITICAL PARTNERS OF BRITAIN

We will place the real and true state of things before the British public and Parliament; and God willing we are sure that they (the British public) will give a hearty ear to it. On your confidence, trust and backbone we (the deputation) took up this responsibility and if you give hearty sympathy and co-operation we are sure to win. Let Lord Sydenham and his party bring obstacles in our way; but we must carry on an agitation in India and not stop unless and until we get what we wanted. Nothing short of our demands would satisfy us. This we must show them by our agitation and I am sure the battle of freedom will be won.

SECOND HOME RULE CONFERENCE

[*Mr. Tilak in his concluding remarks at the Second Home Rule Conference, at Bombay, said*] :–

Last year I had to answer certain objections in the course of my speech at the Home Rule Conference held at Nasik. First I had to tell the objectors that the Home Rule League was not started as a rival institution to the Indian National Congress but as an institution that would help the Congress in carrying out its resolutions into effect. At the Lucknow Congress I tried my best to get the Congress to consent to send a deputation to England, myself undertaking to collect money for the purpose, but my offer was slighted and a couple of dozen trustees were appointed to be in charge of the funds of the Congress. I do not like to blame anybody for what then happened in the Congress about my suggestion. Bengal has hitherto done little work in the direction of Home Rule, and the United Provinces have done less. Some of the Congress leaders have expressed their fear that the Home Rule League will make the Congress work difficult to be done by them. The Home Rulers depend on the purity of their conscience in doing their work in spite of what people opine as regards their efforts. Mr. Montagu may publish his scheme perhaps in

England and India simultaneously, and then the Home Rulers will be on their trial. It is possible that after that scheme is published, the Bureaucracy in India will deceive the people with half a loaf. The Bureaucracy do not want to give the people of India anything, although they echo the sentiment of Parliament that responsible government is the goal of the British Government in this country. The Bureaucracy will not give the right of self-determination to Indians. They say they, as guardians of the Indian people, will exercise their own judgment in the matter of self-determination. Even the ignorant agriculturist in this country now realises what is meant by responsible government being the goal of the British policy in India. Even the agriculturist now knows that the Civil Servant must be under his control.

INDIA'S EMASCULATED MAN-POWER

The map of the world is being changed in this war. India cannot take part in this war because her sons are emasculated under the Bureaucratic policy. I use the expression 'emasculated' because the late Sir Pherozeshah Mehta used it before. Nevertheless India wants to take credit in saving the Empire. No one can now save the Bureaucracy from the consequences of its policy of emasculating the people of this country. It is a great humiliation for the Empire that at this crisis it has to appeal to Japan and America, when it can have availed itself of the crores of Indian subjects, if they were trained for military purposes. Now that the world's history is being changed India must be strengthened in order to strengthen the Empire. The whole constitution of India requires to be modified. Substantial rights must be given to the Indian people. Mr. Montagu came here not on account of the cries of the Congress, but because he was a statesman, who saw danger ahead in India from the changed circumstance in the world's history. In England they have statesmen and in India we have talkers. The people of India should be up and doing and not allow Mr. Montagu to go to England and say he managed the thing successfully though he may not have done anything. Mr. Montagu should not be allowed to go to England and say there that the Indian people are so foolish that he could cleverly manage to delude them. After Mr. Montagu's scheme is published there will be a special Congress here. Indians should now speak fearlessly, because the days of repression are gone. The realisation of the people of Indian's hope for self-government is within a measurable distance. The faith which the deputation has in obtaining Home Rule will take us safe to England and enable us to overcome all obstacles.

INDIAN DEPUTATION AT MADRAS

[In response to Mrs. Besant's invitations to meet Lok. Tilak and Deputation at a Dinner party in Blavatsky Gardens, many were present. Tables were laid out under the banyan tree which was illuminated with electric lights, and the whole scene looked like a fairy land. Mrs. Besant presided at the middle of the long table. The first toast proposed by Mrs. Besant was as usual that of the "King-Emperor" and it was drunk in the usual manner.

LOKAMANYA TILAK

Mrs. Besant next proposed the toast of "Lok. Tilak and the Deputation" and in doing so said: We all know that Lok. Tilak and the other members of the Deputation are going to Great Britain to plead the cause of India, to assert her place in the Empire, and to address themselves especially to the democracy of Great Britain in order to win their assent to the Statute which we hope will soon be passed. I do not propose to stand between you and our guests. I will only ask all of you to drink to their health and to wish them a hearty success, carrying on your wishes for them while they are away until they return amongst us, and I join with the toast the names of Lok. Tilak, the Hon. Mr. Khaparde and Mr. Bepin Chandra Pal.

Mr. Tilak, in reply, said]:—

I thank you, Mrs. Besant, for the honour you have done me and for including my name in the toast. It has been said that we are going outside India to plead the cause of India. Our going outside is necessary at this moment for various reasons. It has been asked why we should go out of India. In fact, I was one of those who thought about ten years ago that by going out of India to plead the cause of India so much cannot be done as by agitating in India. That was my opinion and I dare say possibly some people may quote it against me even now--they have long memories. But times have changed and a man who does not change his opinion with the times is sure to be deceived. Things which were seditious once have ceased to be seditious. The Empire and the Parliament have learnt what the value of India is at present. The administration of the bureaucracy was to a certain extent glittering in the view, but all that glitters is not gold, and it has been found out now that whatever be the appearance of the bureaucratic administration, it carries under it the seeds of decay. Bureaucratic administration was good. It made railways, it made telegraphs, it made post offices, and so on and so on, and then imports and exports were increased, but all that brought about the emasculation of this country, and this was not brought to the notice of the British democracy. And that fact has now been brought to the notice of the British democracy, for they wanted men to fight the battles of the Empire and looked to India, but found that the Indian Government was not ready, and was unable to supply the necessary man-power, although there were thirty crores of people. The people too are willing to work and fight for the Empire. In spite of their willingness and in spite of their numbers, it is now found necessary to appeal to other Nations for help. What is it due to ? I say that it is due entirely to the bureaucratic administration of the country, the object of which was the keeping of the Nation emasculated with a view to carry on the whole administration of the country with a few hundreds or thousands of soldiers, and that India should be kept under military subjection with the aid of the British naval and military power. The Parliament and the British people know that but for this bureaucratic administration during the last 100 or 120 years, they would have been in a position to command a much larger man-power than hitherto from India. So long as this fact is known, and so long as the importance of it is realised, it is our time and opportunity to work for our right. It is this fact that has not been properly noticed even in Indian papers and much less in Anglo-Indian papers, because it is not their business to notice it. The fact is, however, there. But this is exactly the time when we should put forward our demand, not in our own interests but in the interests of the Empire. You will be heard. I am confident that we shall be heard. (Hear, hear). The case is ready. The circumstances are such. These circumstances did not exist ten years ago, but now is the time, and you must strike while the iron is hot. It is our faith. After we go there we hope we shall succeed. This is the best time to urge our claim, not merely on the ground of liberty, not merely on the ground of right. No doubt I said that Home Rule is our birthright, but birthrights are not always recognised and you must work for them. This is the time when we can work with much profit to ourselves. Men to whom we go must realise the need themselves, and then when we press our claim, there is the greatest chance of our prayers, requests or entreaties being heard. That is one reason why our Home Rule League is also sending a deputation. Much has been said that these are times of danger that there are dangers above the surface of water and below the surface of water. But when time comes for work it is for us to stick to that work and not leave it whatever the difficulties are. Dangers there are, and where do you find a place free from dangers ? Do you mean to say that there is no danger where I am now standing ? No one knows when the danger will come. But I hope that with your good wishes, with the blessings of Providence, we shall succeed in this mission and we must succeed. That is our faith, that is our firm conviction. We are carrying with us as I said, not our own fortune but the fortune of the whole of India (Cheers), and when we carry with us that fortune we must feel sure that the case is so strong based on Karma that whatever our individual difficulties may be, whatever the difficulties in the way may be, Providence is with you and you are bound to succeed, or as the Shastras say *Yato Dharma thato Jayah.* We shall do all that we can to attain success, but I may assure you that if we succeed in the end, much depends upon your good wishes, your work here, your sympathy with us, and your unflinching support. We are going as your spokesmen. We are not going for ourselves. We are going for the country. We know what dangers there are on the way, and yet feel that there is a certain call from Providence, from higher sources, and we cannot resist the temptation of responding to the call. I cannot resist. I feel I must go, and so also my colleagues think. We are going on a mission of Dharma. We are going on a mission which involves the fortunes of the whole of India, and there ought to be no hesitation about it. There is a story that when Cæsar was going from Italy to Greece in a ship, there was a storm on the way, and then the sailors refused to carry him farther. Cæsar threw off the mask, and addressed the sailors and said: "You are not carrying your fortunes with you, but you are carrying Cæsar and his fortunes with you." After these words, the sailors carried him to Greece and he succeeded in his plan. Such is the case at present. This is not the place to go into full details to explain what is in my mind and in the minds of my colleagues, and I may tell you once for all that for success in our efforts we depend upon your sympathy and upon your support. So stick to what you have asked for till now. Without that force behind us it is impossible for us to do anything. We hope that we shall derive inspiration, support and strength from that force, and we ask you all to lend us your support as you have been doing hitherto. I thank you again for your good wishes and pray Providence, that is working behind us, in front of us, or as the *Gita* says, on all sides of us, will not fail us, and that if we show sufficient courage, sufficient determination then we are bound to succeed by the grace of God. (Cheers).

REPLY TO THE ADDRESSES OF THE MAHRATTAS AND ANDHRAS

[*In replying to the Presentation of Addresses given by the Mahrattas and Andhras of Madras, Lokamanya Bal Gangadhar Tilak said*] :—

My Andhra and Mahratta Friends :

I join my Mahratta and Andhra friends together for this reason. The principles of administration which were followed by Mahratta Government were as you are all aware borrowed from the Andhra Government at Vijiyanagar. So we Mahrattas owe something to you Andhras. Those principles were eventually copied by Shivaji and his administrators. So there is that link which still exists and I find in the two addresses presented to me a similar combination. That combination still exists and I should say is still working. Though the languages may be different, the one is Dravidian and the other Maharatta, the hearts are one. Both of us, I believe, are actuated by the same feelings for that subordinate naturality which goes to make up the whole Nation. I am one of those who hold that the development of India will be much facilitated if vernaculars are developed and if provinces are redistributed according to language. I expressed that sentiment and opinion long ago, long before the

Andhra agitation commenced. We can appeal to our people better through vernaculars, than in English. English can never become the language of the masses. We must appeal to them through their own vernaculars, and this has been one of the chief objects of my life, and tell you once for all why I devoted more attention to the *Kesari* than to English papers. It appeals to them more. Can a foreign language be the language of this country? English may become a *lingua franca* which will connect different parts of India which are developing themselves. That is my view and I have ever supported that view in my papers and speeches. So you need not have any doubt as regards the sentiments expressed here. India can only be something like the United States, small States all over India, each State having a language of its own, all united together by one common language. But then it is impossible for us to give up our vernaculars and you can never wipe out all vernaculars and make substitutes for them. When Home Rule comes all these provinces are likely to be divided. Now the question is whether we should put this question in front of the question of Home Rule. I should like to place Home Rule in front. If you go and consult the bureaucracy, they say: "We give you the redistribution of Provinces and not Home Rule." For it would increase posts of Lieutenant-Governors and Governors. What we say is: "Grant us Home Rule and we shall look to all these matters." I do not want to put this question in the back ground, for it is safer to ask for Home Rule as it is more comprehensive. Do not press just now for redistribution of the Provinces. It will come in its own time and the development of vernaculars also will come in its own time. All those follow if once Home Rule is granted. Our agitation and our efforts must therefore at present be directed for securing Home Rule for India. Speaking in this hall which bore the name of my friend Mr. Gokhale, I may remind you that when he went to England ten years ago to fight for you, he wanted to get Home Rule but the limitation and the time were not favourable. It is plainly told in Lord Morley's reminiscences that Home Rule for India was aimed at. Lord Morley said that was impossible and India must be content with association with administrators and not participation in administration. You must clearly understand his distinction between association and participation. The English language is wide enough to express all these shades and differences.

At that time the idea which was preached was association. And Lord Morley by his reforms sought to associate Indians with the real administrators, the bureaucratic administrators of the land. That was all that could be done at that time. The times have changed since and the Government have recognised that the goal of British administration should be Responsible Government for India. Now there is greater latitude to work up our ideal. We go under more favourable circumstances and it is quite possible now to realise that ideal, though Lord Morley did not see it at that time and said that as far as he could see, within the range of his vision he could not conceive of Home Rule for India. What was impossible ten years ago became possible now. We are going in that change of atmosphere, change of opinion and change of circumstances, in fact when everything was changed. I am confident that if we are now going with determination, it is not impossible for us to obtain Home Rule. We are working in changed times and altered circumstances. Mr. Gokhale did his best and let us do our best. We are going with determination to fight. The ideal has been worked up, and something must be done that we may get some participation which will lead to the ultimate goal of Responsible Self-Government, that was promised by the Secretary of State and the Viceroy. So what instalment are we to get? The minimum is the reforms we asked for, and the maximum is Responsible Self-Government. What you get depends upon your exertions. They are bound to go beyond what Lord Morley said and they have recognised this in course of time. Now all depends upon your initiative and your exertions If you stick to your ideal, the Congress-League Scheme, then you are bound to get it. If you allow yourselves to be taken away from your goal by allurements, I dare say it will be your own fault. You will be told that now you get as. 2 and then as. 6 and that in 20 years you will get the full rupee. No, you should insist upon the Congress League Scheme as the first instalment. You know that you are working for the Empire. The present conditions in India must be changed; the character of the bureaucratic administration requires to be changed. In the interests of the Empire we must see that we have enough power in our hands to change the character of the bureaucracy. Let us have full power to change the policy and character of the bureaucratic administration and once that character is changed, in 10 or 15 years, India would be as great as Japan. And the English statesmen and the Empire will then have no need to trust Japan; they can trust India. If they trust India, India shall be equal to all the Asiatic nations put together, including Japan. That is our ideal. We are now trying to obtain that power over the administration of the country, financial control, control of the Executive, and sufficient majorities in the Legislative Councils. These three things achieved, everything will follow. They are the master-key. So your demand should now be for the Congress League Scheme. You must not accept less. If you accept anything less, you will in a great degree not only hamper the progress of but ruin the country. We shall be insisting upon the Congress-League Scheme. What will be your demand? Do you say that you are prepared to accept less while we are fighting for the scheme? The Congress has formulated it, the Muslim League has formulated it, the Home Rule League has formulated it, and we of the deputation have taken that as the basis of our work. If you say you accept less, you take away the foundations. Remember that if you support us with your determination, that if you are not prepared to accept anything less, you will enable us to return to India with success. We go relying not on our strength or efforts, but we rely upon the wishes of Providence which are favourable to us. It is no question of age, it is no question of infirmity. We have a call from above. We are simply obeying that call whatever infirmities are. I have no doubt, I am perfectly confident that in following that call we are obeying the call of Providence, and Providence is graciously pleased to lead us to success. (Loud and continued cheers).

HOME RULE

[*The members of the Mahajana Sabah, the Madras Provincial Congress Committee, the Home Rule League, the Madras Presidency Association and the Andhra Peoples Association presented a joint address of welcome to Lok. Bal Gangadhar Tilak—a hearty and sincere welcome—on his arrival at Madras. Mr. Tilak, in reply, said*] :—

I thank you cordially for the honour you have done me and the other members of the Deputation in welcoming us here and in presenting an address which has been signed by almost all the representative bodies in this city. (A friend here suggests "all" representative bodies.) My knowledge of the place is so scanty that I saved myself by introducing the qualification "almost all" but I am prepared to accept the amendment moved by my friend, and I thank you all the more because all the representative bodies of this Presidency have given us their blessing and good wishes for the cause which is the cause of us all, the success of which we have all at heart. As observed by the venerable Chairman, there is one thing which I wish to communicate to you at this moment. No one now requires to be told what Home Rule means. I can safely drop that question. The only question is how Home Rule is to be fought out. The Government of India and the Secretary of State have both declared from their respective places, the one in Parliament and the other through the *Gazette of India*, that Responsible Government or Home Rule shall be the goal of

British administration in India. The King, the Cabinet, the Governor-General and the Secretary of State are all agreed that it is proper and legal for you to ask for Responsible Government, and, secondly, that it ought to be the goal of the British administration in India, but the statement is not as complete as we want it to be. We are told that this Responsible Government will be granted to you by steps which will be decided by the Bureaucracy and not by us. That is not the doctrine of self-determination of which they talk so much in Great Britain. The steps are to be determined by us and not by the present bureaucratic administrators. Self-determination means that one must fix upon these steps, that we must fix upon the time limit and that the matter should not be left to the sweet discretion of bureaucracy which after 150 years of rule have now just come to see what the goal of their administration should be. They worked in utter darkness till now groping in the way, and when the War broke out, and when it was found that the Empire was in a danger they began to see what the goal of their administration ought to be. We do not want to quarrel with them for that. The goal is there and it is no longer seditious to say that we want Home Rule and that Home Rule is our birthright. We are going to England to tell the British Democracy plainly that the question as to what the first step should be and what the time of granting full

Responsible Government should be is no longer a question on which bureaucratic opinion can be tolerated for a moment. We do not want the British Democracy to decide how they should act as an umpire between the Bureaucracy and ourselves. We are going to England for the purpose of convincing the British Democracy that the grant of Responsible Government is the necessity of the hour. It is no longer a question of benevolent generosity or favour. That was the position ten years ago. Now the position is entirely changed. Responsible Government has now become the necessity of the hour, the necessity of the Empire, and, I say, the safety of the Empire. We are going to England for the purpose of convincing the British Democracy that if Home Rule is not granted to India the Empire is in danger of being one day crippled. You all know what the situation is in Asia. India stands alone. Russian influence in Asia is dominated by German influence. Turkey is under the influence of Germany. Japan has the goal of self-aggrandisement. India cannot hereafter be defended by the naval and military forces of Great Britain, naval forces for reasons you all know, military forces, simply because there are none. If India is to be defended in the interests of the Empire, India must be trained to defend herself. Look at the world map—India surrounded by China and Japan on one side, with Siberia on one side, with two Asiatic Turkeys under German influence, with Russia broken up into rival parties. Supposing you have to defend India against a combination inspired from Germany, what will you do? (A cry "we will fight.") I will tell you what my answer is. They say that they will not trust India. They will trust Japan and any other people on the surface of the earth but India. The work of the Deputation is to convince the British Democracy that the gravity of the situation—as the Chairman remarked, the centre of gravity—lies in India and not in England. It is here that the solution is to be found and not in America and Japan. The map of the world is changed and if we do not take the advantage of these circumstances which are providential, we do not deserve to be called citizens, we do not deserve to be called men. Times do not change for you. Time and tide wait for no man and you have to run with them. If you fail to take advantage of the time and circumstances, you fail in the important duties of citizenship. Providence is favourable to you. Why? Because the whole world is changed and it is impossible that there could not be a change. When the world is changed, if you propose to remain stationary, possibly you will be wiped of speedily. You must move along with the times. What is necessary at present is to make the British people realise the position. We are not going to appeal to their generosity, and nothing could be gained by that procedure. We must make them realise that unless they are prepared to raise India, they must be prepared to lose India. If India remains stationary, she will be a dead-weight round the neck of the Empire and there is a danger of both India and the Empire going to the bottom. That is the situation which I wish to point out to the British public. It is not a situation of our making. Providence has brought it about and, as Mr. Pal has said, Providence has been working for us all over the whole world. Providence is working in your own interest. If you have not the ears to hear or the hands to work in consonance with the spirit that is running abroad, I dare say every independent and civilised nation in the world will pass their judgment upon you and that judgment will be against you. Are you prepared to face it? (Cries of No.) After all I am but one individual. Whatever I may hold or whatever I may think will count as the judgment of one man. I appeal to you to think of the situation. I am going to say in England that Home Rule for India is a question of necessity of the hour and that it must be realised. That is the decisive attitude which must be taken, which must be utilised, which must be exploited to its utmost. We want your full support in that work. We are going to represent the cause of Home Rule through the British Democracy as a matter of necessity. We have fixed our demand. You know what happened in the case of Ireland. The British ministers and Cabinet asked the Irish people to meet in a Convention and to settle their demands. We are a bit shrewd people.

We thought that such a demand would be made. We anticipated it and met in the Congress and Muslim League and we have fixed upon the minimum which ought to be conceded to us at once. All that remains is if the British Ministry wishes to treat us on the same footing as they treated the Irish, what we say is, here is our demand, settled at a Convention of the Congress and the Muslim League and no more Convention is necessary, therefore, extend to us the same liberty that you have given to Ireland and carry it through the Parliament. No second reference is necessary. We have our demand ready made. What is that demand? We ask for complete Home Rule within a measurable time. Both of us have agreed happily on that, though the words " within a measurable time" are susceptible of being interpreted in different ways according to the interests of each party. We have fixed upon the first stage or the first step towards Home Rule and that step is that we want financial control. Let me enumerate the principles involved in that. We must have the control of the purse. We must have control over the Executive. The Executive must be prepared to carry out what the Legislature resolves. The Executive must be the servants of the Legislature. Our second demand is that there should be substantial majority of elected members in the Legislative Council. There are minor demands with regard to administration in the Provinces and so on. An attempt will be made—I say it from the knowledge of Bureaucracy—to tempt you to give up a part of your demands. There is no other alternative for the Bureaucracy. They have to accept the goal which has been published all over through the *Gazette of India.* We know where we are. Between Minto-Morley Reforms and complete Responsible Government the Bureaucracy wants small instalments to be fixed at their discretion. That would not do. We say that we are even prepared to accept reforms in instalments but we say that the first instalment should be substantial and should be what we have asked for in the Congress-League Scheme, and that after the payment of the first instalment, the instalments that are to follow should be distributed over as small a number of years as possible. We ask for the control of the purse, control over the Executive and a substantial majority in the Legislative Councils. Without these reforms no improvement in the state of the country will be brought about. We do not want Home Rule so that we may get a few more Government posts, nor is it that we should associate with the Bureaucracy in their costly administrations. We say that the Empire is in danger and that we are willing to save the Empire. We want Home Rule in order that we may be better qualified to render that assistance to the Empire within ten or fifteen years to come. We are anxious to serve the Empire, we are anxious to be a living member, a self-dependent member of the Empire like the other parts of the Empire. Let us have sufficient power that would enable us to achieve this goal within as short a time as possible. Japan became a nation within a comparatively short period. We hope that if we are granted the power and the right that we ask for, the first instalment that we ask for will convert India from a dead-weight into a self-dependent unit of the Empire. Our object is imperial and with that object in view, we press that the Congress demand is the minimum demand that we make. Mind that we are not extravagant. The caution that was necessary to be used and perhaps more than necessary to be used has been set aside and this demand has been fixed with the consent of Hindus and Muhammadans of all shades of political opinion. That is a compromise that we have arrived at. If after bidding farewell to us, after allowing us to work in England for some time, you change your mind, imagine what the consequences would be. It will be a great error, also a disaster, to send us to England and then change your mind behind our back. You had better not send us to England at all if you are likely to change your mind. I wish to take the verdict from you before we are going to England. If you will be content with less when temptations are put before you and when Bureaucracy say that you will ruin your path unless you accept less —they will try to throw the responsibility of the failure on you - it is a very spacious argument, an argument that is likely to appeal to people who have something else in view, be firm at that time. If you really want us to go to England and plead the cause of the country, we expect full and unstinted support from you all (Cheers). If you have no mind to stick to the programme you have made, please let us know about it and we shall know how to act. Otherwise we are going to take the Congress Scheme as the basis of our demand. The Congress Scheme excludes the military and foreign affairs but in the case of military matters the Congress Scheme demands that the Government of India should make a declaration as regards its future policy. We do not ask for control over military affairs because the bureaucracy would suspect that we have some ulterior motive. We still want a definite declaration as to future military policy. We want volunteering to be allowed and military colleges to be opened. In the military matter, it is impossible to utilise the man-power of India without the full consent of the people of India and their full consent to support the Empire. Who can expect any people on the surface of the earth to fight for a country unless the fighter hopes that he will improve his material position in this world? The *Bhagavad Gita* has beautifully expressed that if you die on a battle-field there are gates of heaven open to you. The bureaucracy has refused encouragement to volunteering. There are thousands in this meeting who would declare their willingness to volunteer, who are prepared to defend their country as the Colonies have done. I see a number of young people before me who would come forward with the greatest satisfaction if the Government of India declares their military policy to-morrow. I do not know from what portion of the Empire they can find man-power as much as from India. You will be told that the Government of India is very liberal and that if we accept Responsible Government as the goal of British administration in India everything else will follow. I say, No. I say that the first instalment ought to be such as would make us qualify within 10 or 15 years to take part in the defence of our Empire. The Anglo-Indian Association and Lord Sydenham are saying that India is unfit for Home Rule, that Indian women are not yet liberated, that the caste system is widely prevalent, that Indians have not changed their colour and that therefore Home Rule should not be granted. I do not think that there is any chance of this argument being heard by the democracy. We must be there on the spot. We must be able to say what are the essential conditions necessary to grant Home Rule to India. Have we prevented Government from introducing free and compulsory education among the masses? If the masses are uneducated it is not our fault. There are said to be difficulties in the way of finding funds for educational purposes but funds are easily found for other purposes such as the grant of Exchange Compensation to Civilians and others. We want authority to abolish the bureaucratic policy of administration and we want the whole policy to be changed and the character of the administration to be converted from bureaucratic to responsible power. Let us have your full support, your full sympathy and let us have a continued agitation even more than desirable, for in such a matter excess is not to be condemned. Even more than now keep on your agitation. Let us hear the echoes of your agitation in England. Nothing can be more cheering to us than those echoes. I promise on behalf of the deputation that we shall do our best to carry out the object upon which we go there, not for ourselves but for the country. We are going there in obedience to a call from Providence, from a higher power—an inspiration which we cannot resist. We go in spite of bad health and other circumstances. It is a mission from God, a mission from above, and if we are determined to follow it up with all your power and sympathy, there will be enough energy given to us to carry it out. We feel that times are changed, we feel that it is the will of God to grant Home Rule to India. We possess confidence, that Providence which inspired us in the past, will give us the necessary strength to carry that impulse safely through. I again thank you for the honour you have done to us (Loud Cheers.)

THE PRESENT SITUATION

[*Before a crowded audience, Lok. Tilak made a speech on the 21st April, 1918, at Gowri Vilas compound on "The Present Situation." Mrs. Annie Besant presided. Lokamanya Tilak who was received with deafening cheers, said*] :—

Chairman, Sir Subramanyam and Gentlemen :— You have been already told that whatever conclusions may be formed to-day are likely to be upset by the events of to-morrow. So with this qualification first communicated to you I wish to proceed with the subject. It is an important limitation, for events come one after another so abruptly without notice that I cannot say that what I tell you to-day will be repeated by me to-morrow. Yet there are certain things which we can see through the number of documents that have been furnished by Government recently. When I spoke last here, about three weeks ago, I told you that I was going to tell the British Democracy that India must be granted Home Rule as a War measure, apart from the question of fitness, apart from the question of justice, apart from the question of grace, apart from the question of contentment, Home Rule to India was necessary as a War-measure if the Empire was to be saved. Some papers here took objection to that. I am glad to say that what I have said has been borne out. Home Rule has been granted to Ireland as a War-measure, a War-measure under the necessity of psychological principle, backed up by the pressure from America. Ireland must be granted Home Rule. Why? Because, first, Irish youths must be made to feel that they were fighting for their country, for a principle which is not denied to them at home. That is one reason given. And it is a sound doctrine. Another reason is that it is the desire of President Wilson. Possibly it means that America is not going to take part in this War, unless the Americans are sure, that this War is for establishing liberty and freedom all over the world (cheers). The interest of America is not in the protests of peoples, whether it be Germans or Anglo-Saxons. The American Government are interested in the War and are prepared to help England and her friends, if ultimately the principles of liberty are to triumph and are to be established all the world over, irrespective of colour or continent. That seems to be the reason why America has given its help but not certainly to defend Anglo-Saxon despotism. For these two reasons Ireland will be granted Home Rule immediately.

As regards the situation here created by the War, I must say a few words. It is very clearly acknowledged that the situation is critical. On the Western side the situation is very critical and is getting more and more critical every day and every hour. It is said that if Germans succeed in annihilating the British army during the next two or three months before America can come to their help, the situation will be hopeless. England and her friends believe that that cannot be crushed during that time. They will hold their own. It is not a question of conquest but a question of holding their own till American reinforcements come in and go, together with the man-power of America and of Ireland, to succeed in stemming back German Militarism. The situation in the East is this. The whole of Asia is now open to German invasion. The Pan-Islamic League, and Turkey, the Asiatic Turkestan. Persia and all these countries have been brought under the German influence by the parcelling of the Russian Empire into three or four different compartments, all under Germany. It is quite possible for Germany through some agency to approach the North-Western frontier in a week at best. (A voice "God forbid.") Certainly, but the situation is to be gauged whether God forbids it or not, and unless you are prepared to face it, I do not think, God will come to your help. It must be thought of, taken into consideration and provided for. That is the business of the statesman. When he has done that, you can rely upon Providence. So there is double danger. As regards the danger in the West, one provision made is the application of conscription of Ireland. That cannot be done unless the Irish youths are made to feel that they are fighting for a principle which is not denied to them in their own land. That has been admitted, and they hope to apply conscription to Ireland, even if the Allies are unwilling. England has done all that it could to satisfy Ireland. That is what the Prime Minister has said: We have done what we could and now we are not afraid to apply the law of conscription. In that way they hope to get millions of men, and America says it can give five to seven or ten millions of them in two years. Ireland can give some, if conscription is applied. So is the War situation. But we are not concerned with the whole of it at present.

We are concerned with the Asiatic situation. Now what is the Prime Minister's message? The first document says that this tide of German militarism must be stemmed in the West, but being stemmed in the West, it may find a way into the East—those are not my words—and it will be necessary for Indians to guard their Motherland against any such expected or anticipated danger in future. That is the appeal made to us by the Viceroy. Are you prepared to defend your Motherland, and upon the terms the Viceroy asked you, that you ought to be prepared? If not, you will be forced to prepare without even the psychological consideration shown in the case of Ireland. I want you to read the three documents carefully. One document explains why the deputation is stopped, the second is the Premier's message and the third is the Viceroy's declaration about the Delhi Conference.

GOVERNMENT'S PLAN

Taking all these together, we can read between them a certain plan which seems to be settled and which is being carried out bit by bit. Government have not given out, yet fully, what they propose to do and I do not blame the Government for it, but it is always that they carry on these plans by stages. They have done so. But any man can read for himself. If he reads between the lines he can very easily see, that stopping the deputation is the first scene in the drama which is being enacted. It was not an isolated act. When the passports were granted to us the policy was under consideration it was not settled. Correspondence was then going on between the Viceroy, the Secretary of State and the War Cabinet. By the time we were ready, the question was ready with the solution, what the Viceroy should do, what the Home Government should do and now the first thing to be done was to stop the passage of the Deputation. The second stage was the Conference, whatever that may mean. I do not know what the Conference is to be held for, what conclusions are to be arrived at, or what its procedure is, to arrive at the conclusions. But it was said that one object of the Conference was to consider how to stop the propaganda work in India hereafter, the cessation of all political propaganda. The second is how to utilise the man-power and other resources of India to the best advantage, and the third is to ask the people cheerfully to bear the sacrifices which may be necessary for victory. These are the three objects which have been telegraphed to the newspapers and to the different members invited.

DEFECTS OF THE CONFERENCE

Now what is the nature of this Conference ? All the big Chiefs are invited : I do not know why, because when the question of Native States came for consideration, there was a Chiefs' Conference, and it was there said that the Ruling Princes should not interfere in matters pertaining to the British Administration and we should not interfere with theirs. It is a settled principle that we at present have nothing to do with their administration, we leave them alone. Now in settling the momentous question some of the Chiefs are invited. But why are they invited ? You can deal with them separately. The demands and aspirations of the Princes are entirely different from the demands and aspirations of the British Indian people. If you do not want Home Rule, many Princes will subscribe. Whatever assistance you require from them, obtain it by all means, but do not mix them together, so that the popular element will be invisible in the majority of the Conference. That is one defect in the constitution of the Conference. The second defect is that they have invited all non-official members of the Imperial Council. The third defect is that they have invited such members as would be selected by the Local Governments as representing various interests, (laughter) and then every interest will have one vote, if votes were taken, and there are so many different interests in India that if every interest is given a vote, then there is sure to be a majority of them all, agreeing to the one thing that whatever Government said was good. They will have thus a majority of vote. Being nominated by Government, it will be their duty to accept whatever Government proposed, and are we to be bound by it ? (Several voices "no, no" and "certainly not"). This is the great defect in that Conference. I do not think that the leaders of the Congress are invited. The President of the Congress has yet to be invited. (Cries of Shame.) Mind, she is the President of the Congress throughout the whole year 1918. So this packed-up Conference which is to sit at Delhi is to decide the fate of India and pass final judgment upon the aspirations of the people. It is not even like the Irish Convention. It is something—I do not know what to call it—but, some humbug, to get the Government scheme passed at that Conference.

WHAT IS THE GOVERNMENT SCHEME?

Now what is the Government scheme ? We know that a scheme has been submitted to the Government by various representative bodies—the Congress and League Scheme placed before the Secretary of

State. The majority of the people all over supported the scheme. Is Mr. Montagu going to grant us Self-Government according to that scheme? If so, there is no necessity of stopping any propaganda work. If you grant us Home Rule, we are, quite ready and prepared to support and defend our Motherland to the last (Cheers). Not that we are unwilling to support, but now we are told nothing about the scheme, but there are some indications in the communique on the question of stopping the deputation. What are they? The Government attitude is said to be generous. We have forgotten it. Then it is said that Mr. Montagu has been here and he has heard all our representations,—as if Mr. Montagu is the whole British Nation (laughter),and there is no necessity to carry on the deputation because everything has been heard by the Indian Government. Now that is the argument from which we can see that they are not going to grant us the whole thing. In that communique it was stated that the deputation was going to press their "own Home Rule scheme." What was that? It was nothing more than the Congress-League scheme. If you put these two statements together, the conclusion is that we are going to England to place before the English democracy the Congress-League scheme which Government call our scheme, and that Government are not prepared to go so far. So they have decided something. That something will fall far short of our expectations. It will not amount to even As. 4. There are some who are prepared to say that it will come to As. 8. But I do not think it will come even to As. 4. The bureaucracy have decided what they would recommend the Home Government to grant to you. Their scheme is ready. I do not know whether the scheme will be placed before the Conference. Possibly not. They may possibly ask the Conference to give their consent for the cessation of political activity and propaganda work on the faith that the Government are going to do something in the future.

SOME VIEWS

There are some people who still think that whatever Government is prepared to grant they should accept and rely upon the promises about the future. That is, they say, prudent, statesmanlike and, considering our position, that is what we ought to. You may argue with them as much as possible, but once you find that they are prepared to give you so much and no more, you ought to fall in with their view and tell people that you have done your best to convince the rulers, that you have not succeeded in doing so, and that whatever falls from them should be accepted, with thanks, if necessary. Another attitude is that the times are such that even if you refuse what is being granted to you, Government will be forced in the circumstances to increase what they proposed to grant to you and that eventually you will succeed if you remain firm.

Those are the two schools of thought and I am afraid that the attitude taken up by Government may cause a split in the Nation—I say God forbid it. I say that matters have come to this pass, *viz.*, that some of your leaders who were with us in the Home Rule agitation may be taken away from us, and, relying on their support or pretending that they represent the people, the Government may force their conclusions. It is for you now to decide what course you will adopt.

COMPARE INDIA AND IRELAND

Look at the state of Government. They think that although it is true in the case of Ireland that the man there must be made to feel that he is fighting for liberty, which is not denied to him in his own home, that principle of liberty is not applicable to India. Are we not human beings like Irishmen? It is not a condition imposed by an Indian. Some people say: "Who are you to impose a condition upon Government, and it looks absurd for loyal subjects to impose conditions upon Government." My idea of loyalty is different. We do not impose any condition upon Government, but we bring to the notice of Government the psychological law that you cannot compel a man to do a thing unless you please him at the same time. Before people determine to fight for the liberty of other Nations, they must be assured that they will enjoy that liberty in their own home (cheers). It is not a condition made by us. If any one has made that condition it is human nature, and we are bringing to the notice of Government the law of human nature which will make co-operation effective. I do not think that it is ever considered by any historian or any thinker that to remind the Government of the laws of human nature is disloyal. In my telegram, which I sent from Ceylon to the Viceroy, I set out this principle, *viz.*, that we are prepared to co-operate with Government, that we are prepared to defend our Motherland against any possible danger from the north-west, whether real or imaginary, but at the same time we cannot enthusiastically defend it or zealously defend it, unless in our heart of hearts we are convinced that we are fighting for our own country and not as outsiders in our own country. That is absolutely necessary and that condition must be granted. The bureaucracy do not do so.

A DISTINCTION

Here I must make a distinction between bureaucracy and ourselves. The bureaucracy have a scheme of their own and they will carry it out whether you like it or not. They have settled it during the last two or three weeks, and that is to grant what they think fit, not to consider the principle of self-determination but to treat it as a principle of self-determination *by* the bureaucracy *for* you, because you are yet children. It has been decided to grant you that, to shut up your mouth, to prevent all agitation in the country, and after some months to publish Mr. Montagu's scheme and then to recommend it to the Home Government, as a cut and dry scheme, and not to allow you even to place your views before the Parliament. They think that it is a matter which completely rests with the Government of India and the leaders whom they have called to meet at the Delhi Conference. What they decide there, will be fathered upon you. They forget that the principle of self-determination must be applied to India. You must be made to feel that you fight for your own country. If you have no such feeling, then you will be mercenaries. But ten mercenary men are not equal to one patriot. The Government know it, and they have recognised it in the case of Ireland and they do not want to do it in the case of India (loud cries of shame). The second fact, which must be brought to your notice and which has been already brought in, in the case of Ireland, is the American factor in the situation. In the latest telegram published yesterday, Mr. Lloyd George has plainly admitted that the grant of Home Rule to Ireland was in consonance with the wishes of President Wilson, and he said that unless Home Rule was granted to Ireland, American help would not come forth in such large numbers as it is desirable it should come. The Parliament acknowledges through its Premier that they are forced to take this step in consonance with the wishes of the Americans, whose help is so much necessary at present. Look at India. You probably know in Madras that the matter was represented to President Wilson by one of our leaders (cheers), and what is the response that we got for it? The response is that we were "traitors" to go to America for help, even to inform America what the real situation in India was. They are not prepared to discuss it on merits but any reference to America in the case of India is looked upon as treason by the highest administrative authority in the land, while Parliament openly acknowledges that it is only in deference to the wishes of President Wilson that Home Rule is being granted to Ireland. That is a noteworthy distinction. We cannot go to America. We cannot rely upon the principles of liberty which all the Allies equally proclaim that it is their intention to establish all over the world. But those principles are not to be established in India. The War is not for the establishment of those principles in India. The German Colonies are Black Colonies after all. They say that even in the case of the German Colonies the Allies have agreed that the principle of self-determination will be made applicable. What will Germany say? Germany will say: "If you apply that principle to our Colonies, why not apply it to your own?" Peace negotiations are not to be carried on only by the Allies: they will be on both sides. They now publish to the world that the principle of self-determination is to be applied to the German Colonies. If the Allies do not raise it, somebody else will raise it. What reply will Great Britain give to it? In spite of this War, there can be no reply to the question at the Peace Conference why this principle of self-determination is not extended to India, except the reply that India must be kept aside for the bureaucracy.

THE BUREAUCRATIC SOLUTION

That is the bureaucratic solution of the question. The whole thing has come to this point at present: They are going to hold a Conference which will be followed by the publication of Mr. Montagu's scheme; all political activity will be stopped and possibly a few reforms here and there will be placed before the War Cabinet or the other Cabinet. It seems to me from a reading of these documents that it is intended to settle the question in an arbitrary fashion as soon as possible, under the pretext that the North-West Frontier is in danger and that this is not the time to discuss political reforms. There is ample time to discuss the question of Home Rule being granted to Ireland, though the danger is nearer home there. Here, though we are far away from the theatre of War, danger is apprehended, and all political discussion is to be stopped with a view that the best possible use should be made of the man-power and other resources and that people should be prepared cheerfully to sacrifice. Cheerfulness comes from the heart and if that heart remains untouched, how could that cheerfulness proceed? We might be compelled to work like oxen on the battlefield but that will be an army of mercenaries. India cannot fight a battle for her Motherland unless the sons of India are made to feel that it is for their Motherland that they are fighting and that in that Motherland they possess the birthright of managing their own affairs. This must be said in the Conference. We must muster all our forces together and try to influence as many members of this Conference as possibly could be influenced, so that a protest may be entered in the Conference itself before the Viceroy, that the plan of Government is an absurd plan, a plan that violates the laws of nature, and they must be reminded also that nature is always merciless in enforcing its laws at whatever cost (cheers). If this political agitation is to be stopped, how is it to be stopped? Is it by another legislation, another Press Act, another Seditious Meetings Act, another Ordinance under the Defence of India Act? That seems to be the object. They do not say anything about Home Rule; they forget the fact altogether. They want quiet and peace in India in order that the Government of India may concentrate their thought on a successful prosecution of the War, as if the Government of India are the only people interested in the successful prosecution of the War! If thirty crores of people here are made to feel that it is to their interest to defend the Empire, I think that we can defend it without Government aid. It is not merely the interest of Government. The whole thing seems to be that they want help from you, that they want you to cheerfully help them and at the same time they refuse you your birthright. That is the situation at present. It is being enacted in scenes one after another. Two or three scenes have already been enacted, and we can form an estimate—it may be a mistaken one for the present but not much mistaken—as to what the plot of that drama will be, judging of the scenes we have already witnessed. The Bureaucracy seems to be prepared for smoother public discussion in this land and to represent to the people that you are not fit to get more than they are prepared to give you. Their plan has been arranged and settled in consultation with the Home Government. You will not be allowed to go to England to represent your case. In India you will not be allowed to voice your dissent from the proposals of Government. The whole thing will go before Parliament in the form in which Government have prepared it, and that is all that you are to expect as a result of the War. To my mind, it is the duty of every Indian to fight to the end, and see that India after the War gets the same rights of self-determination as are granted to Ireland. This is the time to work. Providence is with you and is only waiting to see how much courage, persistence and determination you show at this time. Everything will depend upon that.

Do not think that it is a powerful Government and that we must suffer. It is a powerful Government, no doubt, but it does not follow therefrom that we should submit. We must stick to our guns to the last. The only reply to-day is that Government will not give what they are not prepared to give, and that we should not be prepared to take whatever they are prepared to give. I do not care what the Government are prepared to give. If they are going to give us four or eight annas we shall not take it. Even a beggar refuses to take a pie. All of you are better than beggars. If you insist that more *must* be given, more *will* be given. The circumstances are such that they will force the Government to make you feel that it is your case that the Government is fighting. Another argument is that Government may force you to co-operate. If Government pass a conscription law, let them do so, we shall know what to do. If you yield, you give up your case. Another argument is that you must also consider the difficulties of Government. They said that Government is in a very difficult situation and that if you refuse your co-operation you will be playing false to Government. I am not using the word sedition. That argument has no weight. If Government did not care for our feelings for 150 years and at the last moment, at a critical time, comes and appeals to you for help, that Government ought to be prepared to keep aside its own prejudices and concede to us something at this stage. We are not all born for Government that we should so much care for it. The Government is for us and not we for Government. The whole position is absurd. Why should we care for a Government that would not apply the same principle to us that it applies to Ireland? We have that argument, but possibly some of the members of the Conference will excuse themselves on the ground that they are powerless and helpless. True, we are helpless, but there are weapons even in the hands of helpless people. (Cheers). I mean the weapon of Passive Resistance which will make Government come down on its knees (cheers). It must not be thought that we are so helpless because we have no weapon. We must persist and make Government understand that it is impossible to obtain the zealous support of the people unless something is conceded to them. That is the position at present. Government thinks that it can carry out its plan by choosing leaders of the people and nominating them to sit in Conference. That is the principle of self-determination to be applied to us! They will pack up a few leaders and this packed Conference may come to the conclusion that all political propaganda should be stopped.

The British Empire is likely to be threatened in Asia as it has already been threatened in the West. For the West, a provision has been made. For the East, a provision has to be made and that provision is of the nature I have told you. When we appealed to President Wilson from here that letter contained a distinct assurance that India could give 5 to 10 millions of men if the concession is conceded. Take it as a case of the defence of the Empire itself. We can defend the Empire against any attacks in the West and against any attacks in the East. India alone is powerful enough and capable enough to do it. It seems to me that even after this great fight during the War for liberty as it is called colour distinction still lingers in the minds of our Government not willing to grant to India what they are prepared to grant to Servia and to African Colonies because they are German! They are not prepared to extend that principle to India. We have been demanding it. I dare say we do not want to withhold co-operation. We will co-operate but our co-operation cannot be hearty. You may be taken up under the Conscription Act and asked to serve in the Army or go to gaol. You will have to do either of the two. When that Act was passed we shall have to see what we should do. In that way, the thing may be forced and if that does not succeed then must come the grant of Home Rule. The Government of India is trying to see whether the demand for Home Rule can be refused and yet a successful prosecution of the War is carried on. We are interested in the successful prosecution of the War. We are prepared to-day to fight for our Motherland, but it must be our Motherland and not the land of exploitation for other people. Our feeling must be that it is our Motherland that we are asked to fight for. How can you get that feeling? I do not think that the Government of India is so impervious that it cannot understand it. They are far more intelligent than ourselves: that is the reason they are governing us. To attribute to Government a motive or an intention that they are ignorant of all these things is not correct. Bureaucracy generally does not wish to part with power and if I were a bureaucrat I would have acted similarly. The bureaucracy will try to minimise the concession of any political right to you. It is for you to insist that the minimum of the Congress-League Scheme must be granted. We desire to be treated like the men in Ireland and the German Colonies. We desire to be treated as men possessing some sentiments two of which will be enthusiasm and cheerfulness, and if those sentiments are to be evoked, it must be in a psychological way. It is not a condition. It is not disloyal. It is the only right method—right was the word used by Mr. Lloyd George. It is right that people who fight should feel that they are fighting for their right in their own land and not to tie a rope to their own neck. The present political situation is fast changing and after the Conference it will change a bit and if it comes in the way I expect it to do, and if there is a strong protest against the procedure, that procedure is likely to lead to a change in the plan which seems to be already settled. But everything now will depend on your taking the proper step. Do not make any false step. This is a serious time. Our leaders may be led astray, or it may be shown that they are not proper leaders, which is a paraphrase of the same thing. There are men of different temperaments all over the world. There are men who think that they should make easy terms with the rulers. There are others who think that the people are entitled to have something from their rulers, this is exactly the time when the question should be discussed. If the Government of India is going to stop all political propaganda, all questions of national freedom and international freedom will be decided without your knowledge, and then the Government of India will take the gag out of your mouth and ask you to say what you have to say! This is just the time in the country when political agitation and education should go forward. A serious difference of view between you and the Government will arise, and I am afraid it will arise in spite of any protest that may be entered at the Viceroy's Conference, and you will have to keep yourselves ready for that eventuality. Whether you will accept the quarter loaf that will be given to you or insist upon getting the whole loaf is the point. It has been emphasised in several places and also in the newspapers, but the necessity of taking a firm attitude has not yet been insisted upon with that force with which it ought to have been insisted upon.

Some of our leaders are still wavering as to what attitude they should take. I have every respect for them. If they cannot rise to the occasion, let them not ; but let them not cut off the legs of others. If they cannot rise, it is no fault of theirs—they by nature are made short. Perhaps my hand may reach higher and if it does not reach so high I will use some one else's hands, but I mean that my hand should reach higher. This is exactly the time when they should not deter others from going forward. That is the lesson which requires to be impressed upon our leaders. There cannot be unanimity on anything in this world. I am prepared to tolerate difference of opinion, but at the same time the will of the majority must be carried. If the majority of the people feel that they must have Home Rule, Home Rule must be granted in spite of the dissentient voices raised by some people. Let us go to Government, let us place the matter before Parliament. That will have to be done in the near future and everyone must be prepared to understand it and be prepared for the eventuality. My argument is : if I be firm I am sure to get what I want. Let me be firm. Let me not budge an inch, and the circumstances are such that our zealous co-operation, our cheerful co-operation will be necessary. Cheerfulness and zeal will only come when the rights of Home Rule are granted. Even this mighty Government will have to do it (cheers). It was compelled to do so in the case of Ireland. Follow that example. Perhaps you may have the help of America, but then even without that help you must remember that Justice and Providence are on your side. What can Providence do? The favour of Providence enables a cripple to cross a mountain. We shall be assisted in that way only if we have patience, but the struggle is coming. It is begun by Government after hearing all that we had to say, and it now remains to be seen who succeeds in that struggle, the Government or you. We all wish that the people should succeed. We all wish that Justice should be done to us. We all wish that we should be enabled to help the Empire and to defend the Empire against all attacks whether in the East or in the West. Our man-power is very great; that is the only wealth which we now possess, and if you think that it should be wasted, probably you will be left without any resources. It is the only strength we have. Insist that that strength can be made useful in the interest of the Empire only if a psychological condition is fulfilled and not otherwise. That fact must be forced on the attention of Government, and then alone we shall succeed. What will follow hereafter I cannot say. If the Conference decides in our favour, well and good. If it does not, we will have to organise our forces. Possibly the parties will be different then —there will be a Government party and there will be a popular party—the old names will have to be changed—and then in the end, I think, the War circumstances will be such that even if peace be concluded our demands will be granted to us. (Loud Cheers).

NATIONAL EDUCATION

[The following is an article contributed by Mr. Tilak to "New India" in response to the invitation by Mrs. Besant to express his views on National Education]: –

Good Citizenship is the Civic Goal of the members of a Nation generally; and in this respect the older generation is naturally the best guardian of the interests of the younger one. In the language of Wordsworth, "the child is father to the man." If we therefore want our younger generation to attain to the status of full citizenship, we must educate them according to that ideal. In other words, "a Nation that has not taken its education into its own hands cannot soon rise in literary, social or political importance;" and it was this ideal that prompted myself and my colleagues in 1880 to start an independent private English school and soon afterwards an Arts College in Poona. Another attempt was also made in the Maharashtra later on in 1907. But though it is fully recognised that the people of a country must have their education in their own hands, yet there is another principle in Politics which often comes in conflict with it, *viz.*, the Government of the country must also have the education of the people under its control. At first sight, it seems difficult to reconcile these two principles. But I don't think that there is any innate contradiction in these two maxims. What conflict there may arise, arises only from accidental circumstances. Where the people and the Government are one, that is, actuated by the same ideals of citizenship, there can arise no conflict or differences of opinion in the matter of National Education. But where the people and the Government have different ideals of citizenship before them, where the governing class wants to keep the people down in spite of their desire to rise to the status of full citizenship in the Empire, there arises the necessity of National Education as distinguished from governmental education. Viewed in this light, National Education is only a branch or a means to the attainment of Self-Government, and those who demand Home Rule for India cannot but zealously support a movement for the establishment of National Education in this country. The conflict which I have mentioned above can only cease when the people and the Government become one on the higher plane of Self-Government. Till then the authorities will, more or less, come in the way of National Education. But these difficulties must be overcome until National Education becomes the ideal of the governing class, which can be the case only when the Government is popularised.

REFORM SCHEME

[*At the special meeting of the Indian National Congress held at Bombay, under the Presidency of Mr. Hasan Imam, in* 1918, *Mr. Tilak was invited to speak on the Reform proposals, and on rising to speak he was received with great ovation and shouts of 'Tilak Maharajki Jai.' He said*] :—

My first duty is to thank the Government of Bombay for allowing me to open my lips here. I am sorry, however, that the President has not been so kind to me as the Government of Bombay. He has allowed me only five minutes, (Cries of "you may go on.") I shall confine my remarks to a few points on the resolution which has been so ably moved by my friend, the Hon. Pandit Malaviya. What we have tried to do in it is to distil our opinions and it was very difficult to distil in the language of my friend Sir D. Wacha, 'the Golden Cucumber' together. That was the difficulty. It had to be decided and it was a very difficult task and our enemies considered it difficult—I shall not call them enemies but I will call them our opponents. They believed that we were engaged in a very impossible task and that by the beginning of September, the Congress would be nowhere. Unfortunately their predictions did not come true (cries of "fortunately") unfortunately for them, their predictions have not proved true. So long as a spirit of forbearance and a spirit of give-and-take remains in the Congress such a contingency is never likely to arise. We have been awfully misrepresented. We were told, on the strength of stray expressions of thought in moments of excitement and heat that the Congress was going to reject the whole scheme. I could never understand and have never understood what it meant. We are in the midst of our negotiations. If you reject the scheme then you have done with it. What are you going to say to the British people? The British people will say "you have rejected the scheme. What have you come here for. Go back to your country." That would have been their reply. I think that we have learnt enough of politics during the last 15 years under the tuition of our rulers. We have learnt enough of politics to know that it is absurd to take such an absurd action. That should have been made clear. After that there were other difficulties. As I said, fortunately for all, we have been able to place before you a reasoned resolution which combines the wisdom of one party and I may say the tempered temperament of another party—I do not wish to call it rashness. They are happily blended together. The Report on Constitutional Reforms is a very artful, very skilful, and very statesmanlike document. What was the object of that Report? There are two words in vogue, namely Self-Government. We asked for eight annas of Responsible Government. This Report gives us one anna of Responsible Government and says that it is better than eight annas of Self-Government. The whole literary skill of the Report lies in making you believe that one anna of Responsible Government is more than sufficient and more than eight annas of Self-Government. If you read the report over and over again, I do not know what to say but it is a very skilful document—a very statesmanlike document—so as to make you believe that one morsel of Responsible Government is more than sufficient to satisfy your hunger for Self-Government. We have discovered that fortunately. We now plainly say: 'We thank you for the one anna of Responsible Government but that in the scheme we want to embody all that we wanted in the Congress League Scheme.' Rails might be different but the passengers might be carried from one rail to another. That is what we have tried to do and we have tried to satisfy all parties concerned and a very difficult task has been accompanied, as difficult as the task that Mr. Lloyd George is performing in the British Parliament when he means to satisfy the Irish Pacificts and those who want to carry on the War to the end. It is a very difficult task that has been done.The future way is clear and I hope that what we have done will be a material help to us in carrying on the War to a satisfactory end. The Hon. Pandit Malaviya said that we have tried to focus all opinions. Although some of the rails have unfortunately escaped, substantially the resolution represents the opinion of the country. There it is on which we can go. You can utilise it and we can tell the British Democracy that though the Report may be very good and very artfully prepared yet the opinion of the country is that it is unsatisfactory and disappointing. You will ask me what is the good of saying all that. We ask that Self-Government should be completed in 15 years. Our critics say that it is too short a period. I want our critics to remember that unless India is raised to the status of the Colonies, the Empire will be in danger. We ask for Self-Government not for ourselves although there is that self-interest but also for the sake of the Empire. What is the good of developing India in 200 or 300 years. India's status should be raised within the next ten or fifteen years. Those that say that the first step we ask for is too much are I must say the enemies of the Empire; they do not consider the question from a broad point of view. It is not a question between the Bureaucracy and ourselves. We want the right of control over the bureaucracy within the next 10 or 15 years. Then alone India will be ready to take part in that development and strength of the Empire which it must possess and which at the time of the reconstruction of the Empire it should be the duty of British statesmen to bring about by adopting the policy which has been enunciated by them. With these few words, I ask you to accept the resolution unanimously.

THE SWADESHI MOVEMENT

[*At the session of the Indian National Congress, held in* 1906, *at Calcutta, under the presidency of Dadhabai Naoroji the resolution on Swadeshi was moved. Mr. B. G. Tilak, in supporting the same, spoke as follows*] :—

Mr. President, brother-delegates, ladies and gentlemen,—I stand on this platform to-day not to make a speech on the Swadeshi resolution. To deliver a speech on Swadeshism in Calcutta is something like carrying coals to Newcastle! I do not think you want any inspiration or any instruction on this subject. Your leaders, like my friend Mr. Surendranath Banerjea and others, have trained you up in Swadeshism to such an extent that we might imitate you for a long time and yet we may not come to your level (Cries of "No, no.") I stand here to-day to declare that some of the ideas which were not originally incorporated in the resolution and which, unfortunately, I had to suggest, by way of amendment, have been accepted; and we have now unanimously come to the resolution that was read to you by Mr. Anandacharlu. I am glad that you have come to such a solution for one thing, because our Anglo-Indian friends had predicted that the 22nd Congress would probably be the last Congress (Laughter)! And that it would meet with a premature death immediately on attaining the age of majority! That prediction has been falsified (Hear, hear); and falsified under the able, impartial and judicious guidance of our veteran leader, Mr. Dadhabai Naoroji, whom we have in the chair. Our differences have been squared; both parties have approached the question in a spirit of conciliation and not half way. Thanks to my friends, both Hindus and Muhammadans, we have come to an amicable settlement on that point. It is a mistake to suppose that the Swadeshi movement is not favoured by Muhammadans. It is a mistake to suppose that it requires sacrifice from poor people. We, the middle classes are the greatest offenders in this respect (Hear, hear.) The poor *Kumbi* villagers require not many foreign articles at all,—probably none at all. It is we, the middle classes, who are the consumers of foreign goods; and since this Government is not going to stop the drain by imposing a protective duty it becomes imperatively necessary to adopt a measure by which we can do ourselves what the Government is bound to do and what the Government ought to have done long ago. That one point was self-help and another point was determination; and the third, sacrifice. You will find that all this included in this resolution, joined with the declaration made in the Presidential address that Swadeshism is a forced necessity in India owing to unnatural economic conditions in India, makes up a complete case for you. I trust that resolution of self-help adopted this year will form the basis of other resolutions of self-help in years to come. With these few words, and as time is much advanced, and I am not prepared to make a speech on the present occasion, I ask you leave to sit down.

PRINCIPLES OF THE NATIONALIST PARTY

[*On the evening of the 23rd December,* 1907, *Mr. Tilak addressed a mass meeting of over* 3,000 *people including the delegates of all provinces at Surat Below is the text*] :—

We have not come to cause a split in the Congress, we do not want to hold a separate Congress, we want to see that the Congress does not go back. We solemnly say that we want to see the Congress moving with the times, we would not allow it to go back. Our views are misrepresented. It has been told that the new movement is an impediment to progress. Our policy is not destructive, we intend to make an effort to move the Congress on. Times are changed; and so we want some modifications.

Our aim is self-government. It should be achieved as soon as possible. You should understand this. But the people who brought the Congress to Surat, although Nagpur was willing at any cost, are going to drag the Congress back. We are against autocratic movement. These autocrats want to cripple the Congress and so they are against Boycott and *Swaraj* resolutions. The nation is not for the repressive policy. They don't want to say or rather preach boycott openly. They have no moral courage. They are against the word boycott, they are for Swadeshi. If you are to do it, do not fear. Don't be cowards; when you profess to be Swadeshi you must boycott *videshi* goods; without boycott Swadeshi cannot be practised. If you accept Swadeshi, accept boycott. We want this, "don't say what you don't want to do but do what you say."

We are not fighting for men, not for the election of the president, we want men as representative of certain principles. The fight is between two principles, (1) "Earnestly doing what is right" and (2) "Do, but don't displease the Government." I belong to the party who are prepared to do what they think right whether the Government is pleased or displeased. (It is not a question of pleasure or displeasure.) We want to do duty to ourselves, to our country; and working in the path of duty, we should not fear any rational authority, be it ever so high. We are against the policy of mendicancy; for it has been found, this policy would not yield the fruit but would demoralise us. Many young gentlemen in Bengal have gladly suffered for this attitude. Mr. Morley and other Government officials seem to want to make a breach in our camp. They ask us to rally round the Moderates. Are we prepared to do this? It would be impolitic, imprudent, to retrace our steps. The banner of *Swaraj* was unfurled last year at Calcutta by the Grand Old Man of India, Sj. Dadabhai Naoroji. This is our ideal and if we do not stick to this resolution—to this ideal of our Grand Old Man, what will he say? We will be considered traitors to the country. Political regeneration is our goal. No one has any authority to make the Congress recede from this ideal. It will be your sincere duty to see that the name of your city be not associated with this retrograde movement. It would be better if we do not make any progress but we should at least try our best not to recede. In this we want your assistance. It is said by Mr. Morley and by the London *Times* that self-government is impracticable for India. Remember, what is impracticable for Mr. Morley and for the Anglo-Indians is practicable for our countrymen because our interests are conflicting. This our ideal of Swaraj is a distinct goal for the mass to understand. All past ideals are amalgamated into one pure and simple ideal of *Swaraj*, government for the people by the people.

We do not come here to embarass the Moderates. We have determined not to allow the Congress to retrograde. By the grace of God, we will succeed. I am confident of success, for, our cause is a right cause. Whoever he may be, high or low, it will be impossible for him to check the tide of progress. This ideal is our ideal, is the ideal of the younger generation not to damp the spirit of youth. Don't allow them to go far, but don't cripple them. The Moderates are afraid of the word boycott but not of the deed. We feel also as they feel that Swadeshi and boycott had already the effect of vivifying the country. Boycott is the only weapon for the subject nation.

You have heard of the Transvaal Indians. They are not treated as the English King's subjects, but we are asked to be members of the Empire. We don't want to be the slaves of the Empire, we want to be equals or friends with the white subjects not only in India but throughout the whole Empire. The authorities of Transvaal have levied a Jazia-tax on the Indians. 13,000 of our Indians there have met and have determined not to obey the unjust law (hear, hear) while only four hundred form traitors to the country. Do you approve of this attitude of the 13,000 Transvaal Indians? The Congress does approve and the Moderates of the Reception Committee are willing to approve this act and they have drafted a resolution to this effect. If you approve this conduct of the far off Indians you approve boycott, for, the people there have boycotted the unjust foreign laws. This is not inconsistent. The Moderates don't want to please the Government; if that would have been the case, I would have been very glad; but no, no, they fear a civilised government. It is unmanly. If you are not prepared to brave the dangers, be quiet, but don't ask us to retrograde. Pray do not come in the way of the ideals which we have received from the last two Congresses. When the people of the country have no voice in the government of this country, boycott is useful. I implore you, you the citizens of Surat, to help us in our endeavours.

Now we have done with *Swaraj* and Boycott. I

now come to the third ideal—National Education, the resolution which was passed in the last Congress. But the Reception Committee of Surat have not thought it wise to place it among the draft resolutions. It was not allowed in the Provincial Conference held in April here, because certain autocrats did not like this. We don't want to carry this matter high-handedly, as they do ; we will place this before the Subjects Committee and before the Congress delegates. We want to be loyal to the Congress first and in showing our loyalty if our individual interest comes in the way, we will brush this out. It is not a personal question. However high or dignified may one be, respect for him should not come in the way of the Congress. It is a fight for progress. Friction there must be. Where is motion without friction ? And this law holds good in the sphere of politics. We must take care that the friction should not be allowed to go so far as to put a stop to this motion. We have our limits. We want unanimous consent. If not, we will have the resolution passed by the majority and if it is passed, it must be carried. Even the President-elect has no right to change this. A resolution once passed in the Congress must be accepted by all those who join the Congress, whether they like it or not. There will not be any rowdyism there. It is misrepresented. We have come here to fight out constitutionally ; we will loyally fight out ; we will behave as gentlemen even if our opponents do not do so. Our opponents create rowdyism when they fear defeat. We are fighting against foreign autocracy. Why should we allow this home-autocracy? So we want to prevent the autocratic rule in the Congress. The Congress is an organization of all the people and the voice of the people ought to predominate. We should not allow any man, high or low, to ruin the cause of the Congress. Don't recede, even if you cannot progress. Our ideal is practicable. We should stick to our ideal. The policy of the Moderates is destructive. It is a suicidal policy. I don't want you to follow it; we want to progress. Again, I appeal to you. Suratees, Gujaratees, be not led by the threats of the autocrats. Don't fear and we will succeed.—(*Bande Mataram.*)

MEETING OF THE NATIONALIST DELEGATES

[On the 28th December, 1907, under the presidency of Sj. Arabindo Ghose, the Nationalist delegates held a meeting to consider the then situation. The meeting was largely attended. Mr. Tilak in addressing the meeting said]:—

In the course of a lengthy speech, Mr. Bal Gangadhar Tilak said that that meeting represented the middle class Congress, and consisted of those Congress delegates who believed that the possession taken up last year should not be disturbed. There were a number of persons who attempted to disturb that position with the result that a regrettable split had taken place, and the institution, which took 23 years to be built up and on which lakhs of Rupees had been spent, had at last been suspended. One party wanted to go back on last year's resolutions, while others desired to maintain the *status quo*.

The bone of contention between the two parties was that some high persons managing the affairs of the Surat Congress were firmly determined to bring down the Congress from the high pedestal which it occupied a year ago into the lower position of an All-India Moderate Congress (cries of *Shame!*) That was a retrograde move against which the Nationalists had fought during the past few days. The

Surat Reception Committee had brushed aside the claims of Lala Lajpat Rai for the Presidentship on the ground that his election would offend the Government which would throttle the Congress in no time. That was the beginning of the end of the Congress. The dragging of the national movement into a sectional one could not have been accomplished, had not a few individuals been allowed to take the whole power into their own hands and to put forward ideals and methods which fell in with the views of the Government—he did not mean to say that there was a compact between the Government and those individual members. But a creed was enunciated which was least objectionable to the Government. He would not say the most acceptable to the Government, because he did not believe that the Congress creed would ever be acceptable to them.

It might be that they honestly believed that in those days of repression it was prudent, from a worldly point of view, not to go beyond a certain limit, while others were of opinion that repression promoted national growth. There were two schools of thought, one believing that political progress in India could be made only by being in opposition to, and at the same time in association with the Government. There was another school represented by the Nationalists which thought otherwise, and which has received, during the last two or three years, a vigorous impetus. There was a conflict between these two schools, but they have managed so far to carry on the work of the Congress with unanimity by a give-and-take policy. The way in which it had been proposed to go back on the resolutions of last year in regard to Self-Government, Boycott, Swadeshi and National Education, on the ground they did not appeal themselves to the Secretary of State, the London *Times* and the Anglo-Indian papers and officials, was a deliberate insult to the whole Congress, and no one, however eminently placed, had any right to drag back the Congress. The Bombay Moderates wanted the Congress to move a little backwards, to be within the safe line of the boundary, so as not to displease the Government.

Sj. Tilak next explained how it had been proposed to go back on the four questions mentioned above, and how there was opposition to it on the part of the Nationalists, which was as determined as the desire on the part of the Moderates to push back the Congress. That opposition of the Nationalists manifested itself in opposition to the President. When it was settled that Dr. Ghose was to be selected President, merely to please the Government in spite of the unanimous opinion of India in favour of Lala Lajpat Rai, it was considered by the Nationalists to be a wrong step which they were bound to resist. Matters should have been arranged and settled on the principle of give-and-take which hitherto generally characterised the proceedings and resolutions of the Congress. The Bombay Moderates were determined not only to make further compromise with the Nationalists, but also to retract from the position which they had been forced to take at Calcutta by the Nationalists. The Nationalists tried to approach them often, privately as well as publicly, but were kept at arms' length though mutual friends intervened. And the result was the split, which he hoped, would not be permanent, in the Congress camp, just at the time when they ought to have shown a united front. No one regretted the split more than he did. The Nationalists were aware of the harmful effects of the split and the purposes which it would serve. The Government has been asking the Moderates to rally round their standard. It was the duty of every educated man at this particular juncture not to play into the hands of the Government. But, fortunately or unfortunately, because fortunate to one side and unfortunate to the other, the thing had happened, and the Congress autocrats had gained the day, not by attempting to conciliate the other side but by dispersing them (cries of shame), and by even rejecting the most reasonable proposals to maintain the *status quo.* This new spirit in the country was dangerous, and sooner it was destroyed the better. He hoped that the split would only be temporary, and he was quite sure that the experience of the next few years would expose the insecurity of the position taken up by the Moderates.

If it was found difficult for both the parties to unite, the question should have been considered and decided at the meeting of the few leading Congress Delegates before the election of the President. In fact that was the amendment which he wanted to move, an adjournment of the business of election of the President, not of the Congress, in order to allow time for a representative Committee consisting of one Moderate and one Nationalist from each province, to decide the programme of work before the election of the President was taken up, so that they could have unanimously elected the President. That was the suggestion that he had intended to put forward on the Congress platform. if he had been allowed to do so. Though several friends tried to bring about a compromise, their efforts failed, because there was no desire on the other side to yield even an inch. The Bombay Moderates thought that they should take advantage of the exceptional majority of the Moderate delegates which they might command at Surat to force their view on the Congress even at the risk of driving it back. It was that spirit of intolerance that had led to the present situation.

It must be said that the Nationalists should have exhibited forbearance, but there were limits to that forbearance. Would they allow the organisation to move backwards? (Cries of 'no,' 'no.') The result was that a useful organisation had been split up and, as in the case of every partition of the

Hindu family, each had become the weaker for the partition. He hoped that those who desired to have retrogression would soon see their mistake, and soon discover that, although the Government expressed its desire to have the Moderates rallied round its standard, nothing useful could be gained, useful not individually but collectively, until the Moderates were taught by the Government that their position was not only illogical, but suicidal, which according to his belief was yet before the House and was not finally, at least not *properly*, disposed of. Thereon, there was some conversation between Mr. Malvi and Dr. Ghosh on the one hand and Mr. Tilak on the other; and then there was an uproar in which the Congress was declared to have been suspended *sine die*. Now it should be remembered that it is not contended for the Moderate party that any ruling as such was publicly announced upon Mr. Tilak's demand for moving an adjournment and for addressing the House, except perhaps to Mr. Tilak himself and in the conversation referred to above. The fact of Mr. Tilak having asked for an adjournment and permission to address the House, was never openly mentioned to the whole House, nor the Chairman's ruling formally declared to the House. And it is not disputed that from first to last *no question was put* to the House nor votes taken nor even the sense ascertained on the subject matter of Mr. Tilak's chit. Now it is urged against Mr. Tilak that his unconstitutional act consisted of two things—first, in demanding permission to move an adjournment and to address the House on the question of the election of the President, and secondly, in persisting in the assertion of his right to address the House even when he was declared to be out of order by the Chair. And we have, therefore, to consider whether any one or both of these acts were unconstitutional. And as correlated to these questions, we have also to consider the point whether and how far Mr. Malvi or Dr. Ghosh (we will generally say the *Chairman* for either) was acting constitutionally or unconstitutionally in whatever he did on the occasion. What the Chairman apparently did was that he told Mr. Tilak that the latter's chit was considered, but the request therein was held to be inadmissible; and later that he told Mr. Tilak that he had protested enough, that he must no longer speak and interrupt the business and must resume his seat.

The Nationalists had to devise means to keep up the work of the Congress. They must devise measures for keeping up the Congress work, their starting point being the position taken up at the Calcutta Congress. It might be prudent, in worldly interests, to recede from it, but it was not prudent in the interests of the country. Time had come to exhibit more of the resisting spirit in them than the desire to please the authorities, or to advance as cautiously as it might be possible under the rules and regulations, repressive or otherwise, of the

Government of this country. The Nationalists should do what they could do to keep up the fire until the time came when the small light they might be able to preserve might develop into a magnificent blaze. The Nationalists were not met there for the purpose of creating a new organisation which would only advance to the limit up to which the Government would allow it to advance, but for creating an organisation which would have a life of its own, a life that would enable it to grow under the most distressing and discouraging circumstances under the most chilling atmosphere of repression.

How to do it was the question. It was necessary, therefore, to appoint a committee of 30 to 50 members, who would watch the effects of the split, and decide upon the measure to be taken to check the evil effects thereof, and, if possible, make arrangements for the meeting of the Congress next year at some place. The committee to be appointed would work, not in a spirit of rivalry with the other party, but in a spirit of co-operation wherever possible, and he hoped that, within a short time, by the grace of Providence, an opportunity would present itself when both the parties would again be united for the purpose, not only of resisting the repressive measures of the Government, but of advancing towards the goal of self-government unfolded last year.

To

HIS MAJESTY THE KING AND HIS GOVERNMENT.

MR. TILAK'S LETTER TO THE PRESS

Sir,—In view of the exceptional circumstances of the present time, I have to ask you to publish the following in order to remove any possible misunderstanding as to my attitude towards the Government at this juncture. I have already given expression to these views when addressing my friends the other day at the Ganapati gathering at my house. But feeling that a wider publicity to them should be advisable I am addressing this letter to you.

A couple of months ago, when I had an occasion to address those who came to congratulate me on my safe return to Poona, I observed that I was very much in the position Rip Van Winkle returning to his home after a long sleep in the wilderness. Since then I have had opportunities to fill up the gaps in my information as to what has occurred during my absence, and to take stock of the march of events in India during the past six years. And let me assure you that in spite of certain measures like the Press Act—upon which, however, it is not necessary for me to dilate in this place at any length,—I for one do not give up the hope of the country steadily making further progress in the realisation of its cherished goal. The reforms introduced during Lord Morley's and Lord Minto's administration will show that the Government is fully alive to the necessity of progressive change and desire to associate the people more and more in the work of the Government. It can also be claimed, and fairly conceded, that this indicates a marked increase of confidence between the Rulers and the Ruled, and a sustained endeavour to remove popular grievances. Considered from a public point of view, I think this is a distinct gain: and though it may not be all unalloyed, I confidently hope that in the end the good arising out of the constitutional reforms will abide and prevail, and that which is objectionable will disappear. The view may appear optimistic to some; but it is an article of faith with me, and in my opinion such a belief alone can inspire us to work for the good of our country in co-operation with the Government.

There is another matter to which it is necessary to refer. I find that during the six years of my absence an attempt has been made in the English Press here and in England, as for example in Mr. Chirol's book, to interpret my actions and writings as a direct or indirect incitement to deeds of violence, or my speeches as uttered with the object of subverting the British rule in India. I am sorry the attempt happened to be made at a time when I was not a free citizen to defend myself. But I think I ought to take the first public opportunity to indignantly repudiate these nasty and totally unfounded charges against me. I have, like other political workers, my own differences with the Government as regards certain measures and to a certain extent even the system of internal administration. But it is absurd on that account to speak of my actions or my attitude as in any way hostile to His Majesty's Government. That has never been my wish or my object. I may state once for all that we are trying in India, as the Irish Homerulers have been doing in Ireland, for a reform of the system of administration and not for the overthrow of Government; and I have no hesitation in saying that the acts of violence which have been committed in the different parts of India are not only repugnant to me, but have, in my opinion, only unfortunately retarded to a great extent, the pace of our political progress. Whether looked at from an individual or from a public point of view they deserve, as I have said before on several occasions, to be equally condemned.

It has been well said that British Rule is conferring inestimable benefit on India not only by its civilized methods of administration but also thereby bringing together the different nationalities and races of India, so that a united Nation may grow out of it in course of time. I do not believe that if we had any other rulers except the liberty-loving British, they could have conceived and assisted us in developing such a National Ideal. Every one who has the interest of India at heart is fully alive to this and similar advantages of the British Rule; and the present crisis is, in my opinion, a blessing in disguise inasmuch as it has universally evoked our united feelings and sentiments of loyalty to the British Throne.

England, you know, has been compelled by the action of the German Emperor to take up arms in defence of a weaker State, whose frontiers have been violated in defiance of several treaty obligations and of repeated promises of integrity. At such a crisis it is, I firmly hold, the duty of every Indian, be he great or small, rich or poor, to support and assist His Majesty's Government, to the best of his ability; and no time, in my opinion, should be lost in convening a public meeting of all parties, classes and sections of Poona, as they have been elsewhere, to give an emphatic public expression to the same. It requires hardly any precedent to support such a course. But if one were needed I would refer to the proceedings of a public meeting held by the citizens of Poona so far back as 1879-80 in regard to the complications of the Afghan War which was proceeding at the time. That proves that our sense of loyalty and desire to support the

Government is both inherent and unswerving; and that we loyally appreciate our duties and responsibilities under such circumstances.

I am yours, &c.

B. G. TILAK.

Poona, 27th August, 1914.

PUBLIC ADDRESS TO MR. TILAK AND HIS REPLY

[*An address as below was presented to Tilak with a purse containing a hundred thousand rupees on his Sashti Purthi* 61*st birthday, July* 1916, *by his friends and admirers.*]

We, who are a few among your friends in the Maharashtra, have assembled here to-day to congratulate you upon having completed your 60th year and we feel extremely happy to greet you on this joyous occasion.

The last thirty or thirty-five years have proved to be a period of great importance for the Maharashtra and you have during that period of its history rendered special important service to it. In your capacity as a founder of the New English School, as an originator of the Deccan Educational Society, as a Professor in the Fergusson College, as a distinguished author, as the Editor of the "Kesari" and the "Maratha," as a Congressman, as a member of the Legislative Council and, lastly, as the prime leader of the Nationalist movement, you have done service which is invaluable; you have moreover become an exemplar to the people of this country by your prominent ethical virtues such as rectitude, self-sacrifice and courage.

The vow of public service which you have imposed upon yourself is very difficult, in fact, very severe. One is apt to be overwhelmed by the mere thought of calamities which encountered you in the past; and we have nothing but admiration for the determined courage with which you faced all of them, the resourceful struggle with which you won victory in some of them and the cool courage and equanimity of mind with which you bore others which were insurmountable.

The span of life vouchsafed to educated men in this country is unhappily not a large one. To the general causes of this state of things, others of a special nature as indicated above, have been added in your case. It must, therefore, be regarded as a special favour of Providence both upon yourself and upon the people of the Maharashtra, that you have been enabled to see the dawn of your 61st birthday. And we pray to the same benignant Providence to grant you health and long life so that you may be able to render further services to your people.

But how could we greet and congratulate you empty-handed on the present occasion? Considering the self-sacrificing service that you have rendered throughout your life, no present howsoever valuable that we may offer you, can be fit or adequate. But we earnestly entreat you to accept as a present the small purse which we place in your hands along with this address. It is the result of contributions spontaneously made by a comparatively few individuals during the last two or three weeks. Quite a large number of people in the Maharashtra could not participate in the present ceremony as the news thereof was not brought to them in good time. But they will have at least the satisfaction that a few did make a move in time, so that your sixty-first birthday could be celebrated in this manner.

Public-spirited workers like yourself are thoroughly disinterested, and that makes difficult the task of repaying their services. But it is the duty of the people in any nation to be ready to make that repayment at some self-sacrifice lest they should be called ungrateful; and we pray that you will be pleased to accept our small present at least to free us of the Maharashtra from that blame, if not for your own sake.

[*Mr. Tilak, in reply, said*]:—

Esteemed Friends and Gentlemen,—I am aware that any words which I can use to express my heartfelt thanks for your address and gift can but inadequately express my feelings at this moment. The language of joy or emotion is always brief and of the nature of an exclamation and I pray you from the bottom of my heart to make up any deficiency that my words may appear to reveal, so that like the gift which has grown little by little to such a stately sum, my words may in your generous minds grow to the full expression of my feelings. You have all been of the greatest help to me and while I have been anxiously thinking of how to repay your kindness, you have to-day again added to the already heavy debt of gratitude, as if you wish me to be eternally bound to you. I have no doubt that you are actuated by feelings of deep and sincere affection, but I do not think that this makes my task any easier. I only hope that with your blessings Providence may grant me strength to repay this heavy debt of gratitude with which you have overwhelmed me.

Even if I felt a certain embarrassment in accepting the Address, I must formally accept it. But with the purse it is a different thing. I do not know what I should do with the money which it contains. I do not want it for my own sake nor would it be proper to accept it for personal use. I can only accept it in trust to spend it in a constitutional way for national work, and I hope this proposal will meet your wishes. You have entrusted this sum to me in trust and I assure you that I will, after adding my own quota, utilise it to the best of my ability in a manner already indicated and according to rules which will be framed later on. If there is any sense of disappointment with the conditions on which I accept the sum, I hope you will consider my present state of health and mind and extend to me your generous indulgence.

Looking into futurity after completing 60 years one's mind cannot but be filled with misgivings. At any rate I deeply feel this sensation. Memories of storm and suffering rather than those of comparative happiness rise before my mind's eye; and with declining strength one is apt to feel less fortitude in facing them. But I devoutly hope that with your support as heretofore I may be granted life and strength to add to whatever work of public good I may have hitherto done.

The words of high praise which you have bestowed on me in your address remind me of Bhartrihari's lines.

"How many (good people) are there who rejoice in their hearts to make a mountain of the particle of merit they find in others."

To me it is rather a proof of your generous feelings than of any merits in me. But I earnestly pray you not to be content with what little service I could do in the cause of the nation. The National work which faces us to-day is so great, extensive and urgent that you must work together with zeal and courage greater than I may have been able to show. It is a task which is not one that can be put off. Our motherland tells everyone of us to be up and doing. And I do not think that Her sons will disregard this call. However I feel it my duty to beg of you to respond to this call of our Motherland and banishing all differences from your minds strive to become the embodiments of National ideals. Here there is no room for rivalry, jealousy, honour or insult, or fear. God alone can help us in the fruition of our efforts and if not by us, it is certain that the fruit will be gathered by the next generation. And therefore banishing all other considerations from our minds we must unite to work in these National efforts. May God inspire you with this high ideal and I pray Him to grant me life to see with my own eyes your efforts crowned with success!

I again thank you with all my heart for the great honour which you have done me to-day.

SELF-RELIANCE

[Under the presidency of the Hon Mr. Manmohan Das Ramji, a monster public meeting was held on 2nd October, 1917, in Madhav Baug, Bombay, when Mr. Tilak spoke as follows]:—

Gentlemen,—I have chosen to depart from my usual practice of addressing meetings. I have in my hands my written speech and I am going to read it out to you this evening. You will, perhaps, ask me why I have resorted to this unusual method, but I may tell you that I have no wish to tender my explanation for this, astonishing as it may appear to you. But I know you will, without my telling the reason in explicit terms, draw your inferences and I cannot help if you arrive at the truth (laughter). With no much preface I come to the subject of my speech. You are aware, gentlemen, that the Paisa Fund has come out successfully through the severe ordeals to which it was put during the last ten years of its existence. The sphere of action of the Paisa Fund is now no more limited to the four corners of the Bombay Presidency or the Marathi-speaking public. It has now transgressed these bounds and received hospitality at the hands of our Ceylonese brethren across the seas. (Cheers.) The spread of the idea must delight the hearts of all those interested in the cause of the

Paisa Fund, and I have every hope that if you put forth earnest efforts to make the movement popular, it will not take very long before it will lay its hold upon the minds of people inhabiting the several provinces of India. To-day we have got on hand a handsome balance of forty thousand Rupees out of the collections we have made. I have never considered this as a very large amount; for even if we are happily in a position to show a balance of forty lacs of Rupees, I would not regard it as a very prodigious amount, nor look upon it as a greater achievement. We are in absolute need of such large amounts, if at all they are worth to be had. You will, perhaps, say that by indulging in such a talk, we are merely making a show of our inordinate greed. But, gentlemen, remember that such colossal amounts are very badly needed to satiate the appetite of thirty-three million souls of this motherland of ours. No funds can be said to be too large for this purpose.

Now turning to the way in which the funds are disposed of and accounts kept, we may in glowing terms congratulate ourselves on having secured in the person of Mr. Yeshvantrao Nene an Accountant in whose industry, veracity, and business capacity you may safely repose the greatest confidence and trust. If you believe me, I can confidently give my word that Mr. Nene will not allow the smallest error of a pie to creep into his accounts.

The Paisa Fund is an Institution which has a

variety of lessons to give to you. In the first place, it provides you a ground where you can train your young men in the art of organisation with the object of performing civic duties. Selflessness is the first lesson which you are to learn in forming volunteers'-association for the purpose of collecting the Paisa Fund. The Paisa Fund, moreover, teaches you the value of self-reliance. In fact, self-reliance is the very life and soul of the movement. Those that desire to do some kind of service or other to their motherland must necessarily develop these qualities, in order to put forth that service to the best advantage. To the volunteers I have this message to give. Remember all these things, and act up to them. Work with devotion and singleness of purpose for the uplift of the Motherland. You devote only one day in a year for the collection of the Paisa Fund. If you do the work which you have undertaken to do as a part of your duty, with all the zeal and earnestness which you can summon to your aid, I am sure, your devoted efforts will never remain unrewarded by God. If you have faith in Him, remember ever that He is always standing by you. He will certainly crown your efforts with success. Have implicit faith in Him, and be doing your duty even without the reasonable prospect of a suitable reward in return for your exertions.

LOYALTY RESOLUTION

[*In supporting the Loyalty Resolution at the Provincial Conference, held in Belgaum in April* 1916, *Mr. Tilak said*] :—

President and Delegates,—The subject of the resolution I rise to support now is named " War and Loyalty ". At first sight there appears no connection between war and loyalty, and I am going to deal with the subject with a view to see whether there exists a relation between the two and if any such relation exists, to see what duty devolves upon us on that account. Gentlemen, at the outset I must make it plain to you that the demands that we are now pressing upon the attention of the Government, have absolutely no relation to the assistance we have given to them during the present war. We do not make these demands by way of a reward for the services we have rendered during the war. We have been asking for them long before the war, and they have nothing to do with it. They are based on the firm foundation of justice, (cheers). They are not new ones ; we have been dinning them into the ears of the Government for a quarter of a century and more. We are now pressing them with redoubled vigour, and the present time has only afforded us the best opportunity of emphasising them. But for the distrust of the bureaucracy, these demands would have long ago been granted to us. Heretofore they thought that no sooner were the Indians allowed to carry arms, than they would attempt to make use of them in overthrowing the British supremacy in India. But a greater and graver calamity than this supposed or imaginary fear has now arisen in the shape of the present war, and our bureaucracy must now give up all their suspicions about us in view of the loyalty we have shown and the manifold help we have given them. (Cheers). Our cheerful co-operation and willing aid must convince the bureaucracy that we never for a moment harboured any thought of driving the British out of India. We never entertained the idea that the British rule should be supplanted by any other foreign power. On the other hand, in order to strengthen and consolidate the British rule we have shown our willingness to sacrifice to the utmost our blood and our purse (loud cheers). What other proof is needed to demonstrate our genuine loyalty? We request the Government to revoke the Arms Act; but if they are afraid or reluctant to do so now, let them revoke it after the termination of the war. Let them embark upon the experiment a few selected individuals to carry arms without a license, and if the Government is satisfied that the arms are not improperly used, there would be no harm to revoke the Arms Act altogether.

We firmly believe that if there be any people that can sympathise with our legitimate aspirations and help us to realise them, it is the British people, (loud cheers). We are deeply convinced that no other nation than the British can stand us in good stead and promote our welfare (loud cheers). All these things we are quite sure of; but there is no gainsaying the fact that owing to a great many imperfections in the present system of administration a good deal of dissatisfaction and unrest prevails in the country. This dissatisfaction need not however come in the way of conceding our demands. The true reason why our bureaucracy is reluctant to part with its powers is the vain fear that it would lose its prestige. But our services in the war have opened the eyes of the British public to our state and has convinced them more than ever that the suspicions of the bureaucracy had absolutely no foundation in fact. They must have now known that the distrust of the bureaucracy with regard to us Indians was due to their self-interest. Now that the British democracy is aware of the true state of affairs in India, I say the present is the most opportune time to press for our demands being recognised by an Act of Parliament. This, in my opinion, is the relation that subsists between our loyalty and the present war (cheers).

Gentlemen, there are certain people who say that India ought to have supplied more men than have been hitherto despatched from here to the front. But who denies the propriety of this assertion ? But are we to be blamed for not doing something which was not in our power to do ? If we were invested with some authority we could have supplied a gigantic army of ten millions to fight the enemy. And I ask you, in all earnestness, if India is not now in a position to send such a vast force, is it not the fault of our bureaucracy ? History tells us that the great empires of Rome and Greece were ruined on account of the predominance of jealousy in the minds of the ruling classes towards those over whom they exercised their power. Historians say that these horrible vices of jealousy and avarice were peculiar only to uncivilized tribes of the olden times and that they are now fast disappearing. This elimination, they say, is calculated to obviate the down-fall of great empires of modern times. But the behaviour of the belligerents engaged in the present war gives a direct lie to this assertion. These vices, you will note, have not entirely disappeared. They are making themselves felt as fiercely as of yore. So, it is clearly the duty of statesmen who guide the destinies of mighty empires, to guard them against these pit-falls, and in order to do it effectually it is equally clear that all the component parts that comprise the empire must be made strong enough to stand on their own legs. Fortunately the potentialities of India are so great and enormous that it can supply any number of men to the army; so much so that if you make the men stand three feet apart from each other they will form an unbroken line from Calcutta to Berlin! (laughter and loud cheers). But why are not men forthcoming in such large numbers? There is only one reason for this. And it is the distrust of our bureaucracy. Their suspicions might be honest suspicions, but what is honest is not always true (cheers). It has been now proved to the hilt that their misunderstanding about us, though honest, was due merely to a lack of perception on their part of our good intentions. We have shown that we never meant to subvert the British sovereignty. (loud cheers). We never entertained the idea of severing the British connection. We believe that it is only the British that can have genuine sympathies with our national aspirations and can satisfy our needs, (cheers). No one ought to misunderstand us on this cardinal point. We are thoroughly loyal to the person of our Emperor and His Majesty's empire (cheers). We are not against his sovereignty and never mean to sever our connection with his throne. But with all that you must remember that the empire does not mean a bureaucracy. Fighting constitutionally with the bureaucracy for the attainment of certain rights and privileges which we are entitled to as citizens of a great empire does not mean any attempt to overthrow the empire (cheers). If some people try to put such a construction on our endeavours to obtain our legitimate privileges, I should say it is simply wicked to do so. We do certainly want to help our Government. We have practically helped it in several ways and our assistance proceeds in no way from a desire to obtain a reward for it. We help our Government, because it is our duty to do so. (cheers). But while helping them at this moment of their supreme need, I do say that this is the most opportune time to emphasise our demands and you should not swerve an inch from doing both these duties.

Some of our bureaucrats say, " Why do you want arms? We are here to protect you from foreign invasions as well as from internal violence". I ask, however, why should we go to the District Superintendent of Police to request him to protect us from the depredations of a tiger in the jungle? I know a tiger was at large in the jungles of Sinhagarh but the people being quite unable to protect themselves against his rapacity, had to run over to Poona to intimate to the Police Superintendent the danger and obtain a redress of their grievance. The Superintendent, thereupon, came to the place and killed that tiger. Why should we be so much dependent on the help of the authorities even in such petty matters? Does the killing of a tiger mean fomenting a rebellion? (cheer and laughter). But our splendid co-operation in the present war has thoroughly satisfied the Government as to our loyalty. There is now absolutely no doubt about it in any quarters. And there ought to remain no suspicion whatsoever about it. The suspicion having been removed, we have every right to receive from our Government the privileges of carrying arms. The concession will not only promote our welfare but it will go to strengthen the empire as well. It will further secure the peace of the country if all three hundred millions are provided with arms, they will strike terror into the hearts of our foe. He will be afraid of waging war with a mighty power which can muster at a moment's notice millions of armed people to defend the empire. The grant of this concession will make the people strong, bold and manly. It will help to establish a reign of peace all over the world and contribute to universal satisfaction and welfare. It will obviate the necessity of passing the law of conscription. Some of our bureaucrats still assert that they by themselves are eminently powerful to protect the vast British Empire from any danger that might threaten it. But this is a mere idle boast, and has been proved to be so in the present war. The war has shown that you must secure the help of the people in order to defend the empire, and hence our just demand derives an additional force from the necessities of the circumstances. We, therefore, pray to the Government to concede to us the right to carry arms. And request them to strike one from the statute book the pernicious Arms Act which has eaten into the vitals of our country. Such a step will bring delight to the hearts of millions and make them powerful enough to come to the rescue of the empire in the hour of its need. We again assure the Government that this concession will place the loyalty of the people on a more solid foundation; it will make them stronger, and will go a great way in strengthening the empire as well. With these words, delegates, I commend this resolution to your acceptance and I hope you will carry it with acclamations. (" Long Live Lokamanya " " Tilak Maharajkijay ").

INDEX.

INDEX

Tilak Mr —

Published by

Facsimile Publisher
Ashok Vihar, Delhi-110052 (India)
Website: www.facsimilepublisher.com

Distributed by

Gyan Books Pvt. Ltd.
5, Ansari Road, Daryaganj, New Delhi-110002 (India)
E-mail: books@gyanbooks.com, Website: www.gyanbooks.com